PRAISE FOR *Original Sin*

"With extraordinary erudition and just enough lightness of touch to leaven the lump, Alan Jacobs traces the tangled ways that down through the centuries we have tried to think about human cussedness. Are we born with it in us or do we inevitably catch it like the flu? And in either case, what's to be done about it?"

—Frederick Buechner, author of *Secrets in the Dark*

Alan Jacobs presents an engagingly written, eminently humane, and insightful account of an all-important subject that is both timeless and timely.

—George Marsden, author of *Jonathan Edwards: A Life*

"Alan Jacobs's cultural history of the controversies that Saint Augustine's concept gave birth to is fascinating, entertaining, wonderfully researched, and thoroughly even-tempered, giving even the most disagreeable voices their say. *Original Sin* may well become the definitive book on the subject."

—Ron Hansen , author of *Exiles* and *A Stay Against Confusion*

"I do not believe in original sin. I do believe in Alan Jacobs. He is one the smartest and wittiest writers around on matters involving religion, and *Original Sin* is a gem."

—Alan Wolfe, Boisi Center for Religion and American Public Life, Boston College

"In this brilliant account, Wheaton College literature professor Jacobs traces the idea of original sin from the Bibl~~...~~ ent day. . . . In his hands these abstru~~...~~ ngrossing."

—*Publisher~~...~~*

"Replete with example~~...~~ ent cultural expressions, including ~~...~~phy, [*Original Sin*] is intended to introduce ~~...~~road general audience to the complexity of explaining how human beings act evilly toward one another by examining the various cultural manifestations of Augustine's notion of original sin."

—*Library Journal*

"A brilliantly illuminating, deeply thought-provoking intellectual journey."

—*Booklist*

"A strangely entertaining cultural survey . . . Jacobs presents an absorbing history of how mankind has dealt with the fact of its own waywardness. In an easy, fluent style, Jacobs makes the case that we're setting ourselves up for a fall whenever we think that mankind can get things exactly right."

—*The Wall Street Journal*

"Jacobs's discussion is terrifically worthwhile for exposing how the idea of 'evil,' as enunciated within the doctrine, undergoes permutations and translations over time."

—BN.com

"Splendid . . . a book endeavoring to help us say and do something about the sin which so easily ensnares. Jacobs's is not an easy task. Part apologist, part peddler of cultural curiosities, part champion of the doctrinal underdog, he aims to win another hearing for original sin. Strikingly, Jacobs argues that the 'confraternity' of humanity is best grounded not in our being made in the image of God but in our being made sinful in Adam. Truly a revolutionary thought—that the roots of our common humanity might be found, not in our dignity or even our potential, but in our depravity."

—*Books & Culture*

"A deep pool of wisdom . . . an expression of what's wrong with all of us. Jacobs's prose often sings. . . . Careful when you open this book—it could keep you up at nights."

—*Christianity Today*

Original
SIN

A Cultural History

ALAN JACOBS

HarperOne
An Imprint of HarperCollinsPublishers

HarperOne

ORIGINAL SIN: *A Cultural History.* Copyright © 2008 by Alan Jacobs. All rights reserved. Printed in the United States of America. No part of this book may be used or reproduced in any manner whatsoever without written permission except in the case of brief quotations embodied in critical articles and reviews. For information, address HarperCollins Publishers, 195 Broadway, New York, NY 10007.

HarperCollins books may be purchased for educational, business, or sales promotional use. For information, please e-mail the Special Markets Department at SPsales@harpercollins.com.

HarperCollins Web site: http://www.harpercollins.com

HarperCollins®, 📚®, and HarperOne™ are trademarks of HarperCollins Publishers

FIRST HARPERCOLLINS PAPERBACK EDITION PUBLISHED IN 2009

Library of Congress Cataloging-in-Publication Data

Jacobs, Alan.
Original sin : a cultural history / by Alan Jacobs.
    p. cm.
ISBN 978-0-06-087257-1
1. Sin, Original.   2. Sin, Original—History of doctines.   I. Title.
        BT720.J33   2008
    233'.1409—dc22   2008006582

HB 06.01.2021

To those I most love:
my wife Teri and my son Wesley.

Christianity preaches an obviously unattractive idea, such as original sin; but when we wait for its results, they are pathos and brotherhood, and a thunder of laughter and pity; for only with original sin can we at once pity the beggar and distrust the king.

—G. K. Chesterton, 1909

How many volumes have been writ about angels, about immaculate conception, about original sin, when all that is solid reason or clear revelation in all these three articles may be reasonably enough comprised in forty lines?

—Jeremy Taylor, ca. 1650

CONTENTS

INTRODUCTION

All religious beliefs prompt rejection. Souls are reincarnated? Ridiculous. The Bible is divinely inspired? Dangerous nonsense. Muhammad is the prophet of God? Poppycock. Jesus rose from the dead? Absurd. It is the common fate of doctrines to be dismissed; you'd almost think that's what they were made for. But not all beliefs are dismissed in the same way. Some get an airy wave of the hand; others, a thoughtful shake of the head, with pursed lips indicating a tinge of regret; still others, the stern wag of a hectoring finger. But of all the religious teachings I know, none—not even the belief that some people are eternally damned—generates as much hostility as the Christian doctrine we call "original sin."

It is one of the most "baleful" of ideas, says one modern scholar; it is "repulsive" and "revolting," says another. I have seen it variously described as an insult to the dignity of humanity, an insult to the grace and loving-kindness of God, and an insult to God and humankind alike. And many of those who are particularly angry about the doctrine of original sin are Christians. One of the great evangelists of the nineteenth century, Charles Finney, called the doctrine "subversive of the gospel, and repulsive to the human intelligence." A hundred years earlier an English minister, John Taylor of Norwich, had cried, "What a God must he be, who can curse his innocent creatures before they have a being! Is this thy God, O Christian?"

Yet for other Christians this teaching is utterly indispensable. Taylor's outburst prompted book-length retorts from two of the great pastoral and theological minds of that era, Jonathan Edwards and

John Wesley. Blaise Pascal believed that without this particular belief we lack any possibility of understanding ourselves. G. K. Chesterton affirmed it with equal insistence, adding the sardonic note that it is the only doctrine of the Christian faith that is empirically provable. The twentieth-century French Catholic writer George Bernanos wrote, paradoxically but sincerely, that "for men it is certainly more grave, or at least much more dangerous, to deny original sin than to deny God."

What *is* this belief that generates such passionate rejection and such equally passionate defense? We had best begin by saying what it is *not*.

It is not the first human sin. Many people believe that "original sin" refers somehow to Adam and Eve's eating of the forbidden fruit in the Garden of Eden. It's this association that produces countless metaphorical uses of the term, such as the oft-expressed idea that slavery is "America's original sin" or playwright Eric Bentley's claim that "over-complication is the original sin of the intelligentsia." Lord Henry, in Oscar Wilde's *Picture of Dorian Gray*, says, airily: "Humanity takes itself too seriously. It is the world's original sin. If the caveman had known how to laugh, history would have turned out differently." I could cite a hundred other examples. But even in these cases, varying though they are and more or less distant from the Christian doctrine we're concerned with here, there remains something worth looking into—something more than the idea of simple chronological priority.

Let's get at that something more through one more example, this one from a novel I read some years ago. What might it mean to say, as this novel does, that one man's original sin was the purchase of a house? Not that that purchase was his first mistake, or even his first big one, but rather that the transaction somehow set in motion a chain of unpleasant events that could not be arrested or reversed. One might think that what we have here is just a fancy way of saying, "Everything started going wrong then"; but there are actually three further implications of the phrase that most readers will readily perceive. First, after the purchase of the house things *couldn't* have gone right. We also see that once the purchase was made there was no going back—selling the house either was impossible or wouldn't have helped. And finally, we realize that no one could have known in advance how disastrous the purchase of the house would turn out to be; the decision never seemed so consequential.

Once we add up the implications of this one writer's use of the phrase "original sin," we can see that its meaning would have been familiar to the ancient Greek tragedians, since it amounts to little more than the concept of fatal choice—a choice that sets in motion vast irresistible forces of retribution, what the Greeks named Nemesis. The statement "John's original sin was buying that house" occupies the same moral framework as "Oedipus's sin was murdering his father." Since Oedipus doesn't know that it's his father he kills, he can't imagine the full consequences of the act; there's no way to undo his deed, to get back to the life he was living before that moment at the crossroads; and the retribution he has called down upon himself is inevitable.

But if that is all "original sin" means, then that's the oldest of news and has nothing specifically to do with Christianity. And it's certainly possible to read the story of Adam and Eve in this way: the First Couple ate the fruit not knowing how profound the consequences would be, not understanding that the price of their meal would be forced and permanent exile from the garden and then, eventually, death. Read in such a way, it's a disturbing story, perhaps—but not *that* disturbing. However, the doctrine of original sin, as it eventually developed, strikes deeper and challenges or even overturns our usual notions of moral responsibility. Original sin is not mere fatality, the God who oversees it is not the faceless Nemesis, and Adam and Eve do not buy death for themselves only.

In his letter to the Christians at Rome, St. Paul asserts that "sin came into the world through one man," Adam, "and death through sin." Insofar as Paul is saying that Adam brought death upon himself by his sin, he's not being controversial. But Adam is no Oedipus. After all, he was ordered not to eat the fruit of the tree of knowledge of good and evil and explicitly warned that disobedience meant death. An Igbo proverb often quoted by the Nigerian writer Chinua Achebe says, "A man who brings ant-infested wood into his hut should not complain when lizards pay him a visit." Or, as a more familiar vernacular has it, "What goes around, comes around."

But Paul is not content to leave it at that. The whole of Romans 5:12 reads: "Therefore, just as sin came into the world through one man, and death through sin, *and so death spread to all men because all sinned*" (emphasis mine). That is, Adam's sin brought death not just to him, but to "all men"—to all of his descendants: all of us. When we all forfeit our lives because of what one man did at the beginning of human history, "What goes around, comes around" doesn't quite cover it. And do I not have every right to complain about the lizards if it was my first father who brought the ant-infested wood into the hut while I was minding my own business? St. Paul, it appears, does not think so, because earlier in his letter to the Roman Christians he says that those who sin are "without excuse"—which is rather cold of him, is it not?

That most controversial of the church fathers, Augustine of Hippo—with whom we will have much to do in the pages ahead—finds Paul's argument useful in trying to understand a curious passage from the Bible's first book. In Genesis, God makes a covenant with Abraham and explains that a "sign" of the covenant will be the practice of circumcision. But, he warns, "any uncircumcised male who is not circumcised in the flesh of his foreskin shall be cut off from his people; he has broken my covenant." Now, Augustine freely admits, this is pretty strange, for the situation God describes to Abraham "is in no way the fault of the infant whose soul is said to be about to perish. It is not he who has broken God's covenant, but his elders, who have not taken care to circumcise him." And yet the passage clearly says that the uncircumcised infant is the one who has broken God's covenant.

For Augustine this passage meant that "even infants are born sinners, not by their own act but because of their origin"—their origin being the primal fatherhood of Adam. And here we see what is meant by original sin, *peccatum originalis* in Augustine's Latin: sin that's already inside us, already dwelling in us at our origin, at our very conception. Circumcision and the covenant it represents are necessary, because Adam broke faith with God and left all his children amidst the brokenness by somehow managing to transmit to us an irresistible tendency to do just what he did. In another book Augustine writes, "When a man is born, he is already born with death, because he contracts sin from Adam"—*contracts* it, as though it were a disease. Which in a way it is, and in another way it isn't; the categories have a long history of interrelation, confusion, conflation, some of which we will explore. But for now, it's fair to say that most of us feel that sin afflicts like disease and that, like disease, it is easy to acquire and hard to get rid of.

Many of us would also agree that sin, like the more communicable diseases, transfers easily to other people; few of us have strong immunity to its ravages. But we would also agree that the affliction of disease is not moral in character. Although it is possible to act in such a way that one becomes more prone to illness, surely there is no sin in being ill. Disease, we tend to agree, *happens* to us; sin is what we *do*. Yet it is just this simple and familiar distinction that Augustine—drawing on the passages in Genesis and Romans—denies. In his account, an infant who has not "acted" and is "not at fault" has nevertheless, somehow, broken a covenant with God.

This thought takes us far indeed from the Greek tragedians' picture of fatal choice—and from the way that the phrase "original sin" is used in many of the examples cited earlier. That infant described in Genesis 17 has not made a choice. Moreover, although for the man who bought a house he shouldn't have bought or the woman who overcomplicated an issue, there was a time before the affliction, this cannot be said for that uncircumcised boy; he emerges stained from his mother's womb and remains stained unless rescued by whatever mysterious transaction the ritual removal of his penis's foreskin represents. This is the ultimate "preexisting condition," one that can be neither averted nor ignored.

It is, obviously, a belief that violates our most basic notions of justice. No wonder John Taylor of Norwich exclaimed, "What a God must he be, who can curse his innocent creatures before they have a being!" And yet the individual components of the idea are utterly familiar. Everyone knows that some people are born with a malady of some kind: a birth defect resulting from the mistransmission of genetic information, say, or a disorder (HIV, hepatitis) passed from mother to child through the umbilical cord. And we acknowledge that some social circumstances make certain sins all but inevitable. I don't see how I, as a white Southerner raised in the 1960s and 1970s, could have avoided some taint of racism, yet I don't think I should use that upbringing to declare myself innocent. Most of us are also comfortable with talk of "the human condition"—general circumstances shared by everyone, if nothing else "the thousand natural shocks that flesh is heir to." So we comprehend inherited affliction, collective and inherited responsibility, universally shared circumstances. It is the *joining* of these ideas that strains our minds. We struggle to hold together a model of human sinfulness that is universal rather than local, in which we inherit sin rather than choose it, and in which, nevertheless, we are fully, terrifyingly responsible for our condition.

So why would anyone hold to such a strange and, frankly, rather depressing idea? To answer that, we must—well, we must traverse the next three hundred pages or so. But for a capsule answer, you could do worse than invoke Chesterton's comment about the empirical evidence for original sin. Any moderately perceptive and reasonably honest observer of humanity has to acknowledge that we are remarkably prone to doing bad things—and, more disturbingly, things we *acknowledge* to be wrong. And when we add to this calculus the deeds we insist are justified even when the unanimous testimony of our friends and neighbors condemns us—well, the picture is anything but pretty. These are the most truistic of truisms, of course, and I can't imagine that anyone would deny them, but they raise questions, do they not? *Unde hoc malum?* is how it was put long ago: Where does this wrongdoing come from? What is its wellspring, the source of its ongoing prevalence and power? The doctrine of original sin is, if nothing else, an intellectually serious attempt to answer such questions.

It's hard to imagine a more consequential puzzle or one that infiltrates more facets of human experience. I came to the topic when writing a long essay about Jean-Jacques Rousseau—about whom more, much more, later—and discovered that, at almost the same time that Rousseau was declaring the natural innocence of children and articulating a whole philosophy of education based on that innocence, the English preacher John Wesley was preaching sermons on the education of children founded on a belief in the innate and ineradicable corruption of human nature. And it turns out, not surprisingly, that an educational system based on Wesley's beliefs about children differs dramatically from one based on Rousseau's commitments. So, our beliefs about why we so invariably go astray have the most wide-ranging of consequences.

Though many people still echo Rousseau's rhapsodies about the natural innocence of children, his ideas have lost much of their influence. Partly this stems from serious research into child psychology—almost all of which has shown that the psyches of children are lamentably like those of adults—and partly from an increasingly universal skepticism about all things human that is the natural and reasonable response to that foulest of human centuries, the twentieth. As the poet and critic Randall Jarrell once wrote, with a terrifying wryness, "Most of us know, now, that Rousseau was wrong: that man, when you knock his chains off, sets up the death camps. Soon we shall know everything the eighteenth century didn't know, and nothing it did, and it will be hard to live with us." Well, it *is* hard to live with us, hard for us to live with ourselves, because we feel that we have left Christianity and its "baleful," "repulsive" doctrines behind. But we have also left Rousseau's naïveté behind, so where the hell are we? That is, *what* are "we"? What remains of a sense of shared humanity? Do we believe in it anymore? And if so, in what do we ground that belief?

For many scholars and thinkers, especially in the fields we call the humanities, the only thing we all have in common is that we don't have anything *naturally* or *inevitably* in common. The human condition, such as it is, is to be "socially constructed," to be formed wholly by our environments. "Socialization goes all the way down," as the philosopher Richard Rorty used to say. But this view leaves unanswered, and usually unasked, the question of why the social construction of selves is so limited in its range, so unimaginatively and repetitively attached to making us cruel and selfish. Which is why some adherents of this position insist that some societies *have* found ways to construct selves that are uniformly generous and kind—and why they respond with fierce repudiation to any contrary evidence. The classic case study of this phenomenon involves the work of the anthropologist Napoleon Chagnon among the Yanomamo people of the Amazon basin. When Chagnon discovered and reported on the various forms of aggression in Yanomamo culture, he was scorned as a pariah by many of his anthropological colleagues, for whom the natural innocence of the Yanomamo had become an article of faith.

For scholars outside the humanities—the cognitive scientist Steven Pinker, for example—this social-constructionist "denial of human nature" is absurd, largely because it ignores the biological determinants of human behavior, and a common genetic inheritance is something that we all certainly share. Yet although Pinker and likeminded scholars feel they can account pretty well for the prevalence of selfishness and even violence across all human cultures, they have more trouble explaining why we remain uneasy, even guilt-stricken, about our most common tendencies—why *selfish* and *violent* are pejorative terms for us.

In short, some of us have trouble explaining, or even making sense of, common human behavior; others have trouble understanding our common *responses* to that behavior. Yet we all stand here looking back on a century of unparalleled cruelty, dotted with names—Hitler, Stalin, Mao, Pol Pot—that instantly call to mind the worst that human beings are capable of doing to one another. And we could with equal justice mark that century (as well as the one recently commenced) for its cruelty to the natural world, though we lack specific names to associate with *that* foul work. We have never had more need to explain ourselves to ourselves, but we manifestly lack the resources to do so. It may be (I think it is) a propitious moment for reconsidering that curious concept called *peccatum originalis*, the belief that we arrive in this world predisposed to wrongdoing—that this world is a vale of tears because we made it that and, somehow, couldn't have made it anything else.

Again and again the literature and culture of the West have returned to this doctrine, worrying over it, loathing it, rejecting it—only to call it back in times of great crisis or great misery. (It was in the bowels of the Soviet Gulag that Aleksandr Solzhenitsyn came to believe in it.) It repeatedly infiltrates our culture, provoking always the strongest of responses. We cannot make sense of it and yet cannot kill it. The task of this book is to explore the provocation of this single strange idea—a provocation that is located in its combination of repulsiveness and explanatory power. Perhaps no one has understood this better than Blaise Pascal, who wrote in his *Pensées:* "What could be more contrary to the rules of our miserable justice than the eternal damnation of a child, incapable of will, for an act in which he seems to have had so little part that it was actually committed 6,000 years before he existed? Certainly nothing jolts us more rudely than this doctrine, and yet but for this mystery, the most incomprehensible of all, we remain incomprehensible to ourselves."

What follows is an *exemplary* history—so-called not because it embodies excellence that other historians would do well to imitate, but because it makes its case through examples. An exhaustive and systematic cultural history of original sin would probably be impossible; it would surely be undesirable. Though there is a good deal of exposition in the chapters that follow, most of it emphasizes narratives about people, people who engage in a serious and thought-provoking way with the idea of original sin—whether by embracing it, rejecting it, or wrestling with the possibility of it. From my accounts of these people the arc of a story emerges. It is a generally accurate story, I believe, but to tell the *whole* story in a historically responsible way is beyond me and, I think, beyond anyone.

It is also a specifically *cultural* history, not a history of theological ideas. Though theology comes regularly into my narrative—how could it not?—I have tried throughout to write for readers who have little interest in theology. My concern is with the ways in which belief or disbelief in original sin plays itself out in a great variety of cultural forms, from poetry to movies, from psychoanalysis to the rearing of children. But these are all aspects of culture upon which theology impinges. As well it should.

Six Stories

One

When the Greek soldiers burst into the city of Troy, Cassandra—who had prophesied it all, who knew what fate awaited her and all the Trojan women—fled to the temple of Athena. Until quite recently there had stood the talisman of the Trojans, the Palladium, the great statue crafted by Athena herself, the presence of which guaranteed the safety of the city. But one night Odysseus and Diomedes had crept into the city and stolen it. Its theft dismayed and terrified the Trojans, who felt the loss of divine power and protection; they substituted a wooden copy, which under the circumstances was all they could manage. Cassandra threw herself upon this counterfeit, pleading for the divine intervention she knew would not come.

It was Ajax who found her there—Ajax son of Oileus, called "Little Ajax" in contrast to his giant comrade, Telamonian Ajax. All the tales agree that he dragged Cassandra from the temple, as she clutched still the effigy of Pallas; some poets say he raped her first. Later she was taken by the great king Agamemnon back to Argos, where she prophesied and then witnessed his murder before being murdered herself. But Ajax returned to Locris, his homeland, on the north shore of the Gulf of Corinth, where in a storm his ship broke upon the rocks.

Brought safely to land nonetheless by the aid of Poseidon, he climbed out of the surf and boasted that he had saved himself by his own power, overcoming the ill will of the gods. For this Poseidon immediately struck him dead, or perhaps Athena herself executed him with a thunderbolt from the armory of her father, Zeus.

His death was a great tragedy for the Locrians, not because they lost their chief and hero, but because now the wrath of Athena could fall only upon them. Famine and disease overcame them; not knowing that their warrior prince had defiled Athena's shrine—he had been killed before boasting of that—they consulted the great Oracle at Delphi, who told them the story, and told them also that there was a way to atone for Ajax's cruelty. But it was a harsh way.

Athena would ease their suffering under this condition: that each year, for a thousand years, two young maidens of Locris would be sent, as payment and sacrifice, to serve at Athena's shrine at Troy. However, those Trojans who remained in their ruined city considered the very presence of these girls a defilement and would stone them to death and burn their corpses—if they could catch them before their arrival at the shrine. But if the girls could reach Athena's temple, they could not then be touched; they became slaves of Athena's priests. So the Locrians took great care to arrive in stealth at various times of the year. And what the Trojans did not know (so says Aeneas Tacitus, an early Roman military strategist who wrote a survival guide for the dwellers of besieged cities) was that the same secret passage that Odysseus and Diomedes had used to steal the Palladium was the one the Locrians used to sneak this year's maidens into the temple and spirit away the ones they had brought the previous year.

A strange legend; and one with a strange and long life. The Greek historian Polybius, writing in the second century B.C.E., claims to have visited Locris on several occasions. He finds it curious that they trace the lineage of their aristocracy, the "Hundred Families," through the female rather than the male line. He points out that the Hundred

Families had always supplied the girls who were sent to Troy; it was a point of honor for them. And he says that the practice continued even in his own day, though Robert Graves (like other modern scholars) contends that it had ended a century before.

Many historians now believe that a great Trojan War did occur and that Homer's poems may even capture some details of it, though they cannot be sure when it occurred. But by any reckoning, the Locrian maiden tribute had been paid for very nearly a millennium when Polybius visited the city. Once, the story goes, a Locrian slave girl had been killed by an invader of Troy, in Athena's temple itself, and this mirroring of the fate of Cassandra caused the Hundred Families to think that perhaps their debt was now canceled. So the next year they sent no maidens to Troy. But pestilence immediately returned to afflict them; they resumed their tribute and, it seems, never again questioned it.

No one knows for sure when the tribute finally ceased. But generation after generation these people patiently endured the loss of their daughters because of the great sin of their ancestor. They accepted that the goddess's curse had fallen upon them, if not rightly then at least inevitably. Such was the way of the world; the sins of the fathers had to be expiated, even by a thousand years of children. And there was no one else to do it but them.

Two

Of course, this is a particular suffering of a particular people—a historical accident, one might say. The Locrians were unfortunate enough to have had an impious braggart as their prince, just as the Ithacans were fortunate enough to have had a wise and just king, Odysseus. But Greek artists and thinkers sometimes wondered whether the sheer prevalence of impiety and arrogance suggested something—something worrisome—about the very shape or form of humanity. There are, after all, so many more Ajaxes than Odysseuses in the world.

The last and longest of Plato's dialogues, the *Laws*, the only one that does not feature Socrates, begins like a joke: a Cretan, a Spartan, and an Athenian are walking down the road, a road on Crete leading to a cave-shrine dedicated to Zeus, where the Cretan and Spartan, Kleinias and Megillos, plan to worship. The Athenian falls in with them along the way, and we meet the trio in the midst of a debate about the purpose of law and what makes laws good or bad. (It is interesting that the Athenian—to whom the others eventually yield as the wiser man, whose instruction they seek, and who speaks perhaps 90 percent of the words in the dialogue—remains nameless. Could it be Socrates after all? Unlikely. He was known to stick close to Athens.) Their conversation is sober, filled with an awareness that the propensity of humans to do wrong ensures that the making and enforcing of laws will always be difficult work.

At one point late in the dialogue, the three companions discuss the crime of temple robbing—perhaps their minds turn to such matters as they near Zeus's shrine. (In the last few lines of the dialogue Kleinias portentously affirms, "We must take the road along which God himself is so plainly guiding us.") This crime strikes the Athenian as one that particularly needs explaining, and in explaining it he says something curious: the impulse to do such things "comes neither from man nor from God; 'tis an infatuate obsession that is bred in men by crime done long ago and never expiated, and so runs its fatal course."

What could he mean by this? Likewise, what did he mean when, a few lines earlier, he had spoken of "our universal human frailty"?—as though *all* human beings carry within them an inherited curse, a moral "frailty" that we derive from some evil ancestor; as though we were all, in a sense, the Locrian descendants of Ajax, with the added burden that we find ourselves compelled, as the "obsession" runs its "fatal course," to reenact the impious boastfulness of our ancestor.

But what is this crime? And who is this ancestor? The English classicist E. R. Dodds thought that he had found the key in a passage earlier in the *Laws* where the Athenian describes the human love for freedom and what happens when it is given free rein. We strive to "escape obedience to the law," and when that happens, "the spectacle of the Titanic nature of which our old legends speak is re-enacted; man returns to the old condition of a hell of unending misery."

The Titans: the gods who ruled in the generation preceding Zeus and the Olympians; their leader was Kronos, the father of Zeus, whom Zeus overthrew for his cruelty. But why should human beings be said to have a "Titanic nature"? The answer, Dodds claims, is in a story that Plato must have known: the dismemberment of Dionysos. It was a story told—this we know for sure—by practitioners of later Greek religions, the Pythagoreans and the Orphists, to identify the source of evil in humans. At first it keeps to the path of older myths: that Dionysos was born to Semele, a moon goddess, and Zeus; that Hera, Zeus's wife, was jealous and sought the infant's death; and that she commissioned the Titans to carry out the murder, which they did with relish, tearing the child into pieces. But whereas the older versions of the story claimed that Dionysos was rescued and reassembled by his grieving grandmother Rhea, the Pythagoreans and Orphists told a different tale. They said that, seeing what the Titans had done, Zeus hurled a thunderbolt that vaporized them and the remains of the infant god—and then, from the settled dust, there arose human beings, comprised therefore of a large measure of Titanic evil but also a few grains of the truly divine. We have, then, a largely "Titanic nature," but also a Dionysian spark, which prompts us, sometimes, to higher things. This, thinks Dodds, is the story that underlies the Athenian's dark comment on our "universal human frailty" and the "fatal course" on which we have been set.

But as the companions draw closer to the shrine, and as the Athenian expounds more and more fully the system of laws that he believes is best suited to us, their spirits lift. Kleinias, it turns out, has been charged with the establishment and rule of a new Cretan colony, to be called Magnesia; and Megillos says that they must "try every entreaty and inducement" to get the Athenian to sign on as "co-operator in the foundation" of the new city-state. Although the Athenian never formally accepts the offer to guide the shaping of this new colony, it is telling, I think, that in his account of how it should be formed he again and again uses the pronoun *we*. Surely he will help them. The ancient doom still lurks, the crime of the Titans remains not fully expiated; but even in outlining the "fatal course" of the old obsession in our veins, the Athenian counsels his friends to "strain every nerve to guard yourself from it"—which suggests that the course may not prove fatal after all. We go forward to worship Father Zeus at his shrine; a city remains to be built and set on a right path. Law is powerful. All may yet be well.

Three

Meanwhile, not so far away on the Mediterranean's eastern shore, a king of Israel also had sinned, but this was (at first, anyway) largely his own concern. The king, whose name was David, had in his youth been very beautiful; he was now a man, perhaps beautiful still, though with grown children, and he was a great warrior. The chief enemies of Israel in those days were the people of Ammon, whose capital city, Rabbah or Rabbath, lay twenty miles or so east of the Jordan River. David and his general Joab had driven the Ammonites back into their city, and Joab and his troops besieged the city while David remained in Jerusalem—"tarried" there, as King James's translators tartly put it.

It was while thus tarrying that the king took the evening air from the roof of his house, the house that looked out over the town that future generations would call the City of David. And it was from this roof that he saw a woman, in the garden of her own house perhaps, bathing, "and the woman was very beautiful to look upon."

Half a century ago the great literary scholar Erich Auerbach wrote of how peculiarly "reticent" biblical narrative can be; nowhere more so than here. Tersely it records a series of events without once pausing to tell us what any of the people think or feel. David asks who this woman is; someone informs him that her name is Bathsheba, and that her husband Uriah is a soldier in David's own army, serving in the siege of Rabbah. David orders her to come to him, takes her to his bed, and then sends her home. Later she informs the king that she is pregnant, at which point he does something very odd: he calls for her husband.

From Rabbah to Jerusalem Uriah comes. So, how goes the battle? the king asks. Is Joab well? Making progress in the siege? The narrator does not record Uriah's answers, perhaps because a preoccupied David never heard them. But in any case, when the inexplicable interview at last ends, David says to Uriah: It's been a dusty, tiring trip for you; go get cleaned up; go home to your wife. I'll send you some food.

Ah: if Uriah makes love to his wife, her pregnancy will not be suspicious. But the next morning the king's servant remarks that Uriah had in fact not gone home, but had slept in the king's doorway, as a sentinel sleeps, or a faithful dog. Upon learning this, David interrogates the man again and receives this reply: "The ark [of the Covenant] and Israel and Judah dwell in booths, and my lord Joab and the servants of my lord are camping in the open field. Shall I then go to my house, to eat and to drink and to lie with my wife? As you live, and as your soul lives, I will not do this thing." (Shall I lie with my wife? In such times as these?)

David tells Uriah, I'll send you back to Rabbah soon. The next day he invites him to dinner and gets him thoroughly drunk; yet still the man, who could so easily and half-consciously stumble down the hill and into the arms of his beautiful wife, sleeps in the king's house, so strong is the soldier's discipline within him. (Unless, of course, this is not military discipline at all, but rather the shrewdness of a man who knows that he has been cuckolded and is seeking to keep the king in an uncomfortable position, one that could, perhaps, ultimately yield some benefit to himself and his family. If so, Uriah has disastrously misread David.) The next morning David writes a letter to Joab, giving it to Uriah to deliver—who, after all, would more surely deliver the letter without inquiring into its contents? The letter is brief and clear: "Set Uriah in the forefront of the hardest fighting, and then draw back from him, that he may be struck down, and die."

Some time later, after Uriah has been buried and Bathsheba has mourned for him, after the king has made her his wife and she has borne him a son (who would soon die), the Lord sends a prophet named Nathan to visit David. And Nathan tells David a little tale about sheep: about a rich man with many sheep who stole the one ewe lamb of a poor man—a lamb that ate at the poor man's table "and it was like a daughter to him"—killed it, and fed it to a guest. (It is a strange and powerful feature of Nathan's story that it is not the poor man whom the rich man kills, but his ewe lamb—as though somehow David had slaughtered Bathsheba rather than her husband.) To this David replies with all the outrage proper to a righteous king—until Nathan says to him, "You are the man," and launches into an eviscerating catalogue of David's criminal depravities. There is much more to this story, as great a story as has ever been told. But I want merely to notice the single sentence that David offers in response to Nathan's charges: "I have sinned against the Lord."

David was, of course, a great poet, according to the tradition of Israel the nation's greatest poet; and that tradition also says that he composed a psalm upon this occasion, a confession and a plea. Here it is, in the matchless King James Version:

Have mercy upon me, O God, according to thy lovingkindness:
according unto the multitude of thy tender mercies blot out
    my transgressions.
Wash me thoroughly from mine iniquity, and cleanse me
    from my sin.

For I acknowledge my transgressions: and my sin is ever
    before me.
Against thee, thee only, have I sinned, and done this evil in
    thy sight:
that thou mightest be justified when thou speakest, and be
    clear when thou judgest.
Behold, I was shapen in iniquity; and in sin did my mother
    conceive me.

Behold, thou desirest truth in the inward parts: and in the
    hidden part thou shalt make me to know wisdom.
Purge me with hyssop, and I shall be clean: wash me, and I
    shall be whiter than snow.
Make me to hear joy and gladness; that the bones which thou
    hast broken may rejoice.
Hide thy face from my sins, and blot out all mine iniquities.

Create in me a clean heart, O God; and renew a right spirit
    within me.
Cast me not away from thy presence; and take not thy holy
    spirit from me.
Restore unto me the joy of thy salvation; and uphold me with
    thy free spirit.

Then will I teach transgressors thy ways; and sinners shall be
  converted unto thee.
Deliver me from bloodguiltiness, O God, thou God of my
  salvation:
and my tongue shall sing aloud of thy righteousness.
O Lord, open thou my lips; and my mouth shall shew forth
  thy praise.
For thou desirest not sacrifice; else would I give it: thou
  delightest not in burnt offering.
The sacrifices of God are a broken spirit: a broken and a
  contrite heart, O God, thou wilt not despise.

Do good in thy good pleasure unto Zion: build thou the walls
  of Jerusalem.
Then shalt thou be pleased with the sacrifices of righteousness,
with burnt offering and whole burnt offering:
then shall they offer bullocks upon thine altar. (Ps. 51)

Whether David wrote it or not (most scholars today think not), it is as powerful a poem as the story that prompted it. But there is something quite strange about it: this verse: "Behold, I was shapen in iniquity; and in sin did my mother conceive me." It is not just "blood-guiltiness," the murder of Uriah, that he confesses. Looking into his heart—which in Hebrew culture is the seat of the affections and also the will; it is the motive engine of a person—he sees an unclean-ness so deep, so pervasive, that its corruption must have preceded not only his birth, but even his very conception. At the moment that his life first sparked into being, it was somehow already stained. His only hope is that God will take his broken heart, that ruined organ, and replace it with another one: "Create in me a clean heart, O God." But the consequences of his corruption will deepen and extend, like cracks spreading across a pane of glass, until they shatter his family

and then his whole nation, which, it is fair to say, has never fully recovered from the sins of its greatest and most beloved king.

Four

Most scholars believe that David lived in the tenth century B.C.E., by
which time the Locrians had been paying their tribute to Athena for a
hundred years or so. The centuries that followed saw increasing travel
and trade along that longest of roads, the Silk Road, running from
the Mediterranean world that the Greeks and Israelites knew across
the great Royal Road of Persia and ultimately into China. From the
time of David to the time of Polybius, a single dynasty reigned in
China, the Zhou. Though the real power in that land was divided
among six or seven states and the role of the Zhou king was often
nominal or symbolic, yet there remained throughout China, among
the literate at least, a strong sense of a common culture. It was the job
of the political administrators and scholars—these were overlapping
and sometimes identical classes—to maintain that culture. They did
so through the assiduous keeping of court records, through poetry,
and in the end most famously through the discourses and debates of
the great sages, whose ideas are often something like a combination
of administrative manuals and elegant verse.

  If you go to a bookstore looking for the works of the most famous of
these sages, Kong Fuzi—better known as Confucius (551–479 B.C.E.)*—
you will probably find only a single volume, called the *Analects*. This
is a collection of sayings made by disciples of Confucius based on the
recollections of his students. The *Analects* seem to be a random gathering of pronouncements and anecdotes, but from them one can discern

---

* Confucius is the Latin name given him in the sixteenth century by the great
  Jesuit missionary Matteo Ricci.

Confucius's ceaseless concern with the personal disciplines needed to practice righteousness (*yi*) and compassion (*ren*). Through the cultivation of these virtues people not only improve themselves, but also—and this matters more to Confucius—contribute to the improvement of society. Confucius cared above all for the cultivation of political order and harmony, and in fact the great disappointment of his life was his inability to get any political leaders to give him the stature and power of an adviser. "If only someone were to make use of me, even for a single year, I could do a great deal," he laments in the *Analects*, "and in three years I could finish off the whole work"—that is, bring a whole state into lasting order. He did not lack confidence, but in several years of traveling to various Chinese states to offer his services to the local bosses, he never found any takers.

Confucius's belief that he could put a whole society right in such a short time suggests not only self-confidence, but confidence in the malleability of human behavior. About a hundred years after his death was born a man who would become known as the greatest of his followers, the Second Sage, Mencius (372–289 B.C.E.). Mencius was probably one of the compilers of the *Analects*, but in any case from studying the Master's sayings he came to the conclusion that Confucius could be so assured of the success of his schemes because, after all, human nature is essentially good. We come into this world predisposed to virtue, Mencius believed. Notice, he said, the immediate surge of anxiety that we all experience if we see a child about to fall into a well. This is the origin of "human-heartedness" (*jen*). The child may even be completely unknown to us, but our unreflective instinct is compassionate; this testifies to our innate goodness, which we simply need to cultivate, largely by eliminating the corrupting forces of society. This is precisely why Confucians in this tradition believe that political reform can be so effective. Simply by eliminating the negative forces of social disorder or political malformation, the sage-king—the Confucian ideal of humanity—can liberate his people to discover and nourish their own virtue.

But some generations later there came along another great sage, one who also considered himself a faithful disciple of Confucius, who believed that Mencius had gotten it all wrong. His name was Xún Zǐ (310–237 B.C.E.), and it is probably not coincidental that he lived in what has long been called the Warring States Period, when the unifying power of the Zhou dynasty was weakening and the social order crumbling. "The nature of man is evil," Xún Zǐ wrote. "Man's inborn nature is to seek for gain. If this tendency is followed, strife and rapacity result and deference and compliance disappear. By inborn nature one is envious and hates others. If these tendencies are followed, injury and destruction result and loyalty and faithfulness disappear." If we feel a pang of compassion or anxiety for a child falling into a well, that is because the life or death of that child does not affect our interests—we do not gain by it. If we knew we would gain by that child's death, then not only would we feel no anxiety; we'd give the kid a good shove.

But then, someone might say, people often, or at least sometimes, do virtuous deeds. If our nature is evil, where does goodness come from? Xún Zǐ has a ready reply: "I answer that all propriety and righteousness are results of the activity"—this word carries connotations of creativity and artifice—"of sages and not originally produced from man's nature. . . . The sages gathered together their ideas and thoughts and became familiar with activity, facts, and principles, and thus produced propriety and righteousness and instituted laws and systems."

So it would seem that the news from Xún Zǐ is not so bad after all, and not so different from the model of Mencius. Yes, we have an innately evil nature and come into this world predisposed to greed and strife; however, these tendencies are correctable by the judicious enforcement of well-made laws. The one thing needful is that the sages, who have "gathered together their ideas and thoughts and became familiar with activity, facts, and principles," are the ones given charge of "laws and systems." Philosophers rule—or should.

So for Xún Zǐ inborn evil is not so much a curse as an annoyance. Thanks to basic human intelligence, which allows us to see when things aren't working properly and then take the necessary steps to address the problems, we can find sages ("sage-kings," he later says) to establish laws and social structures that mitigate evil and build up good. And, not incidentally, Xún Zǐ believes that "Every man in the street possesses the faculty to know [humanity, righteousness, laws, and correct principles] and the capacity to practice them." Therefore, almost anyone can become a sage; there is no reason why there should ever be a shortage of them.

It's Xún Zǐ's matter-of-factness that's noteworthy here, and really rather attractive. What his philosophy indicates is that one can have a very low view of human nature without being what William James, in his classic *Varieties of Religious Experience* (1902), calls a "sick soul": a person tormented by consciousness of sin and helpless in the face of temptation. James spoke of such people as "these children of wrath and cravers of a second birth," and it was almost axiomatic to him that their personality is antithetical to the confidence and assurance and warmth of what he calls the "religion of healthy-mindedness." But Xún Zǐ, for all his insistence on the depths of our innate sinfulness, seems the very embodiment of healthy-mindedness. How is this possible? It turns out that what matters more than your view of "human nature" is your view of the relative importance of nature and nurture. For Xún Zǐ human nature is evil, but nature is also easily controllable and eminently improvable. All you have to do is put the philosophers in charge.

Five

In south-central Nigeria, in the heartland of the Yoruba people, you may find an extraordinary place called St. Joseph's Workshop. (Or you could have found it fifteen years ago; I am not certain that it still exists, but I assume that it does.) The men of the workshop primarily make furniture—as, perhaps, did their patron, the human father of Jesus who was a carpenter or builder—and quite beautiful furniture too. The workshop was founded perhaps fifty years ago by a Belgian priest who taught the local people the finest techniques of building things from wood. He gave special emphasis to the proper drying and curing of sawn boards of mahogany, something especially important in the humid climate of Nigeria, and something often neglected by other furniture-makers, if I may judge by the wobbly joints and cracked surfaces I have seen in many chairs and tables of that land. Once this priest felt that the people had learned all he had to teach them, he returned to Belgium; they run the workshop on their own now.

The double doors to the small showroom of the workshop are tall and broad and divided into six panels each, and in each panel is carved a scene from the story of the priest's time in Nigeria, from his arrival to his farewell. The carvings are done with extraordinary vividness and skill, and when you go through those doors you see many, many examples of the master carvers' art, including a throne made especially for Pope John Paul II's visit to Nigeria in 1982 richly ornamented with biblical events. At the time of my visit, smaller objects by various carvers lined the walls, but my eye was consistently drawn to the work of one artist in particular, the one who had been primarily responsible for the doors and the throne. His initials are J.A., and I believe his name is Joseph Abada. I was able to buy—for the equivalent of just a few dollars—two of his smaller mahogany pieces. (I couldn't have fit larger ones into my bags.)

One is a Crucifixion, with Mary and John at either side of Jesus, whose eyes are closed and whose navel oddly protrudes above his neat loincloth; the two observers are dressed in recognizable Yoruban costume. Stranger and more powerful is the other piece, an Annunciation. The angel Gabriel, bearing an enormous palm frond that dominates the space, appears before Mary, who, unlike her counterparts in European art, is not sitting peacefully reading the book of Isaiah, but rather standing in the yard of a compound, pounding yams. (It is Gabriel who carries a small book.) She and the angel, like Mary and John, wear Yoruban dress. A chicken on the ground between them pecks grain, and from the top of the scene the Holy Spirit, in the form of a dove, speeds diagonally downwards toward Mary's womb.

The West African yam is a large purplish tuber, so fibrous that it must be pounded into a kind of paste before it can be cooked and eaten. Yoruban woman place the peeled yams in high-sided wooden bowls that look like office trash cans and smash them with a thick stick that is often taller than the women themselves. The image of Mary doing this when Gabriel comes to her is a curious and moving piece of iconography; it represents her humility, her lowness of stature. She is not a queen or a rich woman with servants or slaves to prepare her meals for her; she does the daily work of the ordinary Yoruban woman. We know that her response to the angel's news that she will bear the Messiah of Israel is, "Behold the handmaiden of the Lord," and though this Mary seems well-dressed enough, one suspects that she knows something about being a handmaiden.

I carried this Annunciation back to the school where I was teaching for the summer—the Evangelical Churches of West Africa theological seminary in the small town of Igbaja, a few hours north of the great city of Ibadan—and showed it to my students, almost all of them pastors from various parts of Nigeria. To my surprise, a couple of them, when they saw my beautiful Annunciation, strove with limited success to stifle giggles. I wanted to know what could possibly be funny about this picture, and after some insistence on my part one of them told me.

Traditional Yoruban religion is known for its rich and complex pantheon of gods, with widely varying roles in this world (*Aye*) and in the spirit world (*Orun*). But many Yoruba believe that there is a single creator-god, Olodumare, who became disillusioned and angry with human beings and withdrew from his creation, leaving all the other gods (like the demiurges in Plato) to manage the world with which he had lost patience. But what caused his withdrawal? "When I was a child," my student said, "I was told that the women did it—the women pounding yams. Olodumare lived in the sky, but quite close to us. When the women went out to pound their yams, the noise drove him crazy. And when they lifted their sticks, they poked him in the backside. So in the end he couldn't take it anymore. He went far, far away, and has never returned." He looked at my Annunciation and giggled again. I guess iconography is in the eye of the beholder.

Six

In the same year that I was teaching in Nigeria, 1991, a young anthropologist-in-training named Joel Robbins traveled to Papua New Guinea to live among a people called the Urapmin. There were (and are) only about four hundred of them, comprising half a dozen villages in the far west of the country and near the center of the island. They speak their own language, Urap, but also Tok Pisin, a kind of lingua franca that contains many English words (thanks to a long-standing British and Australian colonial presence), and in school they learn, or are supposed to learn, English.

What came to interest Robbins about the Urapmin was a powerful event that transformed the entire community starting in the year 1977, a mass conversion from their traditional religious culture to Christianity. Much of Robbins's extraordinary book *Becoming Sinners* is devoted to an attempt to understand this conversion, and I can scarcely summarize his complex narrative here. But it is important to note that the Urapmin were of low social status in comparison to neighboring people groups, and such marginal or oppressed communities have historically been fertile ground for the Christian gospel. They had long practiced a form of ancestor worship, but as they compared themselves to their neighbors, it did not seem evident that their ancestors had done them much good, and ultimately they decided to sever their ties.

The bones of the ancestors were kept in string bags hung from the rafters of small houses. Bones, bags, and houses alike were thought to be sacred and spiritually powerful; sacrifices were burned in those houses, and the smoke had blackened the bags. When the Urapmin decided that it was time to abandon the worship of their ancestors, dismantle the houses, and throw away the bones, they did not think the objects powerless; rather, they saw them as repositories of demonic powers. Thus when one of the Urapmin "big men" explained how they had carried out this task, Robbins thought he sounded like someone in the developed world describing a toxic-waste cleanup.

Given the dangers and difficulties of the task, one is moved to ask why the Urapmin did it at all. While acknowledging the people's sense that, socially speaking, they had little to lose, Robbins points out that they thought—if the ancestors turned out to have more power than they guessed—they had a great deal to lose in terms of health and sanity and spiritual well-being. It must simply be said that they took the risk because they believed the Christian story that they had heard. But what specifically was it that they came to believe?

Christianity was not unknown to the Urapmin before 1977. Australian Baptists had made the first serious efforts to evangelize the region in the 1950s, and although they had few direct encounters with the Urapmin, converse among the peoples of the region led to a few Urapmin embracing the new faith. Then in the early 1960s some young men of the villages attended a mission school a few miles away and later became Christian leaders in their home community. But this trickle of Christian influence surged into full flood in 1977, thanks to a great revival that, beginning probably in the Solomon Islands, spread throughout Melanesia in what Robbins describes as a kind of "Great Awakening"—that is, something like the vast revival that swept across Britain and America in the eighteenth century.

The version of Christianity that drove this Melanesian awakening was Pentecostal, characterized by dramatic manifestations of the power of the Holy Spirit to transform people's lives from the inside out, as though the heat of the Spirit life had to force its way to visible expression: ecstatic dance, glossolalia, prophecy, sudden unconsciousness (being "slain in the Spirit"). But what prompted people to fling themselves into the Spirit's powerful but dangerous and unpredictable embrace? If we may judge by the accounts the Urapmin gave Joel Robbins, two interlocking and reinforcing ideas changed their personal lives and the life of the community. The first: that they were sinners, alienated by their sins from God, subject to his fierce displeasure. The second: that Christ would soon—soon!—return in glory to judge the living and the dead. It was therefore vital to accept the saving power of Christ, to confess him as Savior and Lord immediately, so as to avoid the wrath that all unbelievers would encounter if caught by the terrible ruler of All upon his glorious return. So they became Christians, all of them—the whole community of the Urapmin. They destroyed the sacred houses and discarded the bones of their ancestors; they started over.

But what they soon discovered was that their conversion had not put an end to their sins. Still they gossiped about their neighbors or were resentful and envious; perhaps they even lied, or stole. They knew the commandments of God, but somehow managed again and again to disobey them. As they told Robbins, in what apparently was a kind of general confession, "we are too willful, we obey no one but ourselves." They made many confessions; they sought often to make amends and be restored to good relations with their neighbors. Following practices of reconciliation that had belonged to their pre-Christian days, they would bring gifts to "buy the shame" of those they had humiliated or "buy the anger" of those they had enraged.

One Christmas season, when because of certain outside influences tensions among the Urapmin were unprecedentedly high, the Kaunsil—a sort of judge-magistrate—commanded that the entire community, every single one of them, bring a gift to buy the pain of someone else. And once they had done this, Robbins records, "people began to believe that they might be able to control their sinful tendencies enough so that Jesus would take them to heaven when he returned."

This was the heart of the matter. The theology the Urapmin had acquired did not encourage them to think in, say, Calvinist terms: they did not believe in the "perseverance of the saints," in the motto of "once saved always saved." They did not think, as many evangelicals and other Christians (primarily in the Western world) think, that the blood of Jesus covers all our sins, so that our general commitment to the gospel matters, not the precise state of our moral lives at the moment of our death or of Christ's return. For the Urapmin, because he could return at any moment—did he not say that he would come "as a thief in the night," when least expected?—Christians must be ever vigilant, practiced in self-examination, and ready to confess, repent, and, when possible, make amends for all wrongdoing. Did Jesus not himself wonder whether, when he returned, he would find anyone faithful on the earth?

Why do we sin in the first place? Why are we so prone to wrongdoing? Is it because in sin our mothers conceived us? Is it because we labor under the curse of being born with a Titanic nature? Is it because we are born with a lust for gain and for the freedom to grasp whatever we desire? Alas, the Urapmin did not have the leisure for such general and theoretical questions. Every time they looked within, they found more darkness, more willfulness, more disobedience. So they came to the church. In the course of the evening they streamed in, and a pastor stood at the front of the room and prayed:

God, I am praying to you. . . . We want to ask you to send your Spirit down to move us so we can celebrate your name tonight.

That is what I am asking you. You look at each of our hearts. . . . You have the ability to clear away the sins, heavinesses, coveting, and various bad ways that are in our hearts and take us over to Jesus, to your light, and we can give happiness to you. . . .

That is what I am asking. It would be bad if we tried hard at this for nothing. So we must feed this Spirit of yours. You can direct each of us people inside of ourselves, and we can give happiness to your Spirit until we go out and sleep.

That is what I am asking for. . . . So we are ready and have been singing, but our strength is not enough for us to sing with. So we ask you to have the Spirit alone move us and to bring down your strength and put it in our hearts so we can celebrate your name tonight.

TWO

The African Bishop

In the basilica of a North African city called Hippo Regius, the bishop was preaching. The city stood on the rocky Mediterranean coast a hundred miles or so west of Carthage, in what is now the northeastern corner of Algeria. The old curving streets had been laid centuries before by the Phoenicians, and the usual evidences of appropriation by Rome were quite visible: a forum; an enormous theater that seated perhaps six thousand people and served also as a stadium for games; extensive baths; a temple on the hilltop. The church stood in what was called the "Christian quarter," near the villas of the rich; it was perhaps a hundred years old, a big plain hall, and had been expanded a few decades earlier, after Constantine the Great linked the fates of Rome and Christianity.

The bishop's name was Aurelius Augustinus; he's known to us simply as Augustine. A native of North Africa himself, he had come to Hippo in 391, when he was thirty-seven years old—a recent convert to Christianity and a would-be monk—because he had thought Hippo a likely site to begin a monastery. But one Sunday the man who then sat in the bishop's chair, Valerius, spoke warmly of the need for gifted men to serve the church, and the people, having heard that their visitor was a rising young star of the Christian faith, clamored for his ordination to the priesthood and pushed him toward the bishop.

(This was not an uncommon practice in the Christian churches of this period.) "I was grabbed," he later said, ruefully. He wept with fear and shame, though at least some of the people assumed he wept because he thought the role of priest too low for him and wished to be made bishop instantly. Instead, that elevation would wait four years: in 395 he became the bishop of Hippo Regius and served in that role to the end of his life.

When he preached, he sat in his episcopal chair—his *cathedra*—with a book open on his lap, and to the people standing around him he explained the words in the book. It would not have been a Bible as we know it, for Augustine certainly never saw all of the Holy Scriptures bound into a single codex, but rather the particular biblical "book" on which he was preaching that day and perhaps one or two others that he wished to refer to. Though he strove to keep the church plain and relatively unornamented, in keeping with what he believed to be the simplicity of the Gospel, there's reason to suspect that the *cathedra* was one of special dignity, perhaps even made of marble. It's hard to say how many people might have attended any given service; sometimes he comments on the smallness of his audience, or he congratulates his congregation on having come to church when they could have gone to the stadium to enjoy the games. (But he didn't think that Christians should attend the Roman games and races at all.) Once, late in his career, when he wished to address certain uncharitable rumors about the lives that priests and monks lead, he asked for everyone who could possibly attend to come hear him. (This is the sermon in which he tells the story of how he came to Hippo and was "grabbed" and made a priest.) He frequently mentions the tiredness and weakness of his voice, especially as he gets older and when he has to preach on successive days.

A stenographer recorded his discourses—this is how his sermons have survived—and if something unusual happened in the course of the sermon, the stenographer would make a note of it. For instance, when Augustine spoke to his people of the terrible wrath of God, they would actually cry out in terror.* And once Augustine began quoting a verse from Scripture only to have his audience shout the rest of it out loud, after which they applauded themselves for their biblical literacy. Perhaps they knew this verse so well because it was a special favorite of their bishop. It was a verse from St. Paul's letter to the Galatians: "But far be it from me to boast except in the cross of our Lord Jesus Christ, by which the world has been crucified to me, and I to the world."

THE WORST PART of being bishop, Augustine thought, was the requirement that he serve as a kind of magistrate, settling the legal quarrels of the Christians of Hippo. About inheritances they were particularly disputatious, he found. He kept the Scriptures nearby so that he could show them, when necessary, the principles by which they should be conducting themselves. These disputes took up most of his mornings. Far better spent was the time devoted to studying the Word of God, the Word that had changed his life.

What people today think they know about the young, pre-Christian Augustine is that he was an especially wild and licentious fellow, sexually promiscuous, adventurous. But that is to take his own self-description too literally and to misunderstand certain of his key terms. It is true that he spoke and wrote often of the "lusts of the flesh," of "carnal" desires and experiences, and of himself as slave to all these. But for him these were not only sexual: the "flesh" for Augustine is not

---

* Sermon 131: "What then does the Lord say? 'Serve the Lord in fear, and rejoice unto Him with trembling.' So the Apostle too, 'Work out your own salvation with fear and trembling. For it is God who works in you.' Therefore rejoice with trembling: 'Lest at any time the Lord be angry.' I see that you anticipate me by your crying out. For you know what I am about to say, you anticipate it by crying out."

the body, but rather the corrupted will. "Carnal" people are those who (like the Urapmin) obey no one but themselves, who will not submit to God, who insist on getting their own way. Of course, this willfulness often manifests itself in sexual sins or the fulfillment of other bodily desires, but those are but superficial symptoms of a deeper malady, the malady of *cupiditas,* or the orientation of the human will toward its own gratification, as opposed to *caritas,* divine love, which Augustine defined as "the movement of the soul toward God."

What had plagued him all his life, then, was not so much lust in our usual sense of the word as a kind of helpless following along in the wake of his own will's unpredictable changes of direction. In one of the most famous passages of his *Confessions* he describes a sin of his childhood, the theft of pears from a neighbor's orchard, and the tone of the whole passage is befuddlement: *Why in the world did I do that?* This became a recurrent theme for him as he reflected on his life.

As for the body's desires, he certainly knew them well enough; throughout much of his youth he lived with a concubine, who bore him a son. This was a common practice in late Roman culture, at least among the upper classes and those who aspired to raise themselves in the world. It often took families some years to arrange proper marriages for their children—marriages that brought or consolidated wealth and prestige—and young men were not expected to keep themselves chaste during this period. Thus the concubines, who were always of sufficiently low social rank that they could not possibly be thought of as potential brides, were brought in to provide sexual satisfaction, companionship, and domestic service. It was understood that they had to be put aside when an engagement was finally contracted.

Augustine's parents achieved the desired contract when he was close to thirty and had been living with a woman—whom he never names—for perhaps a dozen years. She had even come with him from North Africa to Rome and then Milan. When the engagement was announced and, according to the custom, she and Augustine had to part, she wept and vowed that she would never take another man. Augustine too wept: "My heart which was deeply attached [to her] was cut and wounded, and left a trail of blood." But he acquiesced in the ambition of his parents or perhaps shared it; he sent her back to Africa. He now had two years to wait until his marriage. Rather than spend that time in chastity—he wrote that he was "incapable of following a woman's example" of fidelity—he took another mistress.

Looking back on these events some fifteen years later, he chastises himself for his lust, but seems more concerned with the forking and branching of his will. He loved his concubine, yet he was also ambitious, or at least obedient to his parents' ambitions. He could not restrain himself sexually, yet he preferred life with one woman to the diversions of promiscuity; he never, it seems, played the field. His final comments about this painful scene are very strange. He says that by taking this second concubine he ensured that the "disease of his soul" (lust) would be "guarded and fostered" until his marriage. But he had been "wounded" by the loss of his first concubine, and the wound did not heal. Rather, he says, it "festered," and the resulting pain made him "frigid but desperate" (*frigidius sed desperatius*). It is hard to know what to make of these tortured metaphors, but the suggestion seems to be that he did not find the simple erotic satisfaction with the replacement concubine that he had hoped for. (Does the notion of "frigidity" suggest, as it does to us, sexual impotence? Certainly Augustine always spoke of the "fires" and "cauldrons" of lust.) He couldn't get over his first love, yet he couldn't bring himself to call her back; living chastely was impossible, but the new concubine brought no satisfaction.

Thus his fundamental judgment about himself is not that he is lustful, but that he is internally divided, driven here and there by multiple pressures and desires. And this was the case throughout his pre-Christian life. He was always uncertain where or how to practice his profession as a teacher of rhetoric, trying out options in

Carthage, Rome, Milan. In religion he drifted into the Manichaean orbit—the Manichaeans believed that the world is constituted by a struggle between two great forces, one good and one evil—but wavered in his commitment. He could never get convincing answers to his questions, but, on the other hand, he never found compelling refutations of Manichaean doctrine either. Christianity became more and more attractive to him, but for years he could not acquire the resolution necessary to convert.

The famous conversion scene of the *Confessions*—when he sits under a tree in a garden and hears a child's voice calling "*Tolle, lege,*" "Take it and read"—is the moment of release from this internal torsion. In the pages before that scene we see Augustine encountering multiple stories of people who had given up their whole lives to seek God, sometimes just as a result of reading stories about other people who had given up their lives to seek God, so that, in the climax to a lifetime of self-exasperation, he turns to his friend Alypius and cries, "What is wrong with us?" So he goes outside, sits under the tree steaming with self-reproach, nevertheless continuing in "an agony of hesitation"; he hears the child's voice, determines that this is a "divine command," and runs back inside to pick up "the book of the apostle," which he had earlier been consulting. The first words he reads in that book end his hesitation.

The book contained the most famous and important letter of "the apostle," St. Paul, his teaching to the church at Rome. What Augustine read was the concluding exhortation of chapter 13: ". . . not in orgies and drunkenness, not in sexual immorality and sensuality, not in quarreling and jealousy. But put on the Lord Jesus Christ, and make no provision for the flesh, to gratify its desires." Augustine writes, "I neither wished nor needed to read further." Alypius graciously pointed out to him that the very next words of the letter are, "As for the one who is weak in faith, welcome him."

· · ·

IT IS ONLY PROPER that we should begin and end our biographical overview of Augustine by invoking the words of Paul. For one thing, Augustine's carapace of uncertainty and dividedness—a carapace that simultaneously confined and protected him—could be pierced only by the diagnostic power of Paul's arguments. (I write this as one who was similarly pierced; it was my discovery that Paul understood my inmost griefs and self-loathings that led me to Christianity.) But it is also important to link these two men for the purposes of this book, because Paul and Augustine typically receive the joint credit, or blame, for inventing the notion of original sin as we have come to know it.

It is easy to imagine Augustine, still a relatively young man, sitting hour after hour in his episcopal study and poring over the letters of Paul. It is not likely that he ever relinquished the copy of the letter to the Romans that ushered him into the church; it is easy at least to imagine him clutching it as, in the last days of his life, the Vandals besieged Hippo.* He assiduously studied the whole Bible, of course, and most of his recorded sermons were on the Gospels and Psalms, but one gets the sense that—having been brought into the faith by Paul's incisive interpretation of his divided self—he forever after understood the whole of Christianity in a distinctively Pauline way. As Augustine's great biographer Peter Brown has very shrewdly noted, Augustine was like most learned men of his time in being "steeped too long in too few books." Living as we do in a time of too *many* books, we cannot think that Augustine's scarcity was wholly

---

* Soon after his death the city was captured and largely burned, though his library survived. It fell into the hands of his friend, fellow bishop, and future biographer Possidius, who actually lived for a few years in the ruined city in an attempt to care for the literary remains of the friend he so admired.

a bad thing. But whether for good or for ill, Augustine's mind, after his conversion, was surely "steeped" in the writings of Paul, deeply stained to their color, like the dyer's hand.

As we can tell from the two passages already quoted—the one from Romans 13 and the one from Galatians 6—Paul's command was not so much that we be converted as that we die. The "old man" or "old humanity"—which is governed by the "fleshly mind"— must be crucified so there may be a resurrection, a new birth, a new spiritual mind: a new creation. All of these terms are from the middle chapters of the letter to the Romans. As Augustine studied the complex argument Paul elaborates there, he reflected on these key terms—not in Greek, for he knew little Greek, nor even in St. Jerome's Vulgate, which was then just a work in progress, but in various "Old Latin" translations.*

It seemed to Augustine that the key to Paul's argument came somewhat earlier in the letter, in the fifth chapter, where Paul conducts an extended comparison between the first man, Adam, and the new man, the second Adam, Jesus Christ. Here is what Augustine clearly understood to be the linchpin of Paul's argument:

> Therefore, just as sin came into the world through one man, and death through sin, and so death spread to all men because all sinned—for sin indeed was in the world before the law was given, but sin is not counted where there is no law. Yet death reigned from Adam to Moses, even over those whose sinning was not like the transgression of Adam, who was a type of the one who was to come.

---

* The "old man" is in Paul *palaios anthropos,* but in Augustine *vetus noster;* the "fleshly mind" Paul calls the *phronema tes sarkos,* but Augustine knew it as *prudentia carnis,* or *sapientia carnis,* in contrast to the *prudentia spiritus,* or "spiritual mind"—which for Paul had been *phronema tes pneumatos.*

But the free gift is not like the trespass. For if many died through one man's trespass, much more have the grace of God and the free gift by the grace of that one man Jesus Christ abounded for many. And the free gift is not like the result of that one man's sin. For the judgment following one trespass brought condemnation, but the free gift following many trespasses brought justification. If, because of one man's trespass, death reigned through that one man, much more will those who receive the abundance of grace and the free gift of righteousness reign in life through the one man Jesus Christ.

Therefore, as one trespass led to condemnation for all men, so one act of righteousness leads to justification and life for all men. For as by the one man's disobedience the many were made sinners, so by the one man's obedience the many will be made righteous. (Rom. 5:12–19)

Paul holds up before us the origin of our sin. The name rings out like the blows of a hammer: *sin came into the world through one man; many died through one man's trespass; the judgment following one trespass brought condemnation; because of one man's trespass, death reigned; one trespass led to condemnation; by the one man's disobedience the many were made sinners.* Paul restates his axiom half a dozen times, shading the meaning in various ways, but thereby forging ever more securely the bond that links the first sin of Adam (the one) to the misery of everyone since (the many)—the bond that, for Paul, can only be broken if we crucify the old man and rise again to a new life with Christ and in Christ. We are to "put on" Christ not as a garment (which can be taken off again), but as a new identity. That's how we can say, with Paul, Augustine, and Augustine's parishioners, "The world has been crucified to me, and I to the world."

Read carelessly, Paul could be thought to say that we are in a situation like that of the Locrians, simply laid under a curse by the sin of our ancestor. But none of the Locrians thought that because of Ajax they themselves sinned: they paid for his sin, but they did not repeat it. Yet Paul says—or at least Augustine hears him saying—that the sin of Adam is also our own sin: *all sin; the many were made sinners.* We have inherited from our first father not just a debt, but also a compulsion, a compulsion to reenact his alienation of himself from God.

AUGUSTINE UNDERSTOOD HIMSELF to be reading, quite simply and straightforwardly, Paul's teachings. Scholars who credit or blame Augustine for the "invention" of original sin contend that he misread Paul; and it seems to me that the scholars who make that contention tend to be attached to the Christian faith in some way. If they believe that the Bible is the inspired Word of God and they disagree with Augustine, they must see him as Paul's misinterpreter. But even those with more tenuous or ambivalent connections to orthodoxy seem to prefer not to pick fights with Paul if they don't have to. The theologian and historian Elaine Pagels, for instance, in the course of an extended attack on Augustine's understanding of sin and its effect on freedom of the will, begins her critique by simply asserting that Augustine "invented" a radical new reading of Paul that had never occurred to any previous commentator.*

---

* This is clearly not the place for an extended examination of Pagels's claims, but let me at least note that much pre-Augustinian commentary on Paul bears a close resemblance to Augustine's interpretation. Two hundred years earlier Tertullian (Augustine's fellow North African) had identified each person closely with Adam, in such a way that we seem to be somehow inside the experience of the first man: "our participation in transgression, our fellowship in death, our expulsion from Paradise." True, we are beset by demons, but "the evil that exists in the soul . . . is antecedent, being derived from the fault of our origin (*ex originis vitio*) and having become in a way natural to us." His contemporary Cyprian of Carthage wrote of a "primeval contagion" and of the "wounds" we all receive from Adam. In North Africa, at least, Augustine's reading of Paul is amply anticipated.

Writers with little or no attachment to Christian tradition, however, tend to read Paul much as Augustine did. Freud, for instance, in
Moses and Monotheism, not only perceives that Paul is the inventor of
"original sin," but even sees it as a profound insight from "a man with
a gift for religion, in the truest sense of the phrase." (One suspects,
when reading Freud's reflections on Paul, that Freud saw Paul as
someone much like himself, as his predecessor in discerning the half
hidden, dark secrets of humanity and bringing them to the ruthless
light.) For Freud, this great insight emerged in part from Paul's own
distinctive personality and experience: "Dark traces of the past lay in
his soul, ready to break through into the regions of consciousness."
This past that he drew upon, however, was not just his, but the collective history of Israel: "It seems that a growing feeling of guiltiness had
seized the Jewish people—and perhaps the whole of civilization of
that time. . . . Paul, a Roman Jew from Tarsus, seized upon this feeling
of guilt and correctly traced it back to its primeval source. This he
called original sin; it was a crime against God that could only be expiated through death. Death had come into the world through original
sin." Note that Freud commends Paul for correctly discerning—like
a skilled analyst—the originating moment, the "primal scene," as
Freud liked to say, of our guilt (though Paul does not, *pace* Freud, use
the term *original sin*). Freud says very little, here or anywhere, about
Augustine, but there seems little doubt that he would have thought
Augustine's account of Paul perfectly accurate.

So who was this Paul? A question many have asked. Paul has inspired as much psychoanalysis-at-a-distance as any person in history—more even than Augustine. Yet Augustine has left us much
more self-reflection than Paul. In studying the strange and brilliant
North African we have far more to work with than when we investi-
gate the equally strange and brilliant Jew of Tarsus in Cilicia.

Or so, at least, Luke describes him. The author of the Third Gospel and the Acts of the Apostles is our only source for the claim that

Paul was born with the name of Saul in what was then a great port city, famous as the place where Antony met Cleopatra. (Though there is still a city in Turkey called Tarsus, it bears no resemblance to the great capital of old, whose harbor silted up centuries ago, landlocking it and ending its hopes of recovering its ancient glory.) Luke also tells us that Saul was a Roman citizen, that he left Tarsus to study in Jerusalem at the feet of one of the greatest of rabbis, Gamaliel, and that he led a campaign of persecution against the followers of Jesus before he experienced the most dramatic of conversions while traveling north along the great road from Jerusalem to Damascus. In the letters that he later wrote to Christians throughout the Mediterranean world, he provides less factual detail but more personal insight. We learn that he considers himself a "Pharisee of Pharisees" (stricter than the strict) and that he suffers from some chronic affliction he never names except as his "thorn in the flesh." When he writes in his own hand at the end of one letter—it was his habit to employ amanuenses—he comments on how large his writing is, which suggests either some limitation of motor skills or, more likely, deficient sight. He tells us that he is unmarried.

He also says, in a not uncommon moment of boasting, that with regard to the law he is "blameless"—a curious statement. If he is without sin, then why does he need a Savior? But it would seem that he means that his external observance of the Mosaic code is flawless, for in the greatest of his letters, that to the church at Rome, he writes movingly of how he habitually broke that most internal of the commandments, "You shall not covet." Surely he worshiped only Yahweh, surely he honored his parents and refrained from theft and violence and even lust. But in his heart he—like King David, gazing over the rooftops of Jerusalem—desired what belonged to someone else.

(Shall we pause to speculate? The Talmud records that one of Gamaliel's students was unruly, combative, argumentative: could this have been Saul? The description fits the personality he reveals in his letters, as when he describes a disagreement with Peter, the chief of the apostles, designated as such by Jesus Christ himself: "But when Cephas [Peter] came to Antioch, I opposed him to his face, because he stood condemned." One can easily imagine such a man—especially in his younger and still more pugnacious and confident days—chafing under Gamaliel's authority, thinking that he himself should be the rabbi honored in Jerusalem and far beyond, not a mere and meek disciple. One can even imagine him, after his conversion, feeling some annoyance at the authority granted to Peter, who, though an intimate companion of Jesus, was a mere fisherman who surely lacked Paul's intellectual firepower.)

That covetousness divided him, set him at odds with himself. In a passage that must have struck the endlessly vacillating Augustine as written just for him, Paul sets out the sad facts of his case:

> I do not understand my own actions. For I do not do what I want, but I do the very thing I hate. Now if I do what I do not want, I agree with the law, that it is good. So now it is no longer I who do it, but sin that dwells within me. For I know that nothing good dwells in me, that is, in my flesh. For I have the desire to do what is right, but not the ability to carry it out. For I do not do the good I want, but the evil I do not want is what I keep on doing. . . .
>
> So I find it to be a law that when I want to do right, evil lies close at hand. For I delight in the law of God, in my inner being, but I see in my members another law waging war against the law of my mind and making me captive to the law of sin that dwells in my members. Wretched man that I am! Who will deliver me from this body of death? (Rom. 7:15–24)

Could not King David have said the same? Paul is after all in this very passage quoting the opening of the book of Psalms:

> *Blessed is the man*
> *who walks not in the counsel of the wicked,*
> *nor stands in the way of sinners,*
> *nor sits in the seat of scoffers;*
> *but his delight is in the law of the Lord,*
> *and on his law he meditates day and night. (Ps. 1:1–2)*

And likewise in the longest of the Psalms, 119, the extended and interwoven meditation on Yahweh's gift to Israel of the righteousness that governs the cosmos: "I long for your salvation, O Lord, and your law is my delight." As Paul finds his model in David's Psalms, could not David have affirmed every sentence in Paul's self-diagnosis? Perhaps, then, it is not David alone who was "conceived in iniquity"; perhaps all of us who are likewise split and ruptured ("I do not understand my own actions. For I do not do what I want, but I do the very thing I hate") must wonder whether we came here this way, whether some calamity preceding our birth set us along this broken and wavering path. For what would it be like to be otherwise, to be whole? Can we even imagine it?

THREE

Some Dreadful Thing No Doubt

All this commentary! All this tortured reflection! What prompts it? Just this:

The Lord God took the man and put him in the garden of Eden to work it and keep it. And the Lord God commanded the man, saying, "You may surely eat of every tree of the garden, but of the tree of the knowledge of good and evil you shall not eat, for in the day that you eat of it you shall surely die.". . .

Now the serpent was more crafty than any other beast of the field that the Lord God had made. He said to the woman, "Did God actually say, 'You shall not eat of any tree in the garden'?" And the woman said to the serpent, "We may eat of the fruit of the trees in the garden, but God said, 'You shall not eat of the fruit of the tree that is in the midst of the garden, neither shall you touch it, lest you die.'" But the serpent said to the woman, "You will not surely die. For God knows that when you eat of it your eyes will be opened, and you will be like God, knowing good and evil." So when the woman saw that the tree was good for food, and that it was a delight to the eyes, and that the tree was to be desired to make one wise, she took of its fruit and ate, and she also gave some to her husband who was with her, and he ate. Then the eyes of both were opened, and they knew that they were naked. And they sewed fig leaves together and made themselves loincloths. (Gen. 2:15–3:7)

That's it. Nothing more. This taciturn narration scarcely provides enough information upon which to build such a scaffolding as Paul and Augustine produced—were it not that so many of us share that forking of the will of which they are always so conscious, and wonder what could possibly explain ourselves to ourselves.

AT THE BEGINNING of the fourth book of John Milton's *Paradise Lost*, Satan has made his way to earth, to Eden itself, and now sits "like a Cormorant" on the Tree of Life, which stands in the middle of the garden. He considers for a while the various creatures, but when he sees Adam and Eve—"Two of far nobler shape erect and tall, / God-like erect, with native Honour clad / In naked Majestie"—he is struck dumb by the magnificence of their beauty. (Later, when he ventures to speak to Eve, her glory is such that again he can for a moment neither speak nor act; he is for that instant "stupidly good.") After a time he recovers himself sufficiently to cry—in a rare moment of Miltonic comedy—"O Hell!" For it is to Hell that he hopes to take them.

They are conversing. Satan assumes other forms, of "fourfooted kind," "as their shape serv'd best his end / Nearer to view his prey," and likewise to hear them. Adam speaks to Eve of freedom and of trees; he is amazed and honored by the scope God has given them, their liberty to go and do whatever they wish—with one exception:

Sole partner and sole part of all these joyes,
Dearer thy self then all; needs must the Power
That made us, and for us this ample World
Be infinitely good, . . . he who requires

From us no other service then to keep
This one, this easy charge, of all the Trees
In Paradise that bear delicious fruit
So various, not to taste that only Tree
Of knowledge, planted by the Tree of Life,
So near grows Death to Life, whatever Death is,
Some dreadful thing no doubt; for well thou knowest
God hath pronounced it death to taste that Tree.

And here we must pause, for Milton has set himself an impossible task: to represent how a sinless and deathless sentient creature might envision a condition of sin and death. "Whatever Death is, / Some dreadful thing no doubt"—a nice touch, except how does he know what a "dreadful thing" is? He has lived his whole brief life in perfect unthreatened peace; he cannot know what it means to dread any more than he knows what it means to die.

At this point in the story representation fails, storytelling lapses—or should lapse—into silence. Milton has gotten himself, and us, into a strange tangled corner of thought. How can we, the fallen and fearful, even guess what it might be like to have the easy freedom of sinlessness, to go to one's bed at night anxious for nothing, never suspecting peril in any rustling of the leaves or of the mind? Thus the American poet Donald Justice, in his early poem "The Wall":

They could find no flaw
In all of Eden: this was the first omen.
The second was the dream which woke the woman.
She dreamed she saw the lion sharpen his claw.

A flawless garden would be ominous to us, yes—but why to them? Omens are for those whom suffering has overtaken—those who must look back and ask whether they could or should have seen it coming. The reading of omens is a kind of forward-looking only practiced by those who have looked backward in self-reproach or at least self-doubt. This Adam and Eve knew nothing of. Thus, later in the story, when the archangel Raphael—sent by God to warn the couple against the temptation that is to come—mentions the necessity of obedience, Adam is puzzled: "Can we want obedience then / To him, or possibly his love desert"? Is it even *possible* that we should disobey?*

Moreover, for Justice, the garden itself is pristine, but in the mind of the woman there is a quirk or glitch; no lion sharpens his claw in fact, but only in human dream. But this suggests that something has gone awry within Eve already, in this unconscious imagining of a world without the assurance of peace, a world in which there may indeed be something to dread. Which means that before the Fall that the story (Genesis, and Milton's) tells us of—when the serpent tempts her and she eats the fruit—some purely internal Fall has taken place. But how did that happen? How *could* it have happened? Perhaps Raphael should not have given his warning after all; perhaps they could not have disobeyed, had they not been told that disobedience was an option. At the angel's first hint that other creatures, angelic beings, had rebelled, Adam replies that although he had not previously imagined anything but fidelity to God, "what thou tellest / Hath passed in Heav'n, some doubt within me move." Some doubt—that's not good.

---

* There is a comical moment—perhaps intentional, perhaps not—in a letter of that great eighteenth-century epistolist Lady Mary Wortley Montague, in which, although she admits that she "cannot form an idea of paradise, more like a paradise, than the state in which our first parents were placed," she nevertheless goes on to opine that their felicity "proved of short duration, because they were unacquainted with the world; and it is for the same reason, that so few love matches prove happy. Eve was like a silly child, and Adam was not much enlightened." If only they had been better educated! If only they had been more . . . worldly.

C. S. Lewis—who as a critic was quite aware of the difficulties that Milton created for himself by determining to describe in great detail the unfallen state about which the biblical narrator is so reticent— nevertheless determined, in his novel *Perelandra* (1944), to have a go at the same challenge. Lewis was prompted to tell his story, I think, by two considerations. First, he was always interested in the classic science-fiction theme of alternate worlds. What would happen if event X occurred on Planet Y instead of (or in addition to) our planet? And second, he was interested in what God, in *Paradise Lost*, says about Adam and Eve: that they were "sufficient to have stood, but free to fall." If Milton's God has stated the case accurately, then it becomes possible to imagine a counterfactual, a world in which the first beings resisted the temptation, remained obedient, and remained thus free and happy. Perhaps that's where we need to begin, thinks Lewis: not with striving to imagine how we fell, but striving to imagine how we might have remained unfallen.

It turns out that (no surprise here) such a thought is hard to think. Lewis approaches it with great intelligence and verve, but the results are iffy at best. The setting is the planet Perelandra, known to us as Venus. A man named Weston—or rather Satan occupying the deteriorating body of Weston for this purpose—sets out to persuade the Eve of this world, known only as the Lady, to disobey God, and for a while her chief response is mere puzzlement. Disobedience simply makes no sense to her. She tells Weston (the Un-man, as he is sometimes called, being little more than an animated corpse), "I thought your words had a meaning. But now it seems they have none. To walk out of His will is to walk into nowhere." Sensing that the condition of her mind makes further argument pointless, the tempter changes his tack, and interestingly, he begins to tell her *stories*.

Weston's voice . . . appeared to be telling, with extreme beauty and pathos, a number of stories, and at first Ransom [the novel's protagonist] could not perceive any connecting link between them. . . . From the Lady's replies it appeared that the stories contained much that she did not understand; but oddly enough the Un-man did not mind. If the questions aroused by any one story proved at all difficult to answer, the speaker simply dropped the story and instantly began another. . . . As the endless speech proceeded, the Lady's questions grew always fewer; some meaning for the words Death and Sorrow—though what kind of meaning Ransom could not even guess—was apparently being created in her mind by mere repetition.

Each story, Ransom eventually discerns, concerns a woman who "had stood forth alone and braved a terrible risk for her child, her lover, or her people. Each had been misunderstood, reviled, and persecuted; but each also magnificently vindicated by the event." It is in this light that the Un-man wishes the Lady to consider the temptation he is placing before her. But what is especially interesting here is Lewis's suggestion that before the rational mind can be convinced by argument, the imagination must be shaped and formed so that the person responds in a certain way—with certain *feelings*—to an argument. Only after he has told many, many stories does the tempter return to direct persuasion.

Lewis is not directly telling what happened in our world. But it is obvious that, like Milton and all other retellers of the first chapters of Genesis, he is compensating for the original story's reticence. Though the words Satan spoke to Eve may not have been at all like the ones the Un-man speaks to the Lady, Lewis is clearly inferring that the terse biblical account—the serpent asks a question, Eve answers, the serpent disputes God's story, Eve eats—is not to be taken as reportage, but rather as a summary of a dialectical struggle that could, perhaps, have continued for some time. Perhaps Eve too had to be trained, methodically, in the imagining of disobedience—and again, it's intriguing in this context to meditate on the effect of the story that Raphael tells, even if his intentions are contrary to the Un-man's.

In *Perelandra* the temptation goes on day after agonizing day. It's worth remembering that the seventeenth-century Irish bishop James Ussher—whose calculation of the date of creation established for many Christians, over a period of centuries, the age of the earth—figured that Adam and Eve held out less than two weeks. Creation began, said the bishop, on October 23, 4004 B.C.E., which means that humans were created on October 28. But he also calculated that Adam and Eve were expelled from the garden on November 10. On Ussher's reckoning, paradise was short.* But not as short, it should be noted, as in the bizarre Jewish apocalyptic book known variously as the *Secrets of Enoch,* or *2 Enoch,* or the *Slavonic Enoch.* That book affirms that Adam and Eve resided in paradise for exactly five and a half hours.

---

* Ussher's name is often mentioned with scorn today as an example of rigid and literalistic biblicism, but he found an unlikely defender a few years ago in the paleontologist and evolutionary theorist Stephen Jay Gould, who wrote in an essay that "Ussher represented the best of scholarship in his time." What impressed Gould most of all was Ussher's refusal to make his calculations on the basis of biblical evidence alone. Ussher canvassed every available source of historical information, did serious comparative study of the records of various civilizations, and took into account the idiosyncrasies of the calendar then in use. Though Gould only glancingly notes the point, Ussher's method was strongly countertraditional. For centuries theologians and leaders of the church had affirmed that the key date in human history was March 25, on which date occurred the Fall itself; the angel Gabriel's Annunciation to Mary, which heralded the birth of the One who would undo the effects of the Fall; and the Crucifixion, which defeated the forces of evil, which had been unleashed on this world by Adam's sin. It was with these events in mind that Dionysius Exiguus, the sixth-century monk and calendar-maker, determined that the year itself should begin on March 25, which it did throughout Europe for a very long time. It was England's official New Year's Day until 1752, though by that time January 1 had been celebrated by most English people for hundreds of years. J. R. R. Tolkien, knowing this history very well, made a point of placing the destruction of the Ring and the overthrow of Sauron on March 25.

Thanks in part to Ransom's intervention, the Lady escapes Eve's fate. The story here—and, not incidentally, where was Ransom, or someone like him, when *our* world went to hell in a handcart?—is rather more sober. (Rebecca West's summary of the situation is uniquely terse and apt, I think: "If the whole human race lay in one grave, the epitaph on its headstone might well be: 'It seemed like a good idea at the time.'") Surely even those who cannot believe in the "primeval contagion" of which Cyprian of Carthage wrote will acknowledge that we require no training in the imagining, or acting, of disobedience. The question for us is whether we can conceive of a life without dread or anxiety or self-reproach, a life without omens, the smooth peacefulness of instinctive docility. When Lewis describes the blankness—the slightly curious bewilderment—with which the Lady encounters the suasion of her enemy, can we in any sense entertain her frame of mind? When Milton's Adam speaks of "whatever death is, some dreadful thing no doubt," can we render meaning from that sentence? Or are these just words, words, words? If we cannot understand how humanity got from innocence to experience, from obedience to rebellion, from fellowship with God to alienation from him, we certainly cannot imagine our way *back* into that aboriginal state.

It is for this reason, perhaps, that Samuel Johnson had to announce, along with his admiration of Milton, his disenchantment with the poet's great epic. "*Paradise Lost* is one of the books which the reader admires and lays down, and forgets to take up again," he wrote. "None ever wished it longer than it is. Its perusal is a duty rather than a pleasure. We read Milton for instruction, retire harassed and overburdened, and look elsewhere for recreation; we desert our master, and seek for companions." The fundamental problem is this: "The want of human interest is always felt." Adam and Eve are simply not, in a sense recognizable to Dr. Johnson, human.

In David Maine's recent (alas, not very successful) novel *Fallen* there is an interesting moment. After their exile from the garden,

Adam and Eve wander for a while, and Eve finds herself trying to understand "her own role in the drama." Thinking it through over and over again, wondering how she ever came to follow the counsel of the serpent, she eventually comes to a kind of conclusion: she was herself "born a sinner; or if not born exactly, then created with some flaw that led her astray as surely as a snake, born legless, will crawl on the ground." Yes, that must be it—it's her nature to sin. She came into this world, she thinks, not whole but already wounded.

SO WAS IT ALL *her* fault? Well, many men have said so, starting with Adam, who says to God, "The woman whom thou gavest to be with me"—hey, *you're* the one who put her here—"she gave me of the tree, and I did eat" (3:12, KJV). When it comes her turn, Eve blames the serpent. God is apparently unmoved by both pleas, since he expels man and woman alike from the garden. Milton handles this moment wonderfully: He has God send his Son to judge the erring pair, and to him Adam spins out his tale of self-justification for twenty lines or so. But the Son simply replies, "Was she thy God, that her thou didst obey?" Touché.

Nevertheless, many a preacher over the years has denounced Eve as the cause of the whole mess. She was the weak link, which is of course why the serpent sought her out in the first place. Does this not prove that women are morally and intellectually weaker than men, who therefore rightly have lordship over their wives?

It turns out that this argument, however tempting from the male point of view, is really a trap. Amelia Lanyer, a contemporary of Shakespeare's, offers the proper response in her long poem *Salve Deus Rex Judaeorum*. There she reminds us that it was the *wife* of Pontius Pilate who, enlightened by a dream, warned her husband against allowing harm to come to Jesus. Lanyer has that wife elaborate a brilliant counterargument to the familiar masculine version of the story. "Our Mother Eve," she says, was merely "Giving to Adam what shee held most deare"; she was "simply good, and had no powre to see, / The after-comming harme did not appeare":

> That undiscerning Ignorance perceav'd
> No guile, or craft that was by him intended;
> For had she knowne, of what we were bereav'd,
> To his request she had not condiscended.

She thought she was doing Adam a *favor*. Adam, on the other hand, though he had been given charge over Eve, and indeed over all creation, was at the time of danger nowhere to be found: "Being Lord of all, the greater was his shame." Let's be honest about this, Mrs. Pilate says: "We know right well he did discretion lacke. . . . No subtill Serpents falshood did betray him, / If he would eate it, who had powre to stay him?" And she answers, "Not Eve."

Milton clearly agrees with this general line of thought. Like Lanyer, he agrees that Adam was "not deceived." But when he adds that the poor man was "fondly"—that is, foolishly—"overcome with female charm," you can't help but feel that his theology and his gender are pulling him in opposite directions. Though the text of *Paradise Lost* assigns Adam the greater share of blame, the subtexts seem to be ever working to undermine Eve. The poem sometimes reads like the speech of a hostage faithfully reading the text assigned him by his captors while trying to indicate by facial expressions a very different point of view.

But of course debates like this are themselves consequences of the Fall and indicators that we all share in it. This is why Milton has Adam and Eve immediately begin to trade recriminations, recriminations their descendants are still trading today, with undiminished energy.

. . .

IT WAS THIS TRADITION of which Augustine was the heir: the story of the Fall and the long history of commentary upon it, culminating in Paul's incisive and radical account in the letter to the Romans: sin came into the world through one man; many died through one man's trespass; the judgment following one trespass brought condemnation; because of one man's trespass, death reigned; one trespass led to condemnation; by the one man's disobedience the many were made sinners. But perhaps no one had ever made this core idea so central, had ruminated on it so obsessively, as Augustine. It became the very center of his whole anthropology, and he saw evidence for it everywhere, from the angry cry of a hungry baby to his own tendency to be distracted from prayer, contemplation, or the writing of sermons by the sight of "a lizard catching flies or a spider entangling them in his web."

When scholars studying these matters get angry at Augustine, as they often do, this is often not because of the core idea of original sin, but because of the intensity with which he contemplates it (so unlike the matter-of-factness of Xún Zǐ)—and the inferences he draws from it. Two such inferences in particular stand out to us today and were equally noteworthy to some of Augustine's contemporaries. Augustine believed that the damning stain of original sin could only be removed by the sacrament of baptism, and he believed that the mark of original sin in us today is to be found, primarily and most obviously, in our uncontrollable sexual desires.

Because Holy Baptism alone can remove sin, Augustine was forced to affirm that even newborn infants, if they die without baptism, are eternally damned. It is not clear that he enjoyed contemplating this or that he would have made the same arrangements if he had been Lord of the universe, but he believed that logic demanded that he accept the situation and that we affirm, even in our perplexity, the justice of

God.* As for our sexual nature, St. Paul and St. James alike write of the unruliness, rebelliousness, of our bodily organs ("members," in the King James Bible's rendering), but surely every man, at least, knows of one member that's unrulier than all the others.

Now, this does not mean that Augustine believed that the first sin was sexuality. Certainly he knew that the first sin was prideful disobedience, but for that very reason he understood that our proper punishment—in a kind of poetic justice, or what Dante called *contrapasso*, "counterpenalty"—manifests itself in the prideful disobedience of our sexual organs. In contravention of or just plain indifference to a man's will, his penis lifts its proud head according to its own preferences. Adam covered himself with a fig leaf for shame, but the shame is in being out of control, having to deal constantly with this disobedient part of himself. It is in our sexuality that we can most readily *see* the nature and effects of original sin.

It's probable that Augustine held these views his whole Christian life, but for a considerable portion of his episcopal career he was occupied with other matters. For years a controversy burned throughout the North African church concerning the validity and power of the sacraments. A group called the Donatists contended that sacraments administered by unworthy priests were unefficacious, that is, failed to administer grace; and they further believed that there were many unworthy priests in the church, the heirs and successors of

---

* Abraham Lincoln delivered his Second Inaugural Address in a similar spirit of perplexity—perplexity striving for faith—in the face of inscrutable divine action, or inaction. Quoting the Psalms, he said: "Fondly do we hope, fervently do we pray, that this mighty scourge of war may speedily pass away. Yet, if God wills that it continue until all the wealth piled by the bondsman's two hundred and fifty years of unrequited toil shall be sunk, and until every drop of blood drawn with the lash shall be paid by another drawn with the sword, as was said three thousand years ago, so still it must be said 'the judgments of the Lord are true and righteous altogether.'"

those priests who had compromised or repudiated their faith during the great persecution of Christians by the emperor Diocletian in the first years of the fourth century. (They tended to trust only members of their own party, who could presumably trace their lineage to those who had defied Diocletian's edicts.) Augustine combated Donatism, which he thought pernicious in several respects, with all his rhetorical energy. He preached sermons against them, wrote lengthy theological treatises to defy them, even produced poems in refutation of their ideas. But when these efforts proved insufficient—there was at times actual warfare between Donatists and Catholics, in which people on both sides were killed—he argued for legal prohibitions against the Donatists, which were eventually decreed by the emperor Honorius in the years 408–12: fines, beatings, exile. These laws proved at least temporarily effective, and Augustine, after complaining that in some cases his enemies were being treated too harshly, was able to turn his attention to other matters. (The purge was not complete or permanent, however: there were still Donatists in North Africa when Christians were swamped by the Muslim tide several centuries later.) For during these years life changed in Hippo Regius in some significant ways.

The change was brought about by the arrival of wealthy refugees from Rome. As the barbarians drew closer to the Eternal City, actually sacking it in 410, many members of the Roman social elite fled to safer shores. Hippo Regius was a popular choice; though to many aristocratic families it seemed dully provincial, it was thoroughly Roman, and it was (they thought) safe. Gradually, as Augustine's mind was freed from its obsession with the Donatists, he was able to pay more attention to these new arrivals; and as might be expected it was their theological views that especially interested him. Some of these he had already heard when he had gone to Carthage a few years earlier to lead a great anti-Donatist conference. One point in particular had then troubled him: some people were claiming that the church does not baptize infants for the same reason that it baptizes adults. In the Gospels and the book of Acts we are told that baptism is for the "remission of sins"—but of course, said these people, that does not apply to babies, who are sinless. We baptize them simply in order to consecrate them to Christ.

To Augustine these were deeply offensive words, but, as he later wrote, in the midst of a great ecclesiastical conference concerned with other matters, "there was no opportunity to contradict" the opinion; and in any case the people who held the opinion were not, Augustine thought, of any real influence. But on his return to Hippo Regius, as he heard from more of the refugees and explored these matters more fully, and as he got more letters from friends who informed him of the ideas current in Rome, he discovered that that view of baptism was more commonly shared in Italy than he would have imagined. There was already great controversy surrounding these opinions and others like them, because they were being articulated and promoted by a sincere and learned man, a British Christian living in Rome and then Palestine named Pelagius.

It is not perfectly clear what Pelagius actually believed on every point. Confronted, as he was on several occasions, by hostile inter-rogation in ecclesiastical courts, he gave accounts of his positions, which were often equivocal, sometimes disingenuous, and occasion-ally just plain false. Perhaps he was confused. By all accounts he was a pious man, ascetic in his habits—in writings of the time he is often referred to as a monk, though in fact he was a layman—and eager to see others follow the Christian life with the same dedication and zeal that seemed to come naturally to him. He does not appear to have been a conscious or willing rebel against the church. He even distinguished himself from some of his admirers by admitting that infants should be baptized, and baptized for the remission of sins. But he felt that an overemphasis on human sinfulness, especially on the inherited shackles of original sin, discouraged people from the practice of holiness. Reading accounts of the man's career makes one think of today's motivational speakers. Pelagius seems to have been something like the Tony Robbins of his time, full of exhortation and encouragement: "You can *do* it! You can *be* like Christ!" But, though on some occasions his rhetorical skills got him acquitted in ecclesiastical courts, by 418 the Council of Carthage (effectively led by Augustine) had condemned the major views associated with him, and he faded from public view. He never lacked for followers or defenders, but no one now knows when or where he died.

Pelagius and his followers were zealots impatient for sainthood and intolerant of spiritual mediocrity. Their biblical watchwords were John 14:15 ("If you love me, you will keep my commandments") and Matthew 5:48 ("You therefore must be perfect, as your heavenly Father is perfect"). Pelagius believed that perfect obedience to God is possible and therefore obligatory, or perhaps it would be better to say obligatory and therefore possible. Augustine's emphasis on the corruption of our will, never fully healed in this life, was to Pelagius not just wrong, but absurd. It would make no sense, he felt, for God to ask us to keep commandments that inherited sin would prevent us from keeping, and if Augustine replied that it is precisely in our weakness and failure that we must learn to seek the grace of God, Pelagius countered that the grace of God may be found in our ability to keep the commandments. Grace empowers us to avoid failure, rather than consoling us after we have failed. If Augustine emphasized our utter dependence on God, our permanent status as God's children, Pelagius replied, "Oh, grow up." And he meant it seriously; we should never content ourselves with dependence on God. We are meant to "come of age," precisely as a young man comes of age and is, in Roman legal terminology, "emancipated" from his father. So too we should eventually be *emancipatus a deo*, emancipated from the fatherhood of God—still technically God's children, but adult children.

This we all can achieve, thought Pelagius, because each of us possesses a perfectly free will. At any moment we can simply choose to obey God. As Pelagius's friend and devoted disciple Caelestius wrote, "It is the easiest thing in the world to change our will by an act of will." We live under no inherited curse that constrains and breaks us; that's just making excuses. In fact, he claimed, many people have lived without sinning at all, including people before Christ. To the counterclaim that death is the punishment for sin, and our sinfulness is witnessed by our mortality, Pelagius replied that mortality is a condition of humanity, and Adam would have died, had he never sinned. Moreover, what Adam did has no effect upon us except perhaps as a bad example, which we are free to ignore. And even if we follow that bad example and sin—grossly, repeatedly—our freedom is in no way compromised, and the next time temptation comes we will be just as free to reject it as we ever were. And just as culpable if we do not.

It is in many ways a strange picture of human behavior. As the nineteenth-century theologian Benjamin Warfield wrote, in his detailed account of this whole controversy, in Pelagius's view "After each act of the will, man stood exactly where he did before: indeed, this conception scarcely allows for the existence of a 'man'—only a willing machine is left, at each click of the action of which the spring regains its original position, and is equally ready as before to reperform its function. In such a conception there was no place for character: freedom of will was all." No character because that means (literally) what is *engraved*, set and established. The Pelagian good news is that at every moment you are free to obey; the (unstated, hidden) bad news is that at every moment you are equally free to sin, and at the instant of choice a lifetime of strict spiritual discipline will avail you nothing. And every choice is unimaginably momentous: the clear implication of the claim that perfection is both possible and obligatory is that those who fail to obey—at any point—are in danger of eternal damnation.

As Peter Brown has noted, "It is Pelagius, not Augustine, who harps on the terrors of the Last Judgment." And: "Like many reformers, the Pelagians placed the terrifying weight of complete freedom on the individual: he was responsible for his every action; every sin, therefore, could only be a deliberate act of contempt for God." They did acknowledge—as Mencius did before them and Rousseau would after them—that society somehow gets corrupted and therefore surrounds us with bad examples. But no more than Mencius or Rousseau would they acknowledge the power of those examples. Even an environment of utter iniquity is insufficient to compromise the freedom of a person's will or to excuse anyone who sins.

In the time of Pelagius and Augustine, Christianity had settled into its comfortable place as the official religion of the Roman Empire. In many parts of the Roman world Christianity had become as "normal" and "natural" as it is in America's Bible Belt today. No doubt the spiritual and moral standards for the Christian life had relaxed quite a bit since the days of persecution, when even the hint of Christian faith could cost a person his or her life; no doubt some restored tension, some call for a renewal of holiness, was surely needed. But Pelagianism, like many zealous movements of moral and spiritual reform, writes a recipe for profound anxiety. Its original word of encouragement ("You can do it!") immediately yields to the self-doubting question: "But *am* I doing it?" It makes a rigorous asceticism the only true Christian life—as Brown points out, "Pelagius wanted every Christian to be a monk"—and condemns even the most determined ascetic to constant self-scrutiny, a kind of self-scrutiny that can never yield a clear acquittal. You might have missed something; and in any case you could sin in the next five minutes and watch your whole house of cards crash down.

By contrast, Augustine's emphasis on the universal depravity of human nature—seen by so many then and now as an insult to human dignity—is curiously liberating. I once heard a preacher encourage his listeners to begin a prayer with the following words: "Lord, I am the failure that you always knew I would be." It is the true Augustinian note. Pelagianism is a creed for heroes, but Augustine's emphasis on original sin and the consequent absolute dependence of every one of us on the grace of God gives hope to the waverer, the backslider, the slacker, the putz, the schlemiel. We're all in the same boat as Mister Holier-than-Thou over there, saved only by the grace that comes to us in Holy Baptism. Peter Brown once more: "Paradoxically, therefore, it is Augustine, with his harsh emphasis on baptism as the only way to salvation, who appears as the advocate of moral tolerance: for within the exclusive fold of the Catholic church he could find room for a whole spectrum of human failings." This will not be the last time that the dark word of our "primeval contagion" brings a paradoxical light.

PERHAPS THIS IS AS GOOD a time as any to pause in this exposition and note that the Orthodox church—the church in the eastern part of the world, the Greek-speaking Christians dominated by Byzantium rather than Rome—followed a completely different path than the West on the question of original sin. Some of the greatest of the Eastern theologians can sound very much like Augustine. Maximos the Confessor, for instance, writes of the "ancestral sin" (*progonike hamartia*) that afflicts us all. But the overall Orthodox picture of human sinfulness is quite alien to anything that emerged in the West. Some less than careful historians claim that the Eastern fathers are Pelagian because of their insistence on the freedom of the human will, but that assumes that the conflict that emerged in the Latin world can identify the proper terms for the Greek church—which is not true. In fact, the Greek fathers think differently than the Latin theologians about the most fundamental question of all: what it means simply to be a human being. They tend to see all human beings not as *descen-*

dants of Adam but, in a mystical sense, *as* Adam—Adam is in a way the proper name of humanity. But then Holy Baptism gives us a new life *as* Christ, into whose Being we grow until we achieve our ultimate destiny, *theosis* ("deification"). The great historian of Byzantine theology John Meyendorff argues that although the Eastern fathers would have agreed that infants are not baptized "for the remission of sins," nevertheless they are "in Adam" and therefore subject to death; what baptism does is give them life.* This anthropology would have Pelagius and Augustine alike scratching their heads.

In general, it is fair to say that the conflict between Augustine and Pelagius established certain terms for debating human nature that, in one way or another, we still work with today. Are we tainted or clean, corrupt or integral, bound or free? To most of us in the West the Pelagian debates are quite familiar, and in the last chapters of this book we will see just how fully we are still engaged with the issues that those long-ago Christians wrestled over. Though our culture may not share their theology, it retains a remarkably large portion of their anthropology. In the Eastern world the key theological debates concerned very different matters, and in any event the course of those debates was curtailed when Islam conquered that part of the world. There is no reasonable way to map the experience of Christianity in the West onto Christian life and thought in other parts of the world.

---

* However, Eastern theologians have typically not thought that "all *sinned* in Adam"—that idea is a function of an odd translation into Latin of Romans 5:12—but rather that Adam's sin brought death into the world, which then produced sin. This is how many Greek theologians read Paul's Greek: "As sin came into the world through one man and death through sin, so death spread to all men; and *because of death,* all men have sinned." I must say that I have never found an explanation of this causal claim. Why would mortality *cause* people to sin? Freud has an answer to this, in his theory that the threat of death generates energetic activity—having sex, building, making, writing, whatever—as compensation. But Freud's model of the self is not that of the early Greek Christians; what their account might be remains unclear to me.

• • •

AUGUSTINE MUST HAVE THOUGHT, or at least hoped, that with the condemnation of Pelagian beliefs at the Council of Carthage he had at last put the heresies of purity and heroism to rest. (It's curious that the North African Donatists and the cultured Roman Pelagians, divergent as they were socially, shared this determination to separate the pure sheep from the impure goats.) But it was not to be. In the last years of his life he faced his most skilled and determined opponent, one who ruthlessly exposed weaknesses in Augustine's theology, one he could not defeat or even outlive. This was Julian of Eclanum.

Julian was born around the time Augustine became a Christian, about 386. When Julian was an adolescent and young man, Augustine corresponded regularly with his parents, who wrote from Italy to consult the great African bishop about the son's education. (Julian's father was a bishop himself, but of no intellectual distinction.) In one of his letters to Julian's father Augustine refers to the young man with deep paternal affection:

> As to the other five books, they seem to me scarcely worthy of being known and read by Julian, our son, and now our colleague, for, as a deacon, he is engaged in the same warfare with ourselves. Of him I dare not say, for it would not be true, that I love him more than I love you; yet this I may say, that I long for him more than for you. It may seem strange, that when I love both equally, I long more ardently for the one than the other; but the cause of the difference is, that I have greater hope of seeing him; for I think that if ordered or sent by you he come to us, he will both be doing what is suitable to one of his years, especially as he is not yet hindered by weightier responsibilities, and he will more speedily bring yourself to me.

But Julian did not come to Augustine; instead, he remained in Italy, a more highly cultured land than North Africa and one where the Pelagian influence was much stronger, especially within the upper classes, among whom Julian was raised and to whom he felt he belonged. (His father was a landowner as well as a bishop, and his mother a Roman noblewoman.) Culturally and intellectually, Julian came to believe himself superior to his former mentor, whom in his mature correspondence he referred to, sneeringly, as "the African." Julian—who not only lived among the rich but had acquired learning far beyond Augustine's, especially in Greek language and literature—saw the African as a man whose mind had shrunk to match the provincial backwater in which he lived.

It is hard not to see Julian, as his surviving writings represent him, as arrogant, but I am sure he preferred to think of himself as magnanimous. We know that he was generous. After the Goths had robbed southern Italy of its wealth and produce—having sacked and then grown tired of Rome itself in less than a week—a great famine ensued, and Julian sold much of his land to buy food for the people. But to those who promoted ideas he found dangerous or misbegotten, he was merciless, and Augustine was right, in responding to Julian's first salvos against him, to say that he was being "taunted." And as a veteran of many theological wars, the African was not inclined to respond to taunts with Christlike gentleness. He fired back again and again.

The situation must have been painful for him in several ways. Not only was a family friend whom he had thought of as a son offering him critique and scorn, but the whole controversy erupted after he had thought the Pelagians defeated. Once the Council of Carthage had condemned them, in 418, and Pelagius himself faded from view, the battle seemed over; but these events served only to rouse Julian, who had become a bishop himself just the previous year, to greater and greater anger. He had refused to repudiate Pelagianism and in consequence had been exiled. Fleeing to the protection of a sympathetic fellow bishop in the East (in St. Paul's homeland of Cilicia, as it happened, which Augustine would have found deeply ironic), he wrote from there book after book attacking the African. Augustine was nearly overwhelmed by the sheer volume of mocking response as well its fierceness—Julian's first attack on Augustine was in four books, and his counter to Augustine's response ran eight books further—and it all came at a time when he was worn out and eager to retire from controversy. Nearly sixty-five when the contest with Julian started, he was unable to keep up with the younger man's flow of invective, but not for lack of trying. He eventually managed a six-volume work of his own, but unlike Julian he had constant episcopal duties to attend to. He never finished what he hoped to be his final refutation of Pelagianism; a work in progress, *Contra Julianum*, was found on his desk at his death, in August of 430.

Julian himself lived another quarter century, almost all of it in continued exile from Italy. With every new pope elected and every new council summoned, he prepared himself to make his case, to achieve exoneration, to be restored to his homeland, his estates, his bishopric. Every hope was dashed; the remainder of his career consisted of one unfavorable judgment after another. He died in Sicily in 454, but bishops were still issuing condemnations of his work and views decades later.

Why did Julian fight so passionately, so unyieldingly, at such great personal cost, against the doctrine of original sin? He was obviously not the ascetic type, was rather a kind of mirror image of the abstemious and rigorous Pelagius. Whereas Pelagius and Augustine agreed, in general, about what counted as sin and disagreed mainly about whether we have the power to resist sin's temptations, Julian "defined deviancy down," as it were, and was more than willing to think that a life of wealth, ease, and pleasure was a gift from God to be enjoyed without any pangs of conscience. (Augustine's biographer James O'Donnell has recently emphasized how much the character of the African resembled that of Pelagius; each was an earnest, philosophically minded, ascetically inclined man from the distant provinces. In these respects Julian resembled neither of them.) Such an easygoing theologian seems an unlikely candidate to spend his life suffering exile and scorn, when a simple act of renunciation would have restored him to his ecclesiastical place and his worldly goods. One can only say that he believed Augustine's views to be dishonorable to God and to humanity and inconsistent with the beauty of the Gospel: "You ask me why I would not consent to the idea that there is a sin that is part of human nature? I answer: it is improbable, it is untrue; it is unjust and impious; it makes it seem as if the Devil were the maker of men.... You imagine so great a power in such a sin, that not only can it blot out the new-born innocence of nature, but, forever afterwards, will force a man throughout his life into every form of viciousness." Augustine's views, Julian thought, were equally insulting to God and to us.

Moreover, some Pelagians had been saying for several years that Augustine's theory of original sin made marriage and procreation themselves evil—after all, if sex even in marriage just brings more sin into the world, then how can such sex be good?—and that that theory was therefore inconsistent with biblical teaching that marriage is good. In 419 Augustine wrote a lengthy book, *On Marriage and Concupiscence*, refuting this charge and trying to clarify his (it must be said) extremely subtle views on this matter. It is perfectly clear that Augustine, throughout his career, had no desire to say anything good about sexual desire, even in marriage, but felt compelled to acknowledge that Scripture straightforwardly commends marriage and that Jesus's first miracle, the turning of water into wine, was performed in celebration of a marriage. In light of his need to reconcile his own preferences with the biblical witness, Augustine felt his way toward a delicate and perhaps indefensibly casuistical position: even "honest procreation" will be accompanied or prompted to some degree by lust. Our sexual organs are our *pudenda,* "shameful" members, which is why we cover them in public; they are not exactly evil, but they are "unseemly," and that remains the case even in sex between devout and devoted spouses. Such people "tolerate" lust, but they do not love it.

Augustine's discomfort with, even revulsion toward, the sexual sins he so loathed in his own past (and perhaps his present) appalled Julian. He countered by claiming: "But that pleasure and concupiscence were present in Paradise before the sin, the facts themselves declare. A way was thus paved for transgression through concupiscence, which by the beauty of the apple incited the eyes and spurred on the expectation of a pleasant taste. This concupiscence errs, then, when it does not keep within its bounds, but when it keeps to the limit of the permissible, it is a natural and innocent inclination." But the African lacked common sense in these matters and harped obsessively on one or two crazy ideas, says Julian: "What is as disgusting as it is blasphemous, this view of yours fastens, as its most conclusive proof, on the common decency by which we cover our genitals." "You surely have nothing to sell to inexpert ears except 'natural shame.'" "Truly, what discretion could keep us from laughing when we come to the examples that you supply?"

Again and again Julian speculates (and this must have stung the old man sharply) that Augustine's errors were the product of his Manichaean youth, of a dualism—especially a spirit/body dualism—that he only thought he had shaken off.* Augustine certainly responded as though stung: "You slanderously boast that my words

---

* There could be something to this. In his recent biography of Augustine, James O'Donnell contends that "Manicheanism was the one truly impassioned religious experience of [Augustine's] life. He was the sort of person who has a great love affair when young, sees that it just won't work, breaks it off, then settles down in a far more sober and sensible marriage. What he says and does for the rest of his life will be marked by firm allegiance and commitment to the late-blooming relationship, but the mark of the first never goes away, and some who knew him early will be unable to credit the marriage because they remember the passion."

contradict one another ... as though it could not be true that one and the same evil is inflicted on sinners both by the Devil's iniquity and God's justice."

But he does not use logic alone; he speculates about Julian's motives, as Julian had speculated about his. "You take advantage of the less gifted," he writes, suggesting that Julian's hyperintellectualism leads him to deceive others. (In this debate Augustine consistently presents himself as the plain-spoken ordinary man in contrast to Julian's highbrow.) Julian may not even believe that Augustine contradicts himself, but just "wishes others to think" that. It is not clear to Augustine whether Julian's mistakes stem from "malevolent calculation or deep blindness" (*et maligna calliditate aut tenebrosa caecitate*). In a nice phrase Augustine manages to hint that Julian is both overly enamored of pagan wisdom and unscrupulous in his use of it: "Since it is your custom joyfully to report any conclusions of secular authors which you think will help you ..."

But above all, in response to Julian's challenges he simply stiffens his resolve and, if anything, intensifies his views. To Julian's claim that his views on sexuality are "disgusting" and "blasphemous," he forthrightly asserts in a sermon that the sexual organs are the very site of original sin within us. When Adam and Eve after their act of rebellion become ashamed of their nakedness, what do they cover? "*Ecce unde,*" he cries out, "Look there!" or "Behold the place!"—the place from which original sin is passed on and where its effects may be seen. Adam in Eden, claims Augustine in his greatest work, *The City of God*—which he was working on through his war with the Pelagians—commanded his penis with his own unfallen will to rise when he needed it to rise and to sink into detumescence when its services were no longer required, rather like a drawbridge. But the Fall changed all this. Every involuntary erection, says Augustine, is embarrassing, "shameful," and should therefore remind us of the shame into which our first parents fell. As we have already noted, for

Augustine every involuntary erection reenacts Adam's disobedience. "You like rebellion?" God asks. "I'll show you rebellion." And Augustine insists all the more on these points as Julian continues to mock them. "With deference to your authority," Julian writes in a typical passage, "I say that you evade the point. Rather, learn that truth will remove your freedom to ramble."*

Likewise with Augustine's ever more forceful insistence that unbaptized infants surely are condemned to Hell. Some Eastern theologians—among them the great Origen of Alexandria—while accepting that without the grace of baptism even an infant had to be damned, had speculated that this could be explained by some preexistence of the soul during which damnation-worthy sins had been committed. Augustine denied this. Others thought that perhaps a special place in Hell might be reserved for these infants, a place where, though there was no blessing or union with God, there was also no suffering. Augustine replied that these infants surely descend into "everlasting fire" with all the other sinners. To this Julian howled with outrage:

---

* It is important to emphasize that even for Augustine it is not the body itself that is the source of evil. Augustine understood that when Paul contrasts the "flesh" and the "spirit," he is not speaking of the body and the soul. Paul is capable of designating, with reverence, the human body as "the temple of the Holy Spirit," and when in his letter to the Galatians he gives a list of the sinful "works of the flesh," he includes not just bodily sins like fornication, but also hatred, divisiveness, envy, and even witchcraft—sins that certainly do not have their origin in the body. For Paul, Augustine, and their many followers, the "flesh" is the rebellious will. The Christian picture is not the Gnostic or Manichaean one of an innocent spirit trapped in a corrupt body; it is of a person whose whole being is subject to corruption. Of course, this Pauline sense of balance has often been neglected by Christians who take comfort in Gnostic railings against the evils of the body. A wonderful corrective to that tendency is a poem called "A Dialogue Between the Soul and the Body," by the seventeenth-century English poet Andrew Marvell, in which Body rightly points out that it is often the junior partner, or accessory after the fact, in the enterprise of sin: "What but a Soul could have such wit / To build me up for Sin so fit?"

"Tell me then, tell me: who is this person who inflicts punishment on innocent creatures. . . . You answer: God. God, you say! God!" Julian cites scripture after scripture telling of God's love for us; he reminds Augustine that God loved us so much that he sent his Son to die on our behalf. Yet "he it is who sends tiny babies to eternal flames"? Julian had never imagined that anyone could so doubt the justice and fairness (*aequitas*) of God.

To this Augustine calmly replies with words given to the prophet Isaiah: "For my thoughts are not your thoughts, neither are your ways my ways, declares the Lord" (55:8, KJV). The justice of God is not to be confined to merely human idea of what justice is. (It is noteworthy, I think, that that passage in Isaiah—which follows a verse saying that God "will abundantly pardon"—emphasizes that God's justice differs from ours by being more merciful.) And Augustine would not even admit to any discomfort with a God whose thinking may be so completely alien to ours that when we say "God is just" we are effectively saying "God is we know not what." Rather, he reveled in the very scandal of it. In words the old man left on his desk at his death, he writes, chillingly, "This is the Catholic view: a view that can show a just God in so many pains and in such agonies of tiny babies."

This was not only Augustine's view, of course. Infant baptism for the remission of sins was so deeply ingrained in the life of the Christian church that, as we have seen, even Pelagius accepted it—a point that Augustine seized upon as a mark of Pelagius's inconsistency. Others embraced the doctrine with more enthusiasm. The great nineteenth-century historian W. E. H. Lecky writes of a "theologian who said 'he doubted not there were infants not a span long crawling about the floor of hell.'" Lecky gives no name, and it's possible that he made the story up, but surely there have been theologians who would have endorsed the idea. But Augustine, who was usually the most compelling and dynamic proponent of any view he happened to think was worthy of defense, did more than anyone else in the

Christian church to convince the world that unbaptized infants, because of the sin they had inherited from Adam, would burn in eternal conscious torment.*

The practical consequences of the triumph of this idea were immense. Even after the Reformation it was the stated position of leading English ecclesiastical lawyers that "a child before he is baptized is not a child of God but a child of the Devil"—a position that, as the historian Lawrence Stone has pointed out, is quite disturbing when one considers that as late as the eighteenth century there were many places in Europe where "no less than one-third of all infants died within fourteen days of birth" and "many of these babies ... had almost certainly not been baptized." It was on the grounds of this belief that the baptismal liturgy in the first English Book of Common Prayer (1549), following long medieval practice, included an exorcism:

---

* Just by way of contrast, it's worth noting that that great document of Jewish mysticism the *Zohar*, written in Spain in the thirteenth century, understands the death of infants in almost opposite terms. These children are the "oppressed ones," who are "without sin and without blame," and their sufferings pose a challenge to belief in God's justice. Therefore the *Zohar* insists that "the Holy One, blessed be He, does in reality love these little ones with a unique and outstanding love. He unites them with himself and gets ready for them a place on high close to him." Presumably the author of the *Zohar*—almost certainly a rabbi named Moses de Leon—knew the Christian church's position on the nature of infants and wished to distance himself and his people from it. It is also appropriate at this point to note that it is all but impossible for people raised in Western cultures at this point in history not to feel immense sympathy for the *Zohar* on this point and equally intense revulsion for the Augustinian view. I know that I cannot imagine a just God who does not behave in the way that Moses de Leon's God behaves. I am absolutely convinced that the *Zohar* is right and Augustine is wrong. I also know—notionally at least—that if I had been born in another age and time I might have held the Augustinian position with equal firmness. Yet this notional knowledge does not enable me any more seriously to imagine believing what Augustine believed.

I commaunde thee, uncleane spirite, in the name of the father, of the sonne, and of the holy ghost, that thou come out, and departe from these infantes, whom our Lord Jesus Christe hath vouchsaved, to call to his holy Baptisme, to be made membres of his body, and of his holy congregacion. Therfore thou cursed spirite, remember thy sentence, remember thy judgemente, remember the daye to be at hande, wherin thou shalt burne in fyre everlasting, prepared for thee and thy Angels. And presume not hereafter to exercise any tyrannye towarde these infantes, whom Christe hathe bought with his precious bloud, and by this his holy Baptisme calleth to be of his flocke.

This view led to sheer terror, and sometimes intolerable moral burdens, for generations of European mothers. If a woman struggled in childbirth, she would sometimes ask her local priest to conduct the exorcism while the child was still in her womb, in the belief that the fetus's devilish nature was causing the trouble or in the hope that, if the child must die, its soul could possibly be saved by the cleansing rite. Once a sickly child was born there began a desperate race to get the child baptized—not least because it was also believed that baptism conferred physical health as well as salvation and was therefore instrumental to a child's survival. (On the same grounds it was common for centuries, throughout Europe, to baptize sick pets or valuable farm animals.)

One effect of this doctrine might, however, be commended: churches led the way in pressing for the creation and enforcement of criminal statutes against infanticide. But these too are deep and troubled moral waters, because up until the eighteenth century in England and later in some other European cultures churches also enforced a rite of public shaming on unwed mothers. This meant that an unmarried woman who became pregnant could be forced to choose between infanticide—which, she was told, could damn her child to Hell as well as take its physical life—and a humiliating public exposure that, in rural areas and small towns, was likely to haunt her for the rest of her life.

And so, because a brilliant and devout old bishop could not resist the controversialist's temptation—to take even a caricature of his views and defend it to the death, rather than show dialectical weakness—the whole doctrine of original sin, in Western Christianity anyway, got inextricably tangled with revulsion toward sexuality and images of tormented infants. And there has never been a full and complete disentangling.

But a different vision of what it means to carry the burden of a sin inherited from Adam would, centuries later, emerge.

FOUR

The Feast of All Souls

The Night of the Long Knives, it came to be called: Adolf Hitler's purge, on the last night of June 1934, of potential rivals or dissidents among the *Sturmabteilung*—storm troopers, the military arm of the Nazi party also known as the SA. Two weeks later Hitler took public responsibility for the murders, claiming that they were necessary to the stability and safety of the German state. However, his claim that only seventy-seven died seems to have understated the carnage by a factor of five or perhaps far more. He even made a point of ordering the deaths of the manager and two headwaiters of a restaurant in Munich where, in their eager and ambitious youth, Hitler and the early Nazis had dreamed of power. Perhaps this was meant to erase even the memory of their former weakness.

Emboldened by the success of the purge, less than a month later Hitler ordered (or at least encouraged) an attempted takeover by Austrian Nazis of their country's government. The chancellor, Engelbert Dollfuss, had been pursuing strong-arm policies that resembled those of his neighboring leaders—he counted Musssolini as a friend, and indeed on the day of the attempted *putsch* his wife and children were paying a visit to the Italian dictator in Rome. But for the Nazis all that mattered was that Dollfuss was not himself a Nazi. On July 25, 1934, about a hundred of them broke into the Chancellery in Vienna, hoping to find and execute the whole Cabinet, but only Dollfuss was there. The small party that discovered him immediately shot him twice, once in the throat, and left him to bleed to death on the floor while they meditated their next move. The Chancellery was soon surrounded by Austrian army and police forces; the *putsch* failed as the Nazis panicked and scattered, and many of the conspirators were soon arrested. Hitler and the German Nazis disavowed complicity in or even knowledge of the attack.

Though he had been shot around noon, Dollfuss—a tough, tiny man with a round face and a mustache, not quite five feet tall, and only forty-one years old—remained alive for six more hours, and as his life drained away he continued to plead for a doctor and, more important to him, a priest. A faithful and devoted child of the Catholic Church, he wished to receive the sacrament of Extreme Unction; but the Austrian Nazis ignored him, just as German Nazis had ignored similar pleas from the victims of the Night of the Long Knives. In the trials of the conspirators their treatment of Dollfuss became public knowledge, and later many people would say that this was when they first began to understand the ruthlessness of the Nazis. But it is unlikely that anyone saw the events of June and July 1934 in quite the same light—in quite so lurid and world-historical a light—as a German emigré living in New England named Eugen Rosenstock-Huessy. For him the death of Dollfuss was also the death of a great vision of human community that had been born nearly a thousand years earlier.

BY 1934 ROSENSTOCK-HUESSY had already lived several lives. He was born into a Jewish family in Berlin, but at age eighteen converted to Catholicism. At age twenty-four he was appointed to the faculty of law at the University of Leipzig, thus becoming the youngest *Privatdozent* in Germany. He served as an officer in the German army in the Great War, fighting in the charnel house of Verdun. After the war, he refused to return to the academy, working instead for Daimler-Benz and founding an adult education program in Frankfurt called the Academy of Labor. Finally, he settled into teaching law at the University of Breslau—until the rise of the Nazis. He saw very early on that there would be no place for Jews in Hitler's Germany, or for Catholics either, if they wished to serve only the Christian God. So in 1933 he came to the United States as a lecturer in German art and culture at Harvard. But he soon came into conflict with other faculty, apparently because of his insistence on being openly Christian in his teaching and because of his disdain for supposedly "objective" models of intellectual inquiry. Two years later—just after the assassination of Dollfuss—he accepted a position at Dartmouth, where he remained until retirement, teaching "social philosophy" and writing a series of strange and terrifyingly learned books primarily concerning the intertwined destinies of Europe and Christianity. Though he never entered any intellectual mainstream and fit into no discipline—"I am an impure thinker," he liked to say—his work has inspired something like devotion in its relatively few readers, among them such luminaries as Martin Buber, Reinhold Niebuhr, and W. H. Auden.

For Rosenstock-Huessy, the vicious purge of the SA and the assassination of Dollfuss marked the extension of the Great War. It had not ended in 1919 with the Treaty of Versailles, but was continuing to do its evil work, revealing "its destructive force as the end of a civilization." In a vast book called *Out of Revolution,* which he had conceived while on the front in 1917 but did not write until his first years in America, Rosenstock-Huessy affirmed: "When Dollfuss, the Chancellor of Austria, was deliberately deprived of the comfort of the last anointment, when confession and the solace of a priest were denied to the victims of a German purge in 1934, . . . the Christian democracy of the dead and the dying was no longer real. Modern man believes, perhaps, in equality of birth. But he fancies that everyone dies alone and individually."

What did Rosenstock-Huessy mean by "the Christian democracy of the dead and the dying"? And why did he think it had ended in 1934? These questions can be answered only by going back to the tenth century, to a Benedictine monastery called Cluny, in eastern France. There was created what Rosenstock-Huessy believed to be one of the greatest revolutions in the history of Europe—perhaps the most important of them all, even though (or because) the revolution was not directly political, but rather intellectual and, above all, spiritual. And it would open to the world a wholly new dimension of belief in original sin.

THE KEY FIGURE in this revolution was the fifth abbot of Cluny, Odilo, who came to the abbey in the year 991, when he was not quite thirty years old. His ability and piety were apparently recognized immediately, because only three years later he was made abbot. At some point in his long tenure Odilo got an idea—or, as Rosenstock-Huessy puts it in his characteristically dramatic way, he "discovered world history as a universal order and fact" and made "the first universal democracy in the world." The legendary date is 998; historians think it could have been many years later.

Odilo's hagiographer, Peter Damian, writing just fifteen years after Odilo's death, tells the story of how it happened. A man showed up one day at the door of Cluny with news for the abbot. He had been a pilgrim, he said, a visitor to the Holy Land, and upon his return to Europe had been caught in a terrible Mediterranean storm and cast ashore, as so often happens, on a desolate island. Apparently, as also so often happens, he was the only survivor of the wreck, and—as *invariably* happens—the one resident of the island was a holy hermit. The hermit confided in this pilgrim that there was something extraordinary about the island. In a remote part of it was a chasm, an

opening in an outcrop of rock, from which could be heard the groan-
ing and wailing of tormented souls who had been condemned to that
dark place "for a fixed length of time." As the hermit listened, he heard
complaints from the demons in charge of those poor souls—perhaps the chasm opened onto their break room, where they smoked
cigarettes and shared the frustrations of the job—that the pain of
the sufferers was greatly lessened by the prayers of the faithful. More
specifically, these demons railed against the monks of Cluny, whose
prayers the tormented ones often pleaded for because of their special
efficacy. It was this that the pilgrim especially wanted Abbot Odilo to
know. Upon hearing this news Odilo determined to establish a new
day on his abbey's calendar, a day devoted to prayer for the souls who,
while not damned, had not entered into blessedness: November 2,
later to be called All Souls' Day.

The story of the founding of All Souls' told by Rosenstock-Huessy
and other modern historians is rather different, but all agree that the
holy day began at Cluny and was established by Odilo. The key to its
true meaning is its place on the calendar, immediately following All
Saints' Day on November 1.

Peter Brown, that great historian of early Christianity, has given
the most cogent explanation for the arising of the cult of the saints in
the late Roman world. He explains that the emphasis of early Christian preaching on judgment, on the human need for redemption
from sin, brought to the minds of common people—among whom
Christianity was early successful—their social and political condition. Having strictly limited powers to remedy any injustice they
might suffer or to clear themselves of any charges of wrongdoing,
they turned, when they could, to their social betters in hope of aid.
If a local patrician befriended them—became, for a time, their patron—then they had a chance of receiving justice or at least escaping
punishment. "It is this hope of amnesty," Brown writes, "that pushed

the saint to the foreground as *patronus*. For patronage and friendship derived their appeal from a proven ability to render malleable
seemingly inexorable processes, and to bridge with the warm breath
of personal acquaintance the great distances of the late-Roman social
world. In a world so sternly organized around sin and justice, *pa-
trocimium* [patronage] and *amicitia* [friendship] provided a much-
needed language of amnesty."

As the cult of saints became more and more deeply entrenched
in the Christian life, it made sense for there to be not just feast days
for individual saints, but a day on which everyone's indebtedness to
the whole company of saints—gathered around the throne of God,
pleading on our behalf—could be properly acknowledged. After all,
we do not know who all the saints are. No doubt men and women
of great holiness escaped the notice of their peers, but are known
to God. They deserve our thanks, even if we cannot thank them by
name. So the logic went, and a general celebration of the saints seems
to have begun as early as the fourth century, though it was not until
four hundred years later that Pope Gregory III actually designated
the first day of November as the Feast of All Saints.

It was Odilo's stroke of genius to place his new holiday as the
matching bookend to All Saints'. As the story the pilgrim brought
to Odilo makes perfectly clear, there are suffering souls who depend
on the ordinary mass of the faithful just as the ordinary mass of the
faithful depend on the saints. While the prayers of the pious monks of
Cluny held special power, no prayer by any Christian is useless. Some
are stronger than others, but all can pull on the same rope, and every
little bit of energy helps the cause. The Feast of All Souls became a way
for simple and quite unsaintly Christians to reciprocate, to participate
in the economy of prayer not just as receivers, but as givers.

This is what Rosenstock-Huessy meant when he claimed that the
creation of All Souls' Day marked "the first universal democracy in
the world." The saints have special access to God, they are our patrons

and friends, but then we too may befriend those departed who in their suffering are very far from God.*

Odilo and the succeeding abbots of Cluny were forcibly struck and deeply moved by what they took to be the chief lesson of the pilgrim's story: the power of prayer. It was their excitement over this power that led them to celebrate the new feast with particular exuberance and festivity: no bell at Cluny was left unrung on All Souls' Day. Intercessory prayer became the obsession of Cluny and the many monastic houses (in France and elsewhere) it founded and oversaw. The great historian of medieval monasticism David Knowles says that "the observance and discipline of Cluny eliminated all extra-liturgical activity for the monks following the life of the greater houses, and thus Cluny had little or no share in the educational and intellectual revivals of the period, and her monks produced little artistic work within the cloister." Knowles goes on to note that when a young Englishman with theological interests named Anselm (later St. Anselm of Canterbury) was trying to decide whether to become a religious, he decided against applying to Cluny because he knew that the strict order there (*districtio ordinis*) left no time for the scholarship Anselm loved and meant to pursue. At Cluny prayer was all.

---

* But where are the suffering, exactly? This is not clear from the story the pilgrim told Odilo. As Jacques Le Goff has shown, in his magisterial study *The Birth of Purgatory,* when the first versions of the story appeared purgatory had not yet been invented. There had been for many centuries vague comments by preachers and theologians indicating some kind of intermediate fate for Christians who were not saints but not rebels or unbelievers either, and by the time of Odilo those comments had not grown much less vague—though the original version of the pilgrim's story, recorded by a monk named Jotsuald and copied by Peter Damian, does say this: "For a fixed length of time the souls of sinners are purged there in various tortures." By the time that Jacobus de Voraigne had produced his great compendium of saints' tales, the *Golden Legend,* in the thirteenth century, the idea of purgatory had crystallized, and the story of Odilo and the pilgrim was fit neatly into the emergent myth.

The Cluniac vision of all Christians joined in a vast circle of the prayerful, loving and interceding for one another, is a powerful one. Just as there are saints whose spiritual power and even existence are unknown to us, so too there are poor suffering souls in a place of torment whose names are equally unknown and who are therefore in particularly dire straits. Thus in the *Sarum Primer*—a vastly influential collection of liturgical prayers developed at Sarum, near modern Salisbury, in England—there is a poignant "prayer to God for them that be departed, having none to pray for them." Such poor souls, "either by negligence of them that be living, or long process of time, are forgotten of their friends and posterity"; thus they "have neither hope nor comfort in their torments."

In societies that place a great emphasis on familial duty, a phrase in that Sarum prayer can be stinging: "by negligence of them that be living." Thus an anthropologist named Andrew Orta has recently reported on the way All Souls' Day is practiced among the Aymara people in the Bolivian highlands: they build household altars and pray for all the ancestors whose names they know, and then, when memory fails, they pray for all the unknown ancestors as *laqa achachilas*—"dust grandparents."

Such rites, of course, are not confined to Christian cultures that keep the Feast of All Souls. In China, for instance, there has been for many centuries a festival called Chung Yuan, "Feast of the Hungry Ghosts," which is intended to comfort (and perhaps to placate or appease) the spirits of the dead who have no living descendants to care for them. But this lacks the celebratory element that has always characterized All Souls since the bells first rang for it at Cluny a millennium ago. The celebration arises when people believe that they have the power to lessen the pain and hasten the blessedness of those for whom they pray, whether ancestors or strangers. Thus in many Hispanic countries, where All Souls tends to take the form of the Day of the Dead, a festive spirit typically predominates. In the Philippines, for instance, the holiday—which is exceeded in importance only by Holy Week and Christmas—offers an opportunity for family reunions: whole extended families march to the cemeteries and camp out for a day or two, singing, playing games, and in general just keeping the ancestors company.

Such is the power of this tradition that it can continue in some form long after its original purpose has been forgotten. In his book *Hamlet in Purgatory* Stephen Greenblatt mentions the practice of distributing "soul cakes" on All Souls' Day, which, though violently repudiated by an influential cleric named John Mirk in Shropshire in the mid-fifteenth century, "evidently survived, at least in rural areas, into the eighteenth century." But one L. H. Hayward, writing to the British journal *Folklore,* insists that the practice was still going on in "several villages near Oswestry" in 1937. He even records the rhyme the children of West Felton chanted to get their cakes:

> *Soul, Soul, for a souling cake,*
> *I pray, good missus, a souling cake,*
> *Apple or pear, plum or cherry,*
> *Anything good to make us merry,*
> *Up with your offer and down with your pon,*
> *Give us an answer and we'll be gone.*

It is the same rhyme used four hundred years ago. For all I know some English children use it still. John Mirk must be spinning in his grave.

THE IMPORTANCE OF the All Souls' tradition for our story here is that the "democracy" it promotes is based on nothing more or less than *judgment*—the judgment that each of us stands under because of our inheritance from Adam: original sin. We should not underestimate how countercultural the idea of All Souls' was, and is, and what comfort it could give to people who lived (as almost all Christians did from late Roman times until quite recently) in highly stratified, even ossified, societies. We have already caught a glimpse of this in the picture of the saint as friend and patron for those who could have no intercession from the socially powerful and no hope of rising to a higher place themselves. But also consider the following story, from fifteen hundred years later.

In the middle of the eighteenth century, the great English evangelist George Whitefield (of whom we will hear more later) gained the friendship and patronage of Selina, Countess of Huntingdon, who strove to spread his message to her fellow aristocrats. But Whitefield's relentless emphasis on the universal burden of original sin—it was the point from which he consistently began his preaching—repulsed some of the countess's acquaintances precisely because of its egalitarianism. "I thank Your Ladyship for the information concerning the Methodist preachers," wrote the Duchess of Buckingham, failing to grasp that Whitefield was not a Methodist, but "the doctrines are most repulsive and strongly tinctured with impertinence and disrespect towards their Superiors, in perpetually endeavouring to level all ranks and to do away with all distinctions. It is monstrous to be told you have a heart as sinful as the common wretches that crawl on the earth. This is highly offensive and insulting; and I cannot but wonder that your ladyship should relish any sentiment so much at variance with high rank and good breeding." It must be acknowledged that the duchess, who was rumored to be the illegitimate daughter of King James II, took these high thoughts to an extreme. Sir Horace Walpole wrote, with catty wit, that "she was more mad with pride than any mercer's wife in bedlam." But it is certainly true that the doctrine of original sin is utterly "at variance with high rank and good breeding." The message of All Souls' offends every aristocracy, real or imagined, traditional or inverted—every attempt to separate "us" from "them."

Perhaps when Rosenstock-Huessy identified the death of the "universal democracy" with the rise of the Nazis, he was not aware that a hundred and forty years earlier French revolutionaries had confiscated the relics of St. Odilo and burned them, in public, *sur l'autel de la Patrie*—"on the altar of the Fatherland."

Of course Christians themselves, and not just their enemies, have often acted and spoken as though no universal democracy of sinners under judgment exists. Consider the words of the church's chief Inquisitor in Llerena, Portugal, in the early seventeenth century, on the persistent problem of the *conversos* or Marranos, the Jewish converts to Christianity whose sincerity was to the Gentiles always suspect: "From the moment of its conception, every fetus permanently carries with it the moral attributes—in the case of the Marranos, the moral depravity—of its parents." Such a statement affirms the inheritance of sin, but denies the universality of that inheritance; in it we catch a glimpse of the future of racism, we discern the specter of what would become, centuries later, the eugenics movement and the Nazi cult of pure blood. These new Christians, *cristãos novos,* are but Marranos—swine—and from their parents they inherit only filth; we *cristãos velhos,* old Christians, by contrast inherit *limpeza de sangue,* purity or cleanliness of blood. But this is as much as to say that we old Christians trust in our own merits, not in our Savior's; for if we must trust in him, then we must not be clean, we must be no different from the Marranos. And that cannot be. Our sense of family is offended as deeply as was the Duchess of Buckingham's sense of class and rank. So we purchase our superiority by denying—the case of the Inquisitor almost explicitly—the ancient and crucial doctrine of the church that all have sinned and are in equal need of God's mercy. We sacrifice the Marranos on the altar of family, of blood, of what will one day be called our genes.

. . .

THOSE EUROPEAN CHRISTIANS entering almost any medieval church, or one of later date, would surely have found any number of reminders of their social differentiation—though perhaps not as many as the Duchess of Buckingham would have liked. After the Reformation, in many churches the wealthy had their own pews, "box pews," which were largely enclosed, with locking doors; and there was of course, always, an elaborate protocol of entrances and exits and placements. (It was not uncommon up through the nineteenth century for a church full of people, including the priest, to have to wait to begin the service until the local gentry or aristocracy showed up.) But the architecture of churches often conveyed a message that undermined, or even undid, the hierarchies of this world. That message is contained in one of the last clauses of the Nicene Creed: "He will come again in glory to judge the living and the dead, and his kingdom will have no end."

In the Christian East a common and extraordinarily powerful decoration was the painting, on the ceilings of churches, of Christ returning in this glory. *Christos Pantocrator* such icons are called, "Christ, Ruler of All." In western Europe a more common representation is the "Judgment window" (or wall), usually at the west end of the church—opposite from the altar. Oddly, the most famous painting of the Last Judgment, that of Michaelangelo in the Sistine Chapel, is found at the altar end; but the more usual placement may be seen in the stained-glass windows of many great cathedrals, including Chartres. But it's important to note that such windows were a feature of many relatively ordinary parish churches as well. One of the most vivid and powerful Judgment windows ever produced may be found in England in the rather ordinary parish church of St. Mary in Fairford, Gloucestershire. Ordinary in size and historical importance, that is; extraordinary in its decoration. John Tame, the cloth merchant who paid to have it built in the last decade of the fifteenth century, spared no expense in bringing the best Flemish glaziers and sculptors to Fairford and expected plenty of thanks in return, as a poem on his tomb indicates: "For Iesus love pray for me / I may not pray now pray ye / With a pater noster and an ave / That my payns relessyd may be."

Given that the entrances of such churches were typically near the west end, the parishioners as they entered would have found their Lord looming above them—altogether too close, one might imagine—in his role as cosmic Judge. It must have been something of a relief, at least for those susceptible to powerful visual impressions, to turn their backs on this imposing figure and face the altar, where they could focus on the meal of the reconciled, the Body and Blood given for them. (Though in the Middle Ages, when Communion was rarely given to the laity, their chief hope would have been to catch a glimpse of the Host as it was elevated by the priest on the other side of the rood screen.) But there behind them the great Judge stood, all the same, as though breaking into their world through the medium of the glass. I suspect that for many Christians the experience of seeing such a window in the late afternoon, as the sun flashed the glass into brilliance, was simply terrifying. This was a Judgment the whole world would one day have to face, which in a certain sense is always going on. After all, those whom the hermit heard moaning in their torments had already been judged, and harshly, had they not? (Thus Franz Kafka's famous comment: "Only our concept of Time makes it possible for us to speak of the Day of Judgment by that name; in reality it is a summary court in perpetual session.") No one who walked into that church, of whatever rank or wealth or wit or skill, could claim to be immune to that Judgment or capable of negotiating with the Judge.

It is therefore not surprising that the Feast of All Souls came quickly to be associated with the Day of Judgment, as it also was with Purgatory. The greatest hymn of All Souls' Day is one that is now more familiar to us from requiem Masses, especially in Mozart's setting, the "Dies Irae" attributed to Thomas of Celano.

Judex ergo cum sedebit,
quidquid latet apparebit:
nil inultum remanebit.

Quid sum miser tunc dicturus?
Quem patronum rogaturus,
cum vix justus sit securus?

Rex tremendae majestatis,
qui salvandos salvas gratis,
salva me, fons pietatis.

Recordare, Jesu pie,
quod sum causa tue vie:
ne me perdas illa die.

Roughly and periphrastically: "Therefore, when the Judge sits in judgment, what is hidden shall be revealed; no crime will remain unpunished. Who am I, a miserable wretch, to dictate anything? What patron could I call on, when even one of the just cannot feel secure? King of tremendous majesty, who freely saves your redeemed, fount of pity, save me. Remember, pitying Jesus, that you came because of me: let me not be lost on that day."

THE ORDINARY CHRISTIAN standing—there would have been no pews—in his or her parish church or in a great cathedral would therefore have been bodily poised between Judgment and Mercy. To stand in a church was to occupy a frozen moment, that terrible Second Coming "in glory to judge the living and the dead" paused, as it were, yielding to the sinner just enough time to run to the altar to receive the grace uniquely dispensed there. A vast cosmic tale was being unfolded in the church, and every person had to decide his or

her place in it. And if this message was articulated in the very building itself, it was reinforced by the cycles of feasts and fasts, seasons of
celebration and penitence, that comprised the church year. In space
and time alike, then, a world-historical drama was being enacted, but
at the same time a decision was being pressed on the poor Christian:
what is *your* story, in the midst of this universal Story?

This sense of the Christian life as a drama arose early in the history of the faith, and the conviction of being infected, afflicted, by the
inherited curse of sin was its motive engine. We have already seen how
Augustine described his conversion as the product of a great internal
debate, a volley of argument and counterargument reminiscent of
the rapid-fire exchanges that characterize moments of high tension
in Greek and Roman tragedy. But such tension and uncertainty per-
sisted even among convinced or lifelong Christians, because of the
ongoing sense of dividedness that we discussed in the previous chapter. And the specifically dramatic character of this dividedness, seen
in light of the cosmic story, found a lasting form of expression in the
work of one of Augustine's contemporaries, a Christian Latin poet
from Spain named Prudentius.

Prudentius's magnum opus, the *Psychomachia* ("Soul Struggle"),
though a laughably incompetent work, made the poet lastingly famous. As C. S. Lewis remarked, "While it is true that the *bellum intestinum*"—internal warfare—"is the root of all allegory, it is no less
true that only the crudest allegory will represent it by a pitched battle."
Prudentius knows how important Patience is among the virtues, but
how to represent Patience in battle? His answer is to have a heavily
armored Patience simply stand there, doing nothing, while Ira (Wrath)
attacks wildly, repeatedly, and of course unsuccessfully. Having run out
of ideas but not out of fury—how could Wrath cease to be wrathful?—
Ira simply commits suicide. Patience rewarded, indeed.

Lewis also calls our attention to the poetic difficulty Prudentius is
faced with when he must portray the battle between Superbia (Pride)

and Mens Humilis (Humility). When Superbia falls into a hole in the ground—comical enough in itself—and is thus defeated, "the moment is now come," writes Lewis, "when Humility must triumph and yet remain humble." Prudentius solves this problem by saying that Mens Humilis "uplifts her face with moderated cheer." Lewis's comment: "Nothing could suggest more vividly the smirk of a persevering governess who has finally succeeded in getting a small boy in trouble with his father."

But, in all his haplessness, Prudentius managed to set in motion a great tradition of depicting the life of the sinner-who-would-be-saved as a play, a kind of staged contest among the various forces at work within a divided self—and, on this account of human life, which has created a universal democracy of sinners under judgment, all selves are divided. That's why the most famous play depicting the human condition bears the name it does: *Everyman*.

Everyman (from about 1485) is the most famous of the medieval "morality plays," or "moralities," but not the most typical. Our protagonist is not actually fighting the *bellum intestinum,* because God has sent Death for him, so there's no *bellum* left to fight: game over. There's a comical moment at the beginning when God, on his throne in paradise, rehearses his actions on behalf of humankind and ruefully concludes, "I coude do no more than I dyde, truely." The sinful nature of those humans is tough to overcome. Thus Death says to Everyman: "In the worlde eche lyvynge creature / For Adams synne must dye of nature." So Everyman just has to reckon up his accounts and find out whether he's in the black or in the red. He discovers, for instance, that Goods—his worldly possessions—won't help him. In the end he has Knowledge, who teaches him about his sinful condition and counsels him to seek forgiveness for his "grievous offense," and Good Works, and they turn out to be enough. Luckily for him.

But for those who are not *in articulum mortis*—"at the moment of death"—the more applicable morality play might be the slightly earlier *Castle of Perseverance,* with its protagonist Mankind. Here we see the true inheritance of Prudentius; Abstinence, Charity, Industry, and their teammates are lined up against Gluttony, Backbiter, and—everyone's first pick in the annual fantasy psychomachia draft—Lust-Liking.

But of particular interest to modern readers might be the scene early in the play when the Good Angel and Bad Angel enter and position themselves at either side of Mankind, for this is a theme we know well. Perhaps, if we are of a certain age, we have seen it in a Tom and Jerry cartoon, in *Animal House,* or—if we or our children are of more recent vintage—in *The Emperor's New Groove.* And even as I write these words I have just seen a new incarnation, in an Apple computer ad: as PC looks at the lovely photo book made by Mac, a red-suited devil appears at his left shoulder, urging him to tear the book to pieces, while a white-suited angel at his right encourages him to loosen up and have fun.

But wherever we see or have seen it, we always recognize the theme by its two invariable features. First, the persuasive resources of the good angels seem weak or insipid in comparison to the bold, confident sales pitches of the devils, who always seem to know just what buttons to push and who therefore always win the day. And second, the scene is always played for laughs. But in *The Castle of Perseverance,* Mankind isn't laughing; nor, as we shall see, was the great Doctor Faustus.

Whether played for laughs (as we play it now) or for terror (as our ancestors did), the theme tells us something about original sin, for it is because of original sin that the devils always have a leg up on the better angels of our nature. The angel-and-devil-on-the-shoulders motif seems to tell us that we have a choice. It happens at a moment of decision, it pauses the action (very much as the Judgment windows of medieval churches pause history) and gives us the opportunity to turn aside from our nefarious schemes—but damned if we don't always make the same choice, as though freedom of the will was, well, illusory. And so, now as theatrical or living-room audience rather than as worshipers, we once more confirm our membership in the universal democracy of sinners under judgment. If seeing that can bring us to giggles rather than paroxysms of penitence, that can only be because we don't take sin as seriously as our ancestors did. We don't think it's going to land us in Hell.

FIVE

A Few Words About the Devil

For our purposes in this entangled narrative, there's a telling moment in the 2004 movie *Hellboy*. The story of Hellboy, for the uninitiated, begins near the end of World War II when Rasputin—yes, *that* Rasputin, you only thought he died in 1917—is working with the Nazis to bring about some nightmarish, infernal way to destroy the Allies and rule the world. But the dark scheme is thwarted just in time by arriving American soldiers, the portal to Hell is closed, and all that remains on this side of the divide is a tiny red newborn demon, whom the soldiers nickname Hellboy. He is taken and raised by one Professor Bruttenholm and, sixty years later, is an enormous red demon who files what would otherwise be long curved horns down to flat nubs and contends against the forces of darkness, especially when they invoke supernatural powers. (For us the horns are the definitive sign of devilishness, though earlier generations of Christians thought it was cloven hooves—as Othello is dying he contemplates checking to see if Iago has hooves, but dismisses the idea as a myth—and the thirteenth-century student of Kabbalah Issac of Acre believed that there is one absolutely reliable means of discerning whether a creature is a devil: devils don't have thumbs.)

But in the film Hellboy runs into some trouble. Rasputin is back—never mind how, if you haven't seen the movie—and convinces Hellboy to do what Rasputin says he was made for: to open once more that portal to the demonic realm, so that now the whole world will be destroyed. But just when Hellboy is about to obey—after his great horns have grown in seconds to their full length, their "natural" length, as we might put it—his colleague Agent Myers shouts out, "Remember who you are!" and then throws him a bracelet that Rasputin had earlier torn from Hellboy's wrist. A small cross dangling from the chain burns a white mark in Hellboy's red hand. Myers's imperative seems a strange one, because the events of the moment are *showing* who Hellboy is: a demon. But after a moment of thought, Hellboy turns away from the great lock he's supposed to open and breaks off his horns. When Rasputin asks, "What have you done?" he shoves one of the horns into Rasputin's belly and stage-whispers, "*I chose.*"

At the very beginning of the movie, Professor Bruttenholm had mused in a voice-over: "What is it that makes a man a man? Is it his origins, the way things start? Or is it something else, something harder to describe?" These questions find their answer at the other end of the movie, when Hellboy has destroyed the forces of evil, saved the planet, and brought his beloved back from Hell. Agent Myers thinks these concluding words: "What makes a man a man? a friend of mine once wondered. Is it his origins, the way he comes to life? I don't think so. It's the choices he makes. Not how he starts things, but how he decides to end them."

I'm tempted to say that this is pure Pelagianism—so what if you're the spawn of Hell and the scion of Lucifer? No need to let *that* stop you!—but it isn't, not quite. It's more realistic than Pelagianism, at least as it was articulated by Julian and Pelagius himself, and a good deal more compelling as well. Because they believed that moral perfection is available to everyone, they needed to maintain that the human will is at every moment free to make the choice between virtue and righteousness; years, even decades of sin do not weaken it. If they could not convince their highborn and high-living audiences of this, the task of holiness would have appeared far too strenuous. But Hellboy, after years—decades—of moral training and the practice of service, is still vulnerable to what some might call his "nature," his demonic DNA. He's *Hell*boy, after all. As Professor Bruttenholm says to Myers, "He was born a demon; we can't change that." But then he continues, "But you will help him, in essence, to become a man." So although demonic DNA is not something that can be erased, it can be overcome. But this is not something that just anyone could do, in just any circumstances. The wise and patient fatherhood of Professor Bruttenholm was powerful; so too is the community of "freaks" within which he lives. (As one of them says, "If there's trouble, all us freaks have is each other.") But even this might not be enough for someone with a will less strong than Hellboy's. He's special in that regard; his willpower is, we might say, heroic—or even superheroic. He ain't Everyman, that's for sure.*

---

* Oddly, Hellboy's treatment of these issues echoes quite strongly a more iconic figure in popular culture: Harry Potter. Near the end of *Harry Potter and the Chamber of Secrets,* Harry confesses his fear that he really belongs in Slytherin House with all the Dark wizards. After all, doesn't he speak Parseltongue (snake language) just like Lord Voldemort? Doesn't he share several of Voldemort's personality traits? Don't they even *look* alike? But to this fearful puzzlement Albus Dumbledore, the wise headmaster of Hogwarts, replies, "It is our choices, Harry, that show what we truly are, far more than our abilities." (So what if you've been marked by the powers of the Dark Lord?—etc.)

And I might also add that the nature/nurture position taken by the Potter books is quite similar to that taken by the Hellboy series, though this might not be obvious at first. Hellboy is the beneficiary of good and careful training—careful because his adoptive father knows where he comes from—while Harry gets from his adoptive parents, the Dursleys, nothing but neglect. Yet in Harry's peculiar situation this is also a benefit, because that neglect prevents him from thinking that he's important; it trains him (though the Dursleys never thought of this) in humility. If Harry had been raised as his cousin Dudley was—coddled, praised, every good action overrewarded and every act of cruelty or greed excused—he would have been much easier prey for Voldemort's message of pride and power. Yet with all that said, it's vital to note that what is emphasized about Harry from the first book of the series on, perhaps above all other traits, is his strength of will. In other respects he's an ordinary kid, at least for a wizard, but in that one area he's a superhero—like Hellboy.

But even if Hellboy is extraordinary, superheroic, and all that, nevertheless the prime message the filmmakers wanted to get across, surely, is that origin is not destiny. No matter where you start, it's possible, at least, to choose. If in practice everyone cannot be like Hellboy, there is no theoretical or absolute barrier to what the New Testament calls *metanoia,* repentance, literally "turning around," even if everything in your "nature" seems to be working against you. Hellboy's horns grow of their own accord, but he can file them down, and if things get out of hand, he can even break them off. This is the obvious point of the movie's opening and closing speeches. And it's enough to make one think not just about us, but also about the one we call Satan, formerly known as Lucifer, son of the morning.

A wonderful story is told about St. Martin of Tours, who was born in what is now Hungary about forty years before Augustine and whose early career was as a Roman soldier. Probably when still in his twenties, he had a dramatic conversion to Christianity, abandoned military life, and eventually founded one of the first Christian monastic communities. The story says that because Martin and his fellow monks achieved such deep piety and lived such pure and righteous lives, Satan was angered and began to appear to Martin to tempt him to sin. Failing at that, the Evil One turned, as he so often has throughout his career, to biblical exegesis. Does not the Lord himself counsel us to be perfect (Matt. 5:48)? Does not St. Paul the Apostle simply assume that he and his fellow Christians are perfect (Phil. 3:15)? Does not the beloved disciple John say that whoever abides in Christ does not sin (1 John 3:6)? Yet Martin and his monks still, sometimes, sin; they are therefore damned. The wages of sin is death. They belong to Satan, not to God: it is clearly demonstrated in Scripture itself!

To this Martin replied—so says the tale—O Prince of this world, not only can I and my monks be saved, thanks to the infinite mercy of the Lord Jesus Christ, who died for us, but you too, if you repent, can be saved! It is not too late! Turn from your dark ways, your rebellion, your pride! Turn to the God who loves you, beg his pardon, and He will forgive! And upon hearing these words Satan departed from Martin and troubled him no further.

This is, I think, my favorite story about any saint. Such zeal for the Gospel! And such hopefulness, to think that even the Great Rebel himself is capable of amendment of life! And why not? Is there anything in Scripture or the teachings of the church that makes Martin's hope unwarranted?

Well, yes, there is, at least if the enigmatic book of Revelation is any guide. It tells us that at a certain point in a very complex history, "Satan will be released from his prison and will come out to deceive the nations that are at the four corners of the earth, Gog and Magog, to gather them for battle; their number is like the sand of the sea. And they marched up"—the strange shifts in tense are in the original Greek—"over the broad plain of the earth and surrounded the camp of the saints and the beloved city, but fire came down from heaven and consumed them, and the devil who had deceived them was thrown into the lake of fire and sulfur where the beast and the false prophet were, and they will be tormented day and night forever and ever." But good for Saint Martin all the same. Better to hope too much than too little.

In Milton's *Paradise Lost*, again, God's first speech raises and deals self-justifyingly with three matters of import. (Like God in *Everyman*, he wants to make it clear that he has done his part and that any catastrophe that follows can't be pinned on him.) First he states that, as we have already noted, Adam and Eve were "sufficient to have stood, though free to fall," and that if, being omniscient, he knew that they would in fact fall, that knowledge "had no influence on their fault, / Which had no less prov'd certain unforeknown." Second, he reminds everyone gathered around his throne—and we the audience who overhear—that his plan is to be merciful to Adam and Eve and their descendants, even though justice does not require this of him.

But third, he wants to explain why he has no intention of extending such mercy to Satan and his fellow rebels. "The first sort," he says, not dignifying the devils by giving them a name, "by their own suggestion fell, / Self-tempted, self-deprav'd: Man falls deceiv'd / By the other first: Man therefore shall find grace, / The other none." Case closed.

Unde hoc malum? The ancient question. Where does such evil come from? Why do we possess this "universal human frailty" that Plato's Athenian spoke of? Why do we inflict such terrible and constant damage on others and ourselves? The story of the Fall itself does not answer this question unless it is accompanied by something like a doctrine of original sin, some explanation of why the sin of Adam and Eve is repeated in each generation. But if by *hoc malum* you mean not just the evil that human beings enact, but rather evil anywhere and everywhere in the cosmos, then at that point original sin loses its explanatory power. We know a little bit about how Adam and Eve fell—though, as previous chapters have shown, our knowledge even of that is limited by our inability to imagine their prelapsarian state—and we know that that Fall was aided and abetted by the serpent, the prototype of all subsequent devils perched on all subsequent shoulders. But how the serpent got into that condition is beyond our ken. Genesis only tells us that "the serpent was more crafty than any other beast of the field that the Lord God had made." (It doesn't even identify the serpent with Satan.) But why is his craft devoted to deceit and rebellion? To say that he and his followers were "self-tempted" is not to say much. In the satirical *Political History of the Devil*, which Daniel Defoe wrote in 1726, the question hangs in the air: "How came seeds of crime to rise in the Angelic Nature?"

Here again we might turn to Milton, who, for all his flaws and oddities of mind, meditated more deeply on these issues than anyone. Yet on this particular question he offers little assistance. The story Raphael recounts for Adam and Eve begins with a heavenly decree:

God the Father names his Son as Messiah. Raphael then goes on to explain that Lucifer (as he was then known)—even though he was not himself "the first Arch-Angel . . . in favour and preeminence"— was "fraught with envy" at this announcement. He "could not bear / Through pride that sight, and thought himself impaired." But how did Lucifer become so prideful? How did he come to have what we might call delusions of grandeur, an inaccurate self-image, so that he truly believed himself to be greater and more worthy than God's own Son? What is most significant about this passage is that Raphael makes no attempt whatsoever to explain the situation. He simply and matter-of-factly reports it. Perhaps—and here we might contemplate Milton's strategy of having God use an intermediary to convey the heavenly history to his newest creations—he just does not know. Raphael, like Adam and Eve, is obedient (and unlike them will remain so). There is no reason to think that he truly understands Satan.

It is fascinating, given all the speculative matters into which Milton plunges in the deep waters of this vast poem, that at this point, which we might think to be crucial, he offers us nothing at all. I think this is his way of informing us that the matter is *not* crucial, in fact not even relevant to the story he is telling, which is *our* story. To know our own condition is vital; to know that of other creatures is not. How Adam and Eve moved from obedience to rebellion we must understand; how Satan and his allies made the same move is a matter of indifference. In Defoe's mind the question hangs in the air; Milton dismisses it with a wave of the hand. The story of original sin—the story of this book—is our story; the story of the rebel angels remains to be told elsewhere and by beings quite other than ourselves.

IF THE FIRST TEMPTATION in human history was external—via this inexplicably crafty serpent—none of the subsequent ones have been, at least not straightforwardly. Everyone who read Prudentius in his time or who later watched *Everyman* was surely aware on some level that what is being represented in Superbia or Lust-Liker is a kind of undefined combination or conflation of external, demonic forces and our own now natural sinful inclinations. Where do the devils stop and where does original sin begin? When we read of the devils being "self-tempted," do we not shudder with recognition? Whatever the situation might have been for Adam and Eve, for us the devil on our shoulder is only truly dangerous because of the devil that's already inside us. That's why, in these comical depictions that we moderns specialize in, the angel and the devil alike are almost invariably represented as versions of the particular character who's facing a momentous choice. Little Tom the devil cat and little Tom the angel cat whisper into the ears of big Tom; we know that they are—what's the right word?—facets, or aspects, or moods of big Tom.

A literary example may help us clarify this issue. J. R. R. Tolkien's best critic, T. A. Shippey, points out that a deep confusion between the internal and external dimensions of evil is built into *The Lord of the Rings*, perhaps intentionally. The confusion emerges at its strongest in scenes that focus on the Ring itself, the Ring of Power made by the Dark Lord, Sauron. When, early in the book, Gandalf asks Frodo to hand him the Ring, we are told that "It suddenly felt very heavy, as if either it or Frodo himself was in some way reluctant for Gandalf to touch it." But which was reluctant, Frodo or the Ring? A little later, in the inn called the Prancing Pony, Frodo "felt the Ring on its chain, and quite unaccountably the desire came over him to slip it on and vanish out of the silly situation. It seemed to him, somehow, as if the suggestion came to him from outside, from someone or something in the room." And then later, perhaps most tellingly of all, when, wearing the Ring, he sits upon the seat of Amon Hen and the great Eye of Sauron fixes him, "He heard himself crying out, *Never, never! Or was it: Verily I come, I come to you?* He could not tell." Then he hears the voice of Gandalf (though he does not know that it is Gandalf) commanding him to remove the Ring. The conflict between these two powers—it is fair, and in Tolkien's mythology quite precise, to say that they are an angel and a devil contending for his soul—torments him, until he suddenly, inexplicably, becomes "aware of himself" again and is "free to choose." And he chooses to take off the ring, rather like Hellboy breaking off his horns.

At the end of the story, on the very verge of completing his quest, what Frodo chooses is to put the Ring on one last time and to assume its power. Or does he, in fact, choose? Shippey points out that at that moment Frodo does not say that he chooses anything; rather, he says "I *do not choose* now to do what I came to do." Perhaps choice is no longer available to him. Perhaps, if his will and the will of the Ring could once have been distinguished, they cannot any longer. Augustine believed that we achieve true freedom not by doing what we want, but by conforming our wills perfectly to the will of God, so that nothing in us rebels against him. What Frodo experiences is the demonic counterpart of that freedom, a wholeness of will that is perfect enslavement. But up to that point Tolkien makes it impossible to say whether Frodo's struggles are a function of his own nature or the power of the Ring; rather, he encourages us to think the internal/external distinction may not even make sense.

Tolkien is an unusual writer, in some ways the product of modernity but in the matters we have been discussing quite unmodern. Thinkers shaped by modernity do not treat the question of evil intention the way Tolkien does and can have difficulty reconciling themselves to premodern ways of thinking about these matters. In this light we might consider a famous production of Christopher Marlowe's *Doctor Faustus* (a play first performed not too long before or after Marlowe's murder in 1593). As the drama begins Faustus sits in his study, among his books, and debates which path to wisdom he should choose. One by one he dismisses logic, medicine, law, and theology—"Divinity, adieu!"—and eventually turns to "the metaphysics of magicians": "Necromantic books are heavenly!" At this point the good angel and evil angel appear, the good angel to warn Faustus to "lay that damned book aside, / And gaze not on it, lest it tempt thy soul"; the evil angel, to exhort him to "Go forward," to become, like Jove, "Lord and Commander of these elements." And of course it is the latter advice that excites Faustus's ambitious mind.

Thrice more in the opening scenes of the play the two angels appear. They enter and exit so quickly—no extended debates here, probably because Faustus is so easily won over by the evil angel—that, in early performances, they probably appeared above the stage, stepping forward into light to speak and then backing into darkness once done. Their penultimate appearance, after Faustus has signed away his soul to Mephistopheles, echoes the temptation of Martin of Tours. "God cannot pity thee," whispers the evil angel, to which Faustus replies, "God will pity me if I repent." But to that the evil angel has an unanswerable rebuttal: "Ay, but Faustus never shall repent." Hearing this, Faustus cries out, "My heart's so hardened I cannot repent!" The angels disappear, yet after a few lines return once more, and after a last word of encouragement from the good angel, Faustus actually cries, "Ah Christ my Saviour! seek to save / Distressed Faustus' soul!" But this merely brings on not the insignificant evil angel, but rather a trinity of mighty demons: Faustus's old friend Mephistopheles, Beelzebub, and Lucifer himself, who reminds Faustus of the bargain he has made. Faustus seeks pardon and vows eternal enmity to God— and that's the last we hear from the angels. The evil one need do, the good one can do nothing. Faustus's fate is sealed.

In 1974, the famous theatrical director John Barton staged *Doctor Faustus* for the Royal Shakespeare Company and chose for the leading role an unknown young actor by the name of Ian McKellan. Shrewd move, that. But he made other decisions that are equally interesting and important, though from a different point of view. The directorial problem with which Barton was faced is simple yet serious: how, in the aftermath of Tom and Jerry for heaven's sake, could we possibly take seriously the appearance of the good and evil angels? And his solution was a brilliant one: he made them into hand puppets, held by Faustus himself, their lines spoken by him.

A brilliant solution on more than one count: not only does he avoid sniggers from the audience at the appearance of the debating spirits, but he simultaneously enables an understanding of Faustus that is perfectly commensurate with twentieth-century psychology. For if it was the genius of Prudentius and his followers to reach into the divided self and pull out its voices, giving them bodily substance and individual identity, it was the genius of Freud and his followers to stuff them all back into the box. When Freud sees the good angels and evil angels of our stories as projected externalizations of our own inner conflicts—puppets made by us and able to speak only through our acts of ventriloquism—he is simply returning us to the world of Augustine, in which "the devil made me do it" is scarcely a legitimate excuse. Do we sin because we heed the devilish voice in our ears? Or do we heed that voice because we have already sinned? Whatever answer we might give has little practical significance. The divided self is our inheritance no matter what, and in the pain and disorientation of that experience we may not even care whether we were torn from the inside out or the outside in.

At several points in these past two chapters I have referred to "the divided self," and this is the title of the first book by the odd, once popular, now virtually forgotten Scots psychiatrist R. D. Laing. It was Laing's belief—based in part on his reading of existentialist thought—that various forms of psychosis, especially schizophrenia, often do not indicate illness, but rather are acute insights into what the world is really like. Laing believed that enormous social pressures are exerted on people in order to make them "sleep," that is, become unconscious of the evils of their world. Sleeping people are, in our time, "normal" people. In Laing's writing there are always invisible scare quotes around the word *normal*. ("The condition of alienation, of being asleep, of being unconscious, of being out of one's mind, is the condition of the normal man. Society highly values its normal man. It educates children to lose themselves and to become absurd, and thus to be normal. Normal men have killed perhaps 100,000,000 of their fellow normal men in the last fifty years.") For Laing, the psychotic is the person who can't be put to sleep, who remains on some level aware of the inconsistencies and cruelties of social life and for that matter of his or her own personal life. The schizophrenic hears voices—which normal people do not—but those voices often tell the truth. This is not so far from the Augustinian and Pauline understanding of what it means to be at war within one's person, to be engaged in a *psychomachia*, a soul struggle. Because sin can never be simply eradicated, to be undivided is surely to be lost—normal, yes, but lost.

In one of his books Laing tells the story of a man, a fellow Glaswegian, whose psychosis was treated by medication with some success; the voices he habitually heard were subdued but not silenced. To his doctors this may have been a kind of victory, but not to the man himself. He could be heard on the ward from time to time talking back to them. "Speak up, y'buggers," he would mutter, "I cannae hear ye."

SIX

The Wicked, but Not Very

In the city of Amsterdam, in the year 1635, a great controversy fractured the Jewish community. It was a thriving community in many ways. Most of its members were Sephardic Jews whose ancestors had come to the Netherlands from Iberia more than a century earlier. In 1492 in Spain, five years later in Portugal, Jews had been given the impossible choice of conversion or banishment. Some of those who chose conversion mounted statues of the Madonna on their doorposts, but secretly inserted into them the text of the Shema—the great prayer from Deuteronomy, beginning, "Hear, O Israel: The Lord our God is one Lord" (6:4, KJV)—thus transforming the Madonna into a mezuzah. Many others had truly become Christians. But in Amsterdam, almost uniquely in Europe, Jews could freely be Jews as long as they made no public announcement of their faith and did not attempt to proselytize.

They were a prosperous community too, except for the minority of Ashkenazi Jews from northern Europe among them, whose begging in the city streets embarrassed the Sephardim and led them to contrive schemes of charity for these unfortunates. By the first decade of the seventeenth century they had among them sufficient wealth to build a synagogue, though in 1612 the Reformed Church intervened with the city authorities to prevent them from doing so. The civic leaders of Amsterdam, however, proved to be more than tolerant of the Jews and finessed the anger of the stricter Calvinists; by 1635 there were three synagogues in the city. (Forty years later, combining their resources, the city's Jews built the largest and most lavish synagogue in Europe.)

But of course, the existence of three synagogues in a city, although indicative of the community's flourishing, is also perhaps indicative of certain differences in opinion. The three leading rabbis—Saul Levi Morteira, Menasseh ben Israel, and Isaac Aboab da Fonseca—represented three distinct models of Judaism for their time and place. Menasseh ben Israel, whose piety was deeply shaped by his expectation of the coming Messiah, was nevertheless at ease with the mainstream Dutch culture. One of his books, *De Creatione Problemata*—published in the very year that the dispute we are about to describe culminated—carried a preface by a leading Christian academic in Amsterdam, Caspar Barleus. (Barleus provoked outrage among many of his fellow Dutch Christians by suggesting that Christians and Jews could be on an equal footing in their relationship to God: "Just as I am a son of Christ, you are a son of Abraham," he wrote in his preface.) The Christian leaders of Amsterdam thought Rabbi Menasseh so compelling a rhetorician that, in 1651, they issued an edict allowing him to write whatever he pleased as long as he didn't write it in Dutch. He devoted the years just before his death in 1657 to a mission to England. He wanted Oliver Cromwell, the Lord Protector, to rescind the banishment of Jews promulgated by Edward I back in 1290, in large part because he did not believe that his people's comfortable place in Amsterdam was secure. Though then and later he was the most famous of the city's rabbis, he does not play much of a part in this story.

Rabbi Morteira, perhaps because he alone among the three was Ashkenazi, more closely matches the popular conception of a rabbi from the early modern period. He pointed his people toward the piety of the early rabbinical tradition and considered himself a disciple of the great medieval philosopher Moses ben Maimon, or Maimonides. But Rabbi Aboab was something quite different.

If the messianism of Rabbi Menasseh was one important strain in European Judaism of that period—it is not coincidental that this was the time of the greatest of false messiahs, Shabbetai Zevi—another was the profound renewal of kabbalistic learning and devotion under the influence of the great mystic of the previous century, Isaac Luria. (The followers of Shabbetai Zevi tended to be influenced by Lurianic kabbalism as well, because Luria believed that the increased suffering of Jews around the world—some of the most vicious pogroms in history occurred in these centuries, beginning with the Iberian expulsions—betokened a breaking up of the cosmos that could herald the coming of the Messiah.) And it was the question of the authority of Kabbalah—a series of mystical texts whose revelations of cosmic meaning and pattern went far beyond anything even suggested or hinted at by Scripture or the rabbis—that was at the heart of the dispute among Amsterdam's Jews in 1635. Rabbi Aboab was a fervent disciple of Luria and the chief kabbalist in Amsterdam.

The dispute begins, not with the Kabbalah itself, but with a statement from the tractate called Sanhedrin in the Talmud, that massive compilation of rabbinical wisdom and meditation on Torah: "All Israelites have a share in the world to come." On the surface this seems to say that all Jews will be saved; all Jews will, after the Resurrection that is also taught in the Talmud, come to be with God in the "world to come," that is, what Christians would call Heaven. But Rabbi Morteira insisted that this could not be, because other passages in the Talmud contradict that view. I am not sure which passages he invoked, but there are some likely candidates. For instance, there is heated debate among the rabbis about whether the "ten tribes"—the Northern Kingdom (Israel), which, after the reign of King Solomon, had split from the Southern Kingdom (Judah) and fallen into idolatry—can inherit the world to come. There is near universal agreement that Ahab, the most vicious of the Northern kings, has no share in the world to come. The greatest of all the rabbis, Akiba, insisted that the "generation of the wilderness"—the ones who, during the Exodus, did not have the faith to take possession of the promised land—cannot enter the world to come. And (so says another titan, Rabbi Jose) there was a time when the rabbis of Palestine collectively affirmed: "Who is destined for the world to come? He who is meek, humble, stooping on entering and on going out, and a constant student of the Torah without claiming merit therefore"—which suggests that righteousness is a prerequisite for entry into blessedness.

So, at any rate, was the teaching of Rabbi Morteira, when he learned that there were young men in Amsterdam saying that all Jews would be saved. No, said Rabbi Morteira, only the righteous will be saved; the wicked, like Ahab, will be punished, and punished eternally. But this claim produced cries of outrage from those young men, whom Morteira later called "rebels" and (perhaps more generously) "immature" men who had been "corrupted by Kabbalists." And by "Kabbalists" he primarily meant his rival rabbi, Aboab, who had in fact given these young "rebels" their ideas by teaching that in Kabbalah and in Kabbalah alone could one find the authoritative interpretation of the statement, "All Israelites have a share in the world to come."

Aboab responded to Morteira's critique of his disciples with a powerful counterattack, in a treatise—only discovered little more than thirty years ago by a scholar named Alexander Altmann—called *Nishmat Hayyim*, or "The Breath of Life." "Truly speaking," he wrote, "matters of this kind have been entrusted only to the Kabbalists, illuminated as they are by the light of truth." For Aboab and his followers, Morteira, with his pedantic emphasis on Talmudic scholarship, was simply an old stick-in-the-mud whose opinions, produced in indifference or hostility to the sublime revelations of Kabbalah, were scarcely worthy even to be refuted. Kabbalah never contradicts

Torah, argued Aboab, but it can and does often contradict rabbinical *interpretations* of Torah. The rabbis who commented on Scripture in the Mishnah and the later ones who elaborated Mishnaic teaching in the Gemara, for all their greatness and holiness, were also mortal and fallible; but Kabbalah, which comes from the Lord as does Torah, is perfect and without error. And Kabbalah affirms that all Israelites will be saved. David ibn Abi Zimra, the teacher of Isaac Luria, had written, "All Israelites are a single body"—they cannot be separated, they are "hewn from the place of Unity," and as a unity they are collectively ensured a place in the world to come.

Rebecca Goldstein, in whose curiously discursive biography of the philosopher Baruch Spinoza I first learned about this controversy, says that one of Morteira's chief concerns was to insist that those who remained faithful to Judaism in the midst of persecution would be rewarded, while those who pretended to convert in order to keep their wealth would be justly punished. How can there be no difference in God's eyes between those who remain faithful and those who publicly reject the Covenant? To this telling question Aboab replied by invoking the Kabbalistic doctrine of the *gilgul neshamot*, or cycle of souls—reincarnation. Those who are wicked in this life will be—precisely as Hinduism teaches—sent back into this world again until they learn righteousness. But sooner or later, all Jews will be saved and as a single body inherit the world to come. And this salvation comes not from one's righteousness or anything else, but from the decision of the Lord to make a covenant with these people, to pluck them out and give them the gift of salvation.

The followers of Aboab found Morteira's teachings—especially his teaching that damnation is eternal—deeply offensive, so offensive that they demanded that the community's legal authorities, a group of prominent laypeople known as the *parnassim*, to forbid Rabbi Morteira from saying such things in public. And what reason did they give? That his views were far too reminiscent of the views of the

Christians among whom they lived, the Calvinists, who held strongly to the Augustinian understanding of original sin. "By believing in the eternality of sin and punishment," these rebels complained, "we support the religion of the Christians who say that Adam's sin was eternal and that, on this account, only God, who is eternal, could make atonement for it by incarnation and death."

THE UNIVERSALITY OF SIN is certainly a Jewish belief; there are many statements to this effect in the Scriptures, some of them quite famous. "Who can say, I have made my heart clean, I am pure from my sin?" (Prov. 20:9, KJV); "For there is not a just man upon earth, that doeth good, and sinneth not" (Eccl. 7:20); "All we like sheep have gone astray; we have turned every one to his own way" (Isa. 53:6). But there seems to be nothing in Jewish tradition to support the idea of original sin, of an inheritance of corruption from Adam. The Anglican theologian N. P. Williams, who eighty years ago produced one of the most comprehensive studies of the topic, argues that what loomed far larger in the rabbinical imagination than the consumption of the forbidden fruit was a curious statement from one of the Bible's strangest chapters, Genesis 6. It is here that we learn of the mating of the "sons of God" with the "daughters of men," and of the presence of the *nephilim,* an odd word that (says that gifted translator Robert Alter) seems literally to mean "the fallen ones," but that the translators of the King James Bible rendered as "giants": "There were giants in the earth in those days." Added to this bizarre mix of images is this sentence: "And God saw that the wickedness of man was great in the earth, and that every imagination of the thoughts of his heart was only evil continually." It was the term that the KJV renders "imagination" (Hebrew *yetzer*) that, says N. P. Williams, the rabbis found fascinating. The evil in us, in our hearts—in Hebrew the heart is the seat of will even more than of emotion—can be seen in what we imagine, what we scheme, what we devise. But there is no indication from the rabbis that we scheme so because of Adam. We just do. It is enough to say, with the prophet Jeremiah, that "The heart is deceitful above all things, and desperately wicked: who can know it?"

Samuel Cohon, the scholar most concerned with original sin and Judaism, argues that among Palestinian rabbis, around the time that Paul was writing that sin came into the world through one man, there were indeed debates about the source of human sinfulness and that some concept of an inherited propensity to sin (*yetzer ha ra*) was considered. But even among the proponents of such an idea, the rabbinical ideas "have the character of random, informal and private opinions without any dogmatic import whatever." That is, the question of the origin of sin was not one the rabbis believed had implications that the pious and observant Jew needed to worry about.

The young "rebels" of Amsterdam's Jewish community were not so different; for them, our scheming or lack of scheming has nothing to do with anyone's inheritance of the world to come. Salvation is God's gift to Israel, period. Whether he does or could extend that gift to those whom the rabbis call "righteous Gentiles" outside the covenant does not seem to concern the followers of Aboab; their emphasis is on the eternal benefit to be received by the children of Israel. And it is hard to imagine that this is not a response to a Dutch Calvinist theology, which sees—and strongly emphasizes—the Christian Church as the New Israel, and Christian faith and baptism as the new circumcision.

Dutch Calvinism, like many forms of Christianity, takes what theologians call a "supersessionist" view of Judaism. Because the Jews refused Jesus, their true Messiah, the covenants that God made with Abraham, Jacob, and Moses have been "superseded." Gentiles who accept Jesus as Savior now take the place of the disobedient children of Moses, and the church becomes the new Israel. Its rite of initiation, Holy Baptism, replaces the rite of circumcision, and even the story of

Noah and the Flood is reinterpreted as a prefiguration of the passage of Christ's church, the true ark, through a dying world. The historian Simon Schama has written eloquently of the "Hebraic self-image" of the Dutch Republic, and of the habit Dutch preachers had of speaking "as though the congregation were itself a tribe of Israel." One can easily imagine how well this went down with Amsterdam's Jews.*

For the Dutch Christians, as for all those in the Augustinian tradition, original sin is the problem of all humanity, and Jews and Gentiles do not differ in this affliction. God's one remedy for sin is the redemptive death of his Son, and our proper response to this remedy is simply to accept it, to lay claim to it, to place all our hope in it; and here too Jew and Gentile occupy the same boat. (Thus the Apostle

---

* The origins of supersessionism are in the Gospels and in Paul's letters, but it's worth noting that Paul struggles mightily to understand the status of Jews who reject Jesus. In chapters 9–11 of his great letter to the Romans he gnaws away at this problem in a kind of agony. At one point he seems to say quite clearly that the vast majority of Jews have simply rejected what he takes to be the gospel message, that we may be saved only by faith in the Savior, Jesus. Having chosen instead to be judged by their works, they will be so judged and found wanting, whereas those Gentiles who never even sought to keep the law of Moses, because they seek to be judged only by their faith in Jesus, will be saved thereby. But near the end of his meditation Paul pivots suddenly and asserts that "all Israel will be saved. . . . For the gifts and the calling of God are irrevocable." Then, perhaps knowing that he at least appears to have contradicted himself, he concludes this tortured meditation with an outcry, a kind of rhetorical throwing up of the hands: "Oh, the depth of the riches and wisdom and knowledge of God! How unsearchable are his judgments and how inscrutable his ways!" For Paul's later Christian followers, though, including almost all the Reformers, the matter was much simpler: they focused all their attention on Paul's words about the Jews' rejection of their Messiah. Thus Martin Luther, though early in his career he had been something close to a philo-Semite, was maddened by their unresponsiveness to his own preaching of the gospel and ended by recommending that they be exiled from Germany or, failing that, that their houses and synagogues be burned to the ground, their books taken from them, and their rabbis threatened with death if they preached or practiced their religion.

Paul: "For there is no distinction between Jew and Greek; for the same Lord is Lord of all, bestowing his riches on all who call on him. For 'everyone who calls on the name of the Lord will be saved.'") So we have one disease—Rosenstock-Huessy's "universal democracy" of sinners once more—for which there is a unique and invariable cure.

The young Jews of Amsterdam would surely have known this teaching very well. Most of them would have been born in the city and would have interacted regularly with Dutch Christians. (Such freedom of movement was unusual, almost unique, among Europe's Jews; but—as one Rabbi Uziel wrote a generation earlier, in 1616—the one significant prohibition was that a Jew "may not openly show that he is of a different faith from the inhabitants of the city." This policy would have increased the likelihood that these young men would have heard the "Hebraic" rhetoric of Dutch Christianity without being able to respond to it in any way, at least publicly.) And it seemed to them, as they compared the local form of Augustinian Christianity with Rabbi Aboab's kabbalistic revelation of the place that all Jews have reserved for them in the world to come, that the root of the division was to be found in the doctrine of original sin. Rather than contest the Christians' prescription, they questioned their diagnosis. For if there is no inherited curse of original sin, there is no universal problem to be solved, no universal disease to be cured. Yes, God gave his law to the people of Moses, and yes, that law is to be followed, and yes, to disobey that law is to incur the wrath of God. But none of this has anything to do with the ultimate disposition of the souls of the children of Israel: whether upon completion of this incarnation or as reward for some future life of righteousness, all Israel will truly be saved. Again, what might happen to the Gentiles is no concern of Kabbalah.

And there was another issue as well. Rabbi Morteira had been born and circumcised a Jew in Venice and marked, it would seem, from childhood as a scholar of Torah, but Rabbi Aboab had been born in Portugal as a Marrano; the rite with which he had been brought into this world was not circumcision, but Catholic baptism. He had very good reason, then, to say along with St. Paul that in relation to the people of Israel "the gifts and the calling of God are irrevocable" (Rom. 11:29). If his parents or grandparents had repudiated Judaism and accepted Christian baptism, while others had suffered exile rather than renounce their faith, that did not deprive him or his family of Jewish identity and of a full share in the world to come. Aboab, by the time of writing *Nishmat Hayyim*, had already been stung by one of Morteira's arguments. Morteira claimed that if you deny that sins are eternally punished and insist that all Israelites are saved, then many ex-Marranos might return to the "impure land" of Portugal or Spain and even take up again the "abomination" of professing Christian belief. Why shouldn't they? Aboab replied that such an idea is nonsensical; no Jews would do such a thing if they knew it could mean repeated incarnations and great, prolonged suffering. But in any case, whatever punishment the Lord chooses to decree, in the end all Jews share the same fate. Aboab ends his treatise with these words: "This is what our rabbis, of blessed memory, meant when coining the phrase, 'Though he sinned, he is still an Israelite.'"

THE PROTESTANT REFORMATION did not bring about any substantially new teaching regarding original sin. The leading theologians of the movement, with the partial exception of the great Swiss reformer Ulrich Zwingli, forcefully reaffirmed the Augustinian teaching, which they believed had been diluted by medieval theologians and all but forgotten in the devotional practices of the common people of Europe. (And by the testimony of most modern historians, medieval Christians, when they thought of their own sins at all—which they probably did no more often than we late moderns do—tended to imagine them with the kind of urgency that we saw, in this book's

Chapter One, among the Urapmin of Papua New Guinea. For the person terrified by the prospect of dying unshriven, in a state of mortal sinfulness, there is little time to reflect on how the whole miserable situation got started. In such panic Adam and Eve come to mind simply as people to be blamed, vaguely, for screwing everything up.) Luther in Germany, Calvin in Geneva, Cranmer in England all spoke with nearly one voice on this matter. The great confessions and catechisms of the Reformation traditions—the Augsburg Confession, the Heidelberg Catechism, the Church of England's Articles of Religion, the Westminster Confession of England's Presbyterians—all clearly endorsed and reinforced the Augustinian view.

But they did so in a time—rather like Augustine's time—when multiple cultural and social forces mounted increasingly strong resistance, if not (at first) to belief in original sin itself, then at least to its doctrinal and practical importance. The great Dutch humanist scholar Erasmus clearly affirms the reality of original sin (for instance, in his dialogue *The Pilgrimage of Pure Devotion*); but in his most famous work, the *Praise of Folly* (1511), he elaborates a long list of absurd "mysteries" that theologians occupy themselves with—for instance, whether the Second Person of the Trinity could have taken the form of a donkey, or a woman, or a devil, or a gourd, instead of a man's form—and among the items on the list is the question of how original sin is transmitted down through the generations. For Erasmus such theological trivia simply distract us from the difficult task of living a faithful Christian life.

Some seventy years later the great English poet Sir Philip Sidney, a devout Protestant but also an heir of Erasmus's humanistic tradition, wrote that "our erected wit"—our God-given and intentionally developed power of reason—"maketh us know what perfection is, and yet our infected will keepeth us from reaching unto it." This way of phrasing the point emphasizes sin's power to bind us and limit our ability to achieve what our rational minds can conceive, but it is easy to imagine a relatively slight altering of the balance that would emphasize the ability of our "erected wit" to compensate, and more than compensate, for the binding power of our "infected will"—rather as that heir of Confucius Xún Zǐ believed that, though we are indeed born with a sinful nature, it can be trained and disciplined by the wise counsel of sages and the proper implementation of that counsel by princes.

In or around the year that Odilo of Cluny died (1049), an Irish monk composed a dream-vision narrative, the *Vision of Tondal,* which was widely read throughout the Middle Ages. (As late as the fifteenth century Margaret of York commissioned the Netherlandish artist Simon Marmion to produce an illuminated version of it.) In his dream Tondal is given an angel-guided tour of the afterlife, in which he sees various rewards and punishments. Among the groups he is shown something like a place of mild punishment—obviously a full-fledged Purgatory is on its way, though not yet arrived—whose inhabitants the angel describes. "These," he says, "are the wicked, but not very." This strikes me as a lucid and brief summary of the view of original sin that grew stronger and stronger throughout the sixteenth and seventeenth centuries. Despite all the Reformers could do to emphasize our utter depravity and consequent absolute dependence on the grace of God, increasing numbers of people, while acknowledging the reality of original sin, preferred to minimize its consequences: we are all the wicked, but not very.

IN THE YEAR 1656, while Menasseh ben Israel was immersed in his great (and ultimately successful) campaign to get Jews admitted once more to the country of England, France was occupied with a very different religious controversy, one in which the doctrine of original sin was nowhere mentioned, but everywhere of the first importance. The dispute is enormously complex and therefore almost impossible to summarize, but the key elements of it may, without too much distortion and oversimplification, be listed. In 1638, Cornelius Jansen, the bishop of Ypres, completed a large treatise on the theology of Augustine and then promptly died. It was Jansen's belief that the church had lost sight of Augustine's great insight that, in our miserable condition of bondage to sin, we are utterly dependent on God's grace. Jansen further believed that the church—the Roman Catholic Church, of which he was a bishop—was in some danger of relapsing into Pelagianism.

In 1641, the Holy Office of the church condemned Jansen's book and forbade the reading of it, further declaring that the church's views on grace were not at all inconsistent with Augustine's and that Jansen had attributed to Augustine views the saint did not hold. A year later, Pope Urban VIII issued a bull, *In eminenti,* reaffirming the condemnation of Jansen.

But this did not end the affair, especially in France, where Jansen's book and theology had become compelling to people who saw in it a just condemnation of the worldliness of the church in France, deeply implicated as it was in affairs of state and the cultural life of the aristocracy. A theologian named Antoine Arnauld took up the banner of Jansen, celebrating Augustinian theology and criticizing or satirizing the prelates of the church and (most forcefully) members of the Jesuit order. Arnauld and his fellow Jansenists believed that the Jesuits were particularly culpable, because they had employed their dialectical skills to water down Christian moral teaching and thereby allowed the cultural elite to live in deep sinfulness untroubled by pangs of conscience.

But few of these critics, least of all Arnauld, wished to be at odds with Rome; and given the condemnations of Jansen, they found themselves in a tight spot. Arnauld solved the problem—to his own satisfaction anyway, though not ultimately to that of the church—by agreeing that the specific propositions that the pope and the Holy

Office had condemned were surely pernicious, but denying that Jansen had actually affirmed any of them. In other words, Arnauld applauded the theological instincts of Mother Church while questioning its leaders' ability to read texts well. (This was a nice quid pro quo, since the church had accused Jansen of misreading Augustine.) So the debate continued, growing more and more heated, throughout the 1640s and well into the 1650s, as Arnauld and the Jansenists lost every round institutionally—with the church proper and with the theological faculty at the Sorbonne—but gained more and more approval popularly. And then Blaise Pascal got involved.

It was soon after the first condemnation of Jansen that Pascal began to be drawn to the bishop's teachings, when he was in his early twenties (he was born in 1623). His first fame was as a scientist and mathematician, and had he never written a theological word, he would still be famous today for the work he did in those spheres. But he had a kind of calling. His attraction to Christianity, more particularly the strict Jansenist emphasis on the corruption and depravity of our wills and God's unique power to heal those wills, varied in intensity. When in 1652 his sister Jacqueline became a nun at the convent of Port-Royal, the very epicenter of Jansenist spirituality, he was dismayed. (He was a man living much in *le monde* at the time.) But then one night in 1654 everything changed for him. He recorded the night's events and, famously, sewed the *Mémorial*, as it came to be called, into the lining of his everyday coat. Here it is:

The year of grace 1654,

Monday, 23 November, feast of St. Clement, pope and martyr, and others in the martyrology.

Vigil of St. Chrysogonus, martyr, and others.

From about half past ten at night until about half past midnight,

FIRE

GOD of Abraham, GOD of Isaac, GOD of Jacob
not of the philosophers and of the learned.
Certitude. Certitude. Feeling. Joy. Peace.
GOD of Jesus Christ.
My God and your God.
Your GOD will be my God.
Forgetfulness of the world and of everything, except GOD.
He is only found by the ways taught in the Gospel.
Grandeur of the human soul.
Righteous Father, the world has not known you, but I have
  known you.
Joy, joy, joy, tears of joy.
I have departed from him:
They have forsaken me, the fount of living water.
My God, will you leave me?
Let me not be separated from him forever.
This is eternal life, that they know you, the one true God, and
  the one that you sent, Jesus Christ.
Jesus Christ.
Jesus Christ.
I left him; I fled him, renounced, crucified.
Let me never be separated from him.
He is only kept securely by the ways taught in the Gospel:
Renunciation, total and sweet.

Two years later he decided to enter the fray in support of Arnauld and the Jansenists and (ultimately) in condemnation of the Jesuits. He had begun to make spiritual retreats at Port-Royal and came to know Arnauld—and his whole large family, almost all of whom were connected with Port-Royal in some way—very well. Pascal, like his sister, came increasingly to identify Jansenism with authentic Christianity itself, with the true condition of miserable humanity desperate for the loving grace of God; and Arnauld and the other leading Jansenists very much wanted their brilliant and learned friend to become, somehow, their advocate.

Pascal's intervention came in the form of a series of letters—the *Provincial Letters,* as they came to be called—written supposedly by an ordinary man observing the great debates in Paris and reporting on them to his friend in the provinces, professing throughout a bemused naïveté that Pascal himself most certainly did not possess. They are brilliant letters, corrosively witty and sardonic, not at all what you might expect from a man who fairly recently had been caught up in an ecstatic, visionary, consuming encounter with God. But it was that encounter and that God that Pascal wished to justify by writing his letters. And undergirding his whole participation in the debate was a deep conviction that this vision of God—and its corresponding sense of the "grandeur of the human soul"—is utterly dependent on the Jansenist and Augustinian understanding of original sin.

The *Letters* begin in a tone reminiscent of Erasmus. Our narrator is amused, in his slightly befuddled way, that the extremely technical theological terms surrounding the Jansenist controversy (terms that, let it be noted, I have spared the readers of this book) can provoke such passion on both sides. The whole of the first letter is occupied with the narrator's attempts to find a religious authority who can tell him what the word *proximate* means—as in "the proximate power of the believer to keep God's commandments"—and why it is important to use that word in just the right way. (I see that I have just brought in one of those terms after all, may I be accursed.) Eventually he grows exasperated and cries, "Now, for the last time I ask you, Reverend Fathers, to tell me what I must believe to be a Catholic," to which the priests ("in unison") reply that he must "say that all the righteous have proximate power, leaving aside all question of meaning." It is when he learns that he must pronounce certain syllables without claiming or even seeking to know what they mean that our provincial letter writer loses his patience.

Between the publication of the third and fourth letters—each was at first published individually in pamphlet form—an event occurred that changed the tone and approach of the whole series. In February of 1656 Antoine Arnauld was definitively condemned and expelled from the Sorbonne. In the campaign against him the Jesuits led the way—not surprisingly, since Arnauld and before him Jansen had been vocal opponents of Jesuit power and worldliness—and so Pascal decided to train his extremely powerful satirical guns directly on them. The remainder of the letters constitute a nearly vicious, but often quite funny, exposure of the hypocrisies and thoroughly unchristian positions of the Jesuits. For instance, there is the carefully argued claim that, despite the biblical prohibition of murder, it is permissible to kill someone to prevent that person from insulting you. Also the even more nuanced view of a famous Jesuit theologian named Vasquez that, though the church teaches that rich Christians should give "from superfluous wealth to relieve the needs of the poor," nevertheless, "what persons in high society retain in order to improve their status and that of their relatives is not called superfluous." Indeed, Vasquez contends, it's almost impossible for aristocrats and royalty to have *any* superfluous wealth—once the concept of superfluity is properly understood. Several of these letters are occupied with reports of conversations with a particular (imaginary) Jesuit, who, quoting repeatedly from the works of leading figures in his order, produces a kind of *summa* of Jesuit doctrine that culminates in his proud claim that, through the skillful and subtle theological arguments known as casuistry, "our Fathers have dispensed men from the irksome obligation of actually loving God."*

At this point (the end of the tenth letter) our narrator turns from the good Father in horror and talks with him no further; in the next installment he addresses real Jesuits, who complain that he has made fun of sacred things. But here our bumbling naive narrator disappears, and Pascal seems to speak chiefly in his own voice. Though he wittily corrects those who think the opinions of Jesuits are "sacred things"—"Is no one to be able to laugh at . . . the fantastic and unchristian decisions of your authors, without being accused of scoffing at religion?"—he is at pains seriously to respond to the charge, precisely because he believes with all his heart that the Jesuits themselves are the ones who have cheapened the truly sacred things, human sin and divine grace, and deprived them of the fear and awe they should naturally command. It is they through their casuistry (the rich have no superfluous wealth, one may murder to avoid having one's pride insulted, Christians need not love God) who have mocked the sacred and deserve mockery in return. Pascal's specifically Christian defense of satire is a marvelous thing.

As we saw earlier, in our discussion of Pelagius and his followers, the theologian who wishes to minimize the effects of original sin— who wishes to deny that our power to do good has been impeded or

---

* Most Jesuits and many other Catholic theologians have claimed that Pascal didn't play fair in his quotations from Jesuit theology, that his selections distort. In some cases this is true. But he was surely right in seeing that the practice of many French Jesuits in his time, especially those who heard the confessions of the aristocracy, was to weaken and dilute biblical and formally endorsed church teaching about sin and grace alike. Søren Kierkegaard writes in his journal that most people believe that the commandments of Scripture—for instance, "You shall love the Lord your God with all your heart and all your mind and all your strength, and your neighbor as yourself"—are intentionally oversevere, the moral equivalent of setting your clock ahead by ten minutes. Pascal gives ample evidence to show that this was the characteristic French Jesuit view in his time.

diminished by our inheritance from Adam—must reckon with what seems to be the obvious fact that we don't do nearly as much good as his theory says we can, that we consistently fail to keep many (most? all?) of the commandments of Scripture. Pelagius's own way of reckoning with this was to insist that no matter how strict and forbidding the moral law seems, we remain capable of keeping it and culpable for not doing so. Therefore every Christian should live the kind of disciplined and holy existence that monks and nuns strive to live, lest he or she suffer the pains of eternal punishment. But the Parisian Jesuits of Pascal's day knew that such a message would scarcely earn them credit from what Vasquez called "persons in high society"; so they went the opposite route, "defining deviancy down" so that the great forbidding cliff of Mount Sinai was reduced to a scarcely noticeable rise of ground. If all that is meant by the commandment to love God is that we should not actively hate him, then I believe that's a peak almost all of us may scale. So, in the view of the Parisian Jesuits, original sin impedes us little or not at all in our quest for righteousness, in part because the righteousness we seek is such small beer.

For Pascal this model of the human condition insults humans and God alike. The God whom he encountered on the night of the Feast of St. Clement was a God of "FIRE." "Our God is a consuming fire," writes the author of the letter of the Hebrews, remembering the words of the prophet Malachi: "But who may abide the day of his coming? and who shall stand when he appeareth? for he is like a refiner's fire, and like fullers' soap: And he shall sit as a refiner and purifier of silver: and he shall purify the sons of Levi, and purge them as gold and silver, that they may offer unto the Lord an offering in righteousness" (3:2–3, KJV). Similar images are everywhere in the Bible. They suggest simultaneously that God is somehow in himself firelike (bright, hot, pure), but in relation to us, or to our corrupt natures, something utterly destructive. In the refiner's fire—the hottest of fires—everything that is not pure gold or silver will melt and evaporate. What remains is precious metal, ornamental in the highest degree and variously, wonderfully useful.

Likewise, the wheat will be saved and stored, says Jesus, but the weeds will be burned to ash and blown away on the wind. This is an image with at least double meaning: those who are but weeds, whose sin has made them but weeds—who have lost the power to choose—will be burned in the fires of Hell; but also, all of us are encumbered by the useless chaff of sin, the dehumanizing husks of pride and rebelliousness, which are our portion from our first father and which must be reduced to ash and cast aside so that our truly nourishing grain may be saved.

For a Christian like Pascal these metaphors go to the very heart of Christianity. "It is a fearful thing to fall into the hands of the living God," says the writer to the Hebrews; "The fear of the Lord is the beginning of wisdom," say the Psalms and Proverbs. This fear arises when we recognize—as Pascal did that night in 1654—the enormous chasm that separates the pure fire of God and the corruption of our debased natures. But for Pascal that fear, and *only* that fear, yields proper wonder at the love and mercy of God. Those who, like his Jesuit enemies, compromise the holiness of God and elevate the stature of fallen humanity do not know—and therefore prevent others from knowing—the miracle of divine grace.

In the extraordinary *Pensées*, "Thoughts," which he wrote in the last years of his life—sometimes scribbling madly, sometimes working through a point methodically, filing and organizing stacks of related ideas, all in hopes of producing a great book in defense of true Christian faith—Pascal returns to these concepts and images again and again. He strenuously works out the implications of his *nuit de fer*, "night of fire." But he would not live to write his book. In November of 1661 the nuns of Port-Royal were forced to sign documents unequivocally denouncing Jansen, Jansenism, and the writings of Arnauld. A month before this dark ceremony Pascal's sister Jacqueline died, by all accounts simply of a broken heart; death was to her less fearful than the choice between denouncing her own most heartfelt beliefs and being excommunicated from the church she loved and sought to be wholly obedient to. Her brother's health was already declining, but from this point on the decline accelerated. He died in August of 1662, in agony. He was only thirty-nine years old.

In the *Pensées* he left behind there is continual testimony to what we have been calling the divided self: "Is it not as clear as day that man's condition is dual? The point is that if man had never been corrupted, he would, in his innocence, confidently enjoy both truth and felicity, and, if man had never been anything but corrupt, he would have no idea either of truth or bliss. But unhappy as we are ... we have an idea of happiness but cannot attain it." But Pascal believed that this duality is a temporary condition, one that will ultimately be resolved into simplicity. "It is clearly evident that man through grace is made like unto God and shares his divinity"—which we were originally made to do—"and without grace he is treated like the beasts of the field." Divinity and bestiality are the futures available to us, says Pascal, and each of us will inherit one or the other.

But while we are in this condition of duality, there is one key that will unlock our mysteriousness to ourselves, that will explain both our misery and our ambition for happiness: original sin.

It is ... an astounding thing that the mystery furthest from our ken, that of the transmission of sin, should be something without which we can have no knowledge of ourselves. Without doubt nothing is more shocking to our reason than to say that the sin of the first man has implicated in its guilt men so far from the original sin that they seem incapable of sharing it. This flow of guilt does not seem merely impossible to us, but indeed most unjust. What could be more contrary to the rules of our miserable justice than the eternal damnation of a child, incapable of will, for an act in which he seems to have had so little part that it was actually committed 6,000 years before he existed? Certainly nothing jolts us more rudely than this doctrine, and yet but for this mystery, the most incomprehensible of all, we remain incomprehensible to ourselves.

THE YEAR 1656 was a curious and, if one cares for emblematic moments, also an exceptionally eventful one in European religious history. In April King Jan Kazimierz of Poland staged the coronation of an icon, Our Lady of Częstochowa, the "Black Madonna," as queen and protector of Poland, believing that she had miraculously thwarted an attack on the monastery of Jasna Góra by a Swedish army. In October the English Quaker James Nayler reenacted Christ's triumphal entry into Jerusalem by riding into Bristol on a horse, a donkey apparently not being available, with disciples surrounding him singing hosannas. Menasseh ben Israel spent much of the year in London, consolidating his work in gaining for Jews readmission to England by writing and publishing his *Vindiciae Judaeorum*. Thus Rabbi Menasseh was absent from Amsterdam during the summer, when the Jewish community there formally and fiercely excommunicated a brilliant young scholar named Baruch Spinoza for unnamed "abominable heresies" and unspecified "monstrous deeds."* And in November came Pascal's *nuit de fer*.

---

* "By decree of the angels and by the command of the holy men, we excommunicate, expel, curse and damn Baruch de Espinoza, with the consent of God, Blessed be He, and with the consent of the entire holy congregation, and in front of these holy scrolls with the 613 precepts which are written therein; cursing him with the excommunication with which Joshua banned Jericho and with the curse which Elisha cursed the boys and with all the castigations which are written in the Book of the Law. Cursed be he by day and cursed be he by night; cursed be he when he lies down and cursed be he

It was also the year in which another brilliant literary career commenced, though with no fanfare at all. In Bedfordshire, England, there lived a half-educated tinker named John Bunyan, who in 1656 was twenty-eight years old. As a teenager he had been a soldier in Cromwell's Parliamentary Army and after his discharge had married and resumed work in and around his native Bedford. But throughout this period the chief concern of his life was his spiritual condition. As a younger man he had read some Christian books—in his autobiography he mentions the most popular devotional manual of that time, Arthur Dent's *Plain Man's Pathway to Heaven*—but did not feel any particular conviction to amend his life until one Sunday afternoon when, in disregard of the Puritan conviction that Sundays were days only for rest, prayer, and worship, he was playing a kind of lawn game called "cat" and heard a voice within him: "Wilt thou leave thy sins and go to heaven, or have thy sins and go to hell?"

Almost paralyzed by this unexpected intervention—"leaving my cat upon the ground, I looked up into heaven"—Bunyan began a long period of prayer, self-doubt, and spiritual terror. Almost immediately he began living a more outwardly Christian life, but looking back on that period in his life, the best he could say for himself was that he was now a "brisk talker . . . in matters of religion." True heartfelt conviction of sin was not yet his. That conviction eventually came, though along with it came a deep fear that he was irretrievably

when he rises up. Cursed be he when he goes out and cursed be he when he comes in. The Lord will not spare him, but then the anger of the Lord and his jealousy shall smoke against that man, and all the curses that are written in this book shall lie upon him, and the Lord shall blot out his name from under heaven. And the Lord shall separate him unto evil out of all the tribes of Israel, according to all the curses of the covenant that are written in this book of the law. But you that cleave unto the Lord your God are alive every one of you this day."

damned; and with such a fear he struggled for some years before, in 1654 or thereabouts, he settled his mind that he was truly a Christian and joined the small independent congregation in Bedford. According to the records he was the twenty-sixth member of that body.

The congregation's leader was a pious and energetic preacher named John Gifford. Bunyan had talked with him often during his long period of fear and confusion. But Gifford died in 1655, not long after Bunyan had joined the congregation, and almost immediately it was discovered that this young tinker was not just a passionate believer, but also a gifted speaker. In this culture where—in dramatic contrast to the established Church of England—the line between clergy and laity was virtually nonexistent, there were no barriers to Bunyan taking a leading role among his fellow "professors" (as those who "professed" saving faith in Christ called themselves). Soon he was known throughout the area around Bedford for his strong preaching, and this local prominence led him into more and more contact with other idiosyncratic religious groups in the area—of which there were many—and especially with Quakers. And it was Bedfordshire's Quakers who turned John Bunyan into an author.

It is very difficult to say with any specificity what Quakers—more properly, the Society of Friends, "Quaker" being a scornful nickname that later Friends wore as a badge of honor—actually believed, because Quakerism is essentially nondoctrinal. Even the pacifism that is now so closely associated with Quakerism was not originally a part of the movement; when Bunyan first came into conflict with them, many leading Quakers, including the aforementioned James Nayler, had like him served in the Parliamentary Army. (A quasi-official renunciation of violence came in 1661, when the most famous and influential Friend, George Fox, was deeply disillusioned by the restoration of the English monarchy.) But it's probably fair to say that all Quakers believed in the "inner light"—or "inward light," as it was first called by Fox, who also referred to it as the "Christ within."* Fox believed and taught that people have "no need of any teacher but the Light," because that light is accessible to anyone who has the patience to wait for it to manifest itself. Does not the first chapter of John's Gospel say that Jesus is "the true light, which enlightens everyone"? This is why Quaker meetings are without preaching and filled with silence; people speak only when illuminated by the light or, to shift the metaphor from the visual to the aural realm, when the Christ within speaks clearly to them.

Bunyan found such beliefs and practices repulsive. For one thing, he knew what it was like to hear voices "within," and in his case they had often been voices that drew him toward wickedness or persuaded him that he was damned. In these matters the Quakers, thought Bunyan, showed no discernment: they were perfectly happy to take any voice they heard as the "Christ within." And for Bunyan this could only be because they understood neither the power and glory of what we might call the Christ without—the Christ who died on the cross, rose from death, ascended into Heaven, and is seated at the right hand of the Father—nor the depths of their own wickedness. The Quakers were too credulous; they lacked the suspicion, the wariness proper to sinners, who are always being besieged by the forces of evil who seek our destruction.

Nayler did in fact write, in the year of his triumphal entry, that Christians placed far too much emphasis on the Bible as the Word of God—which, Nayler said, it most certainly is not—and on the historical Jesus. What Jesus did hundreds and hundreds of years ago

---

* Though Fox is now universally held to be the founder, during the 1650s Nayler was commonly thought to be the leader of the movement, and in fact he did write the first Quaker books. It was only after Nayler's disgrace and death that Fox's authority became undisputed.

is meaningless, thought Nayler, in comparison to what the Christ within can do and say now in each and every one of us. He called his ride into Bristol a "sign," and what he sought to signify by it was simply that every time a person who listens to the Christ within enters a town, that is effectively the Triumphal Entry all over again. It is vital to understand—Leopold Damrosch, Jr., forcefully demonstrates this in his wonderful book *The Sorrows of the Quaker Jesus*—that Nayler never for a moment succumbed to any delusion, never imagined that he was Jesus of Nazareth. His "sign" may have been the product of a disturbed mind, and perhaps Nayler was also driven by a sense of rivalry with Fox, with whom he had recently and seriously quarreled. But the sign was also the product of a clearly thought-out, if unorthodox, theology, one that was characteristic of most Quakers, even if they did not endorse Nayler's rather dramatic way of enacting it. When, after his "sign" got him thrown into prison and brought before interrogators, he was asked whether he was the only Son of God, his reply was, "I am the son of God, but I have many brethren." Fox on several occasions said almost the same.

In all the buzzing confusion generated by Nayler's strange behavior and by the provocative statements of many other Quakers, Bunyan saw what the real issues were and immediately sat down to write a book. In the typical style of the time, he gave it a title so exhaustive it all but substitutes for the book itself:

SOME GOSPEL TRUTHS OPENED, ACCORDING TO THE SCRIPTURES; OR, THE DIVINE AND HUMAN NATURE OF CHRIST JESUS, HIS COMING INTO THE WORLD, HIS RIGHTEOUSNESS, DEATH, RESURRECTION, ASCENSION, INTERCESSION, AND SECOND COMING TO JUDGMENT, PLAINLY DEMONSTRATED AND PROVED;

And also, Answers to several questions, with profitable directions to stand fast in the doctrine of Jesus the Son of Mary, against those blustering storms of the Devil's temptations, which

do at this day, like so many scorpions, break loose from the bot-
tomless pit, to bite and torment those that have not tasted the
virtue of Jesus, by the revelation of the Spirit of God.

So the first step in Bunyan's career as a writer was a polemic against
those who would narrow the gap between Christ and us, between
God and humanity, by diminishing the uniqueness of Christ's work
and person. For Bunyan, if the absolute uniqueness of Jesus Christ,
both in who he is and in what he does, goes, then the whole of Christianity goes with it.

But Bunyan also saw that the Quakers were playing a double game.
Even as they diminished the role of Jesus they uplifted the power of
humanity. Quakers have never formally denied original sin as such,
but then that is not the Quaker way; they lack any institutional mech-
anism through which even to make such decrees. Some Quakers have
endorsed it, while others have rejected it forcefully, among them
many in Bunyan's own time. A rejection of this doctrine was one
of the ways Quakers could most easily and unmistakably distinguish
themselves from Calvinist-Augustinian "professors" like Bunyan.
Christopher Hill, perhaps the greatest scholar of the many hetero-
doxies of the seventeenth century, mentions Quakers in Bunyan's
era who believed that a deep awareness of inherited and inescapable
sin—an awareness absolutely central to Bunyan's Christianity—was
simply the result of a hyperactive imagination. One even argues that
such awareness is the product of religious melancholy and therefore
should be treated as an illness, especially through manipulations of
the "sick soul's" diet. Presumably he would have prescribed Prozac,
had it been available.

These were actually common views among the various religious
groups who rejected the doctrine of original sin, some of them
more socially respectable than Quakers. In Bunyan's masterpiece,
The Pilgrim's Progress (1678), when Christian is encountered by

Mr. Worldly-Wiseman—clearly meant to represent broad-church Anglicanism—what the stranger immediately notices is the great weight Christian is carrying about on his back (which makes sense, since that's the first thing Bunyan tells us about his protagonist). He looks at poor Christian and cheerily cries, "How now, good fellow, whither away after this burdened manner?" (It is only later, when Christian looks upon Christ hanging upon the cross, that the burden instantly and without any effort on his part drops away.)

If Worldly-Wiseman is a portrayal of any particular person, the likeliest candidate is one Edward Fowler, the rector of the Anglican church at Northill, just outside of Bedford, and therefore a neighbor of Bunyan's. (Bunyan's brother Thomas lived in Northill.) In 1670 Fowler began to write books in defense of what he called "The Principles and Practices of Certain Moderate Divines of the Church of England," or what would later be known as Latitudinarianism. Fowler was at pains to insist upon "the reasonableness of the Gospel precepts" and to suggest that what did not seem to him reasonable could not possibly be Christian. Like Pelagius, he believed that God would not have commanded us to do anything that we cannot do; and if it ever seems that he has done so, that is only because we have misunderstood the nature of those commandments or have taken them too literally. People like Bunyan, with their emphasis on the corruption of our nature and our absolute dependence on grace, have become so fixed in their irrational convictions that they cannot even be argued with; they are not "men of tender consciences"—that is, they are not malleable—and should not be "dealt with" as such. Fowler was all for the forcible silencing of men like Bunyan, and indeed Bunyan spent a great deal of time in jail as a result of the policies that Fowler advocated.

In superficial matters and in certain others as well, men like Fowler scarcely resembled the Quakers. Like Bunyan and his fellow "professors," the Quakers thrived chiefly among the poor, whose dignity they upheld and whose cause they pleaded. Comfortable Anglicans like Fowler saw all the varying Dissenters as fanatics, extremists. Conversely, all the Dissenters, however much they may have disagreed on other matters, would have seen Fowler as a time-serving toady of the powers that be, which as far as I can tell he certainly was. Fowler managed to keep his living at Northill throughout the tumultuous years of the Restoration of the British monarchy by cheerfully conforming to whatever the dominant views happened to be. ("A glorious Latitudinarian," mocked Bunyan, "that can, as to religion, turn and twist like an eel on the angle; or rather, like the weathercock that stands on the steeple.") Fowler was actually quite open in his view that "Christian liberty" allows us to believe or practice whatever happens to be "commanded by the custom of the place we live in, or commanded by superiors, or made by any circumstances convenient to be done." In other words, Christian faith could never call for civil disobedience; to the contrary, such disobedience is always culpably "unpeaceful." (To which Bunyan replied, "How then if God should cast you into Turkey, where Mahomet reigns as Lord?") No wonder Fowler eventually rose to be Bishop of Gloucester.

English Quakers would have been just as appalled at all this as Bunyan was, and for the same reasons. Yet to Bunyan, on matters deeper and more important than these—which is to say, at the level of core doctrine—Fowler's views are "the self-same which our late ungodly heretics the Quakers have made such a stir to promote." Fowler and the Quakers alike denied the Augustinian picture of human beings coming into this world already carrying on their backs the burden of sin and helpless to shuck it off. That the Latitudinarians thought this view of human nature an affront to rational religion, while the Quakers thought it an affront to the mystical power of the inner light was to Bunyan irrelevant. What mattered was that he was surrounded, from the beginning of his career as a writer to his death in London in 1688, by people who denied and obscured what he believed to be the single most important truth of the human condition and thereby hid from people their only avenue of escape. There was but one path to the Celestial City, the path that Christian, the Pilgrim, takes.

Critics have also associated another character in *Pilgrim's Progress* with Edward Fowler: Ignorance. (For Bunyan, ignorance and worldly wisdom can scarcely be distinguished.) Ignorance is a man with a clear conscience. When Christian asks him why he thinks he is going to make it to Heaven, Ignorance answers, "My heart tells me so." When Christian reminds him that the book of Proverbs says, "He that trusts his own heart is a fool," Ignorance blithely counters, "That is spoken of an evil heart, but mine is a good one." When Christian asks him how he knows *this*, Ignorance says it is because his "heart and life agree together." When Christian asks him how he knows this, Ignorance simply circles back to his starting point: "My heart tells me so," and when Christian challenges this further, he simply says, "I will never believe that my heart is thus bad."

Eventually Ignorance grows tired of this conversation and leaves Christian and his friend Hopeful. But we have not seen the last of him. When Christian and Hopeful are being welcomed by angels into the Celestial City, they happen to catch a glimpse of a man knocking at the gates. It is Ignorance. And so the last words of Bunyan's story are not words of celebration or praise, but warning, warning to the Edward Fowlers of the world that there will come a time when neither their easy consciences nor their episcopal robes will save them. "The King . . . commanded the two shining ones that conducted Christian and Hopeful to the City to go out and take Ignorance and bind him hand and foot, and have him away. Then they took him up, and carried them through the air to the door that I saw in the side of the hill, and put him in there. Then I saw that there was a way to Hell, even from the Gates of Heaven as well as from the City of Destruction. So I awoke, and behold it was a dream."

SEVEN

More Hateful than Vipers

Our story so far has inscribed a clear pattern. From time to time in Western history, a vision of the greatness of human moral potential emerges or arises, only to find an immediate counter in an equally potent and vivid picture of human bondage to the sin we all inherit from Adam. Occasionally someone holds in a single conception these competing visions, no one more profoundly than Shakespeare. Thus Hamlet's outcry of praise: "What a piece of work is a man! how noble in reason! how infinite in faculty! in form and moving how express and admirable! in action how like an angel! in apprehension how like a god! the beauty of the world! the paragon of animals!" But, his voice and countenance dropping, he continues: "And yet, to me, what is this quintessence of dust?" Likewise that extraordinary moment in *The Tempest* when young Miranda sees a party of her fellow human beings for the first time: "O brave new world, that hath such people in it," she cries, and for a moment we too see ourselves as the miracles that we truly are, extraordinary creatures made in God's image. We remember, perhaps, Milton's brief lamenting catalogue in Book III of *Paradise Lost* of all that has been lost to him in his blindness: "Thus with the Year / Seasons return, but not to me returns / Day, or the sweet approach of Ev'n or Morn, / Or sight of vernal bloom, or Summer's Rose, / Or flocks, or herds, or human face divine." *Human face divine:* that is what Miranda sees, and we rejoice with her, until we hear her father's laconic and knowing reply to her celebration of the brave new world: "'Tis new to thee." A world of hurt lurks in that phrase. These humans do not improve with acquaintance, my child, he hints. And we think, that's true too.

But in the main the celebrants of human potential go to verbal war with the denouncers of our corruption. A Pelagius rises up only to be met by an Augustine. The Renaissance's praise of what that extravagant Italian scholar Pico della Mirandola called "the dignity of Man" finds its refutation in Calvin's insistence on our "total depravity." Comfortable Parisian Jesuits get lashed by an anonymous letter writer who in his private journals praises the doctrine of original sin as the one teaching able to reveal us to ourselves. Quakers and Latitudinarian Anglicans, in their placid insistence on the ease with which we can please God, inadvertently provoke one of the most brilliant and lastingly consequential literary careers in English history, a career prompted simply by the desire to reaffirm humanity's dire condition and helplessness to address that condition.

The pattern, then, is clear. But the two parties do not always have equal success. Indeed, it would seem that the Depravity Party had its greatest success in the time of Augustine, when the Pelagian forces were clearly routed. A millennium later the Reformers fought their humanist opponents to a draw, perhaps—the Augustinian picture of humanity prevailed in some parts of Europe, was scarcely influential elsewhere. In France the Jansenists were routed more decisively than the Pelagians had been in the Roman world and became a tiny sect that continued a few more decades, primarily in a small corner of the Netherlands. And in England the Latitudinarian movement grew stronger and more widespread, while Bunyan's descendants dwindled; the great historian of English Dissent, Michael Watts, argues convincingly that in the fifty years after Bunyan's death the general population of England grew considerably while the numbers of Dissenters declined.

But then came the Great Awakening. This great revival of the Christian faith, under the leadership of George Whitefield and John Wesley, transformed Anglo-American Christianity, initiating the evangelical movement, which still flourishes today and—thanks to its vast army of missionaries—has brought the Augustinian model of original sin to the whole world. It is, I think, fair to say that the continued existence of a strong doctrine of original sin depends upon the evangelical movement; where that movement has not flourished, neither has Augustine's understanding of human nature. The Great Awakening and its consequences will govern much of the rest of this story—but not all of it. The later history of original sin holds a few surprises.

George Whitefield was born in Gloucester in 1714, the son of an innkeeper who died when George was two, leaving the family near poverty and a gifted young man with few prospects. In light of his later career as an orator it is significant that Whitefield's first love was acting, but ultimately he realized that any real distinction in life would come to him only if he attended university. He came to Oxford's Pembroke College in 1732 as a "servitor"—that is, a student whose tuition was waived or reduced in exchange for his acting as a servant to other students. Four years earlier another great-man-to-be, Samuel Johnson, had come to Pembroke under precisely the same circumstances, but had left after a single year because of his complete destitution. Whitefield managed to stay the course, and in the process met and fell under the influence of a pious Fellow of Lincoln College named John Wesley.

Wesley was eleven years older than Whitefield and had had a wavering kind of spiritual career marked by crests of holiness followed by troughs of indifference, but by this time had settled himself on a steady commitment to piety coupled with deep scholarship. The young men he gathered around himself were known derisively as the "Holy Club," but they accepted the name. Wesley repeated this practice with a name a little later when people started referring to him and his followers as "Methodists" because they pursued a "method" for achieving a righteous life. The first thing Wesley wanted his friends to know was that true Christian holiness depends on an awareness of our own helpless captivity to the "sin in our members" with which we are born. This was not a message the exuberant and outgoing Whitefield took to immediately; but in his last year at Oxford, 1735, he accepted both his condition and Christ's remedy for it and forever after marked this as the moment of his conversion. (Years later he wrote, "Whenever I go to Oxford, I cannot help running to the spot where Jesus Christ first revealed himself to me, and gave me the new birth.")

He had now found not only his salvation, but also his vocation. A year later he was ordained as a minister of the Church of England and almost immediately—after only a few months of going back and forth between London and Oxford in various minor clerical roles—began the career that would make him one of the most famous men of his time, that of itinerant outdoor preacher. This was not so much a deliberate choice on his part as a kind of groping for an expedient in curious circumstances. Whitefield's love of performance was gratified by the task of preaching; his love of the Gospel was gratified by the positive responses he got, right from the beginning. His association with Wesley, a deeply suspicious figure in an Anglican world dominated by Latitudinarians, made him unwelcome at many churches, but the few vicars who allowed him to preach typically found their buildings overstuffed with eager listeners. Outdoor preaching seemed, then, to commend itself; he needed no churchman's approval, and, given the great power of his voice, virtually anyone who wished to hear him could do so.

And many, many people did so wish. Whitefield quickly crossed the Irish Sea to preach in Ireland, then, in 1739, made the greater adventure of coming to America. There he happened to meet one

Benjamin Franklin, whose commentary on his relationship with Whitefield is both funny and illuminating. Franklin's first interest in the preacher was more or less scientific. He had heard tales of Whitefield preaching to thousands of people and doubted whether a single human voice could possibly be heard by so many. So when Whitefield was preaching in Philadelphia, Franklin took the opportunity to circumnavigate the crowd, trying to ascertain the farthest distance at which the preacher's words could still be discerned. After doing some rough calculations Franklin came to the conclusion that "he might well be heard by more than thirty thousand," as indeed he often was.

But Franklin, though he liked Whitefield and admired his concern for the welfare of humanity, wasn't much interested in the evangelistic message. When Franklin offered to host Whitefield in his own home and the preacher expressed his gratitude that such an offer was made "for Christ's sake," Franklin corrected him: "Don't let me be mistaken; it was not for Christ's sake, but for your sake." Nevertheless, Franklin could not but admit, ruefully, that even he was subject to the suasive power of Whitefield's oratory:

> I happened . . . to attend one of his sermons, in the course of which I perceived he intended to finish with a collection, and I silently resolved he should get nothing from me. I had in my pocket a handful of copper money, three or four silver dollars, and five pistoles in gold. As he proceeded I began to soften, and concluded to give the coppers. Another stroke of his oratory made me asham'd of that, and determin'd me to give the silver; and he finish'd so admirably, that I empty'd my pocket wholly into the collector's dish, gold and all.

But this occurred when Whitefield was appealing for funds to support a charitable project of his, an orphanage he wished to build in

Georgia. Franklin's confession of weakness, in this context, is also a sly bit of self-praise: his heart was too tender to resist such a humanitarian cause. Whitefield's core evangelistic message, on the other hand, left Franklin not only cold, but baffled, because of the preacher's repeated insistence on the curse of original sin. "The multitudes of all sects and denominations that attended his sermons were enormous," wrote Franklin, "and it was matter of speculation to me, who was one of the number, to observe the extraordinary influence of his oratory on his hearers, and how much they admir'd and respected him, notwithstanding his common abuse of them, by assuring them that they were naturally half beasts and half devils."

It's likely that Franklin could have heard such "abuse" at almost any of Whitefield's sermons, because the great evangelist believed and repeatedly stated that an awareness not just of certain particular sins, but of the burden of original sin, was essential to true conversion. Here is an extended passage from a typical sermon, to give us just a taste of what it would have been like to hear Whitefield:

When the Comforter comes into a sinner's heart, though it generally convinces the sinner of his actual sin first, yet it leads him to see and bewail his original sin, the fountain from which all these polluted streams do flow.

Though every thing in the earth, air, and water; every thing both without and within, concur to prove the truth of that assertion in the scripture, "in Adam we all have died"; yet most are so hardened through the deceitfulness of sin, that notwithstanding they may give an assent, to the truth of the proposition in their heads, yet they never felt it really in their hearts. Nay, some in words professedly deny it, though their works too, too plainly prove them to be degenerate sons of a degenerate father. But when the Comforter, the Spirit of God, arrests a sinner, and convinces him of sin, all carnal reasoning against original corruption, every proud and high imagination, which exalteth itself against that doctrine, is immediately thrown down; and he is made to cry out, "Who shall deliver me from the body of this death?" He now finds that concupiscence is sin; and does not so much bewail his actual sins, as the inward perverseness of his heart, which he now finds not only to be an enemy to, but also direct enmity against God.

And did the Comforter, my dear friends, ever come with such a convincing power as this unto your hearts? Were you ever made to see and feel, that in your flesh dwelleth no good thing; that you are conceived and born in sin; that you are by nature children of wrath; that God would be just if he damned you, though you never committed an actual sin in your lives? So often as you have been at church and sacrament, did you ever feelingly confess, that there was no health in you; that the remembrance of your original and actual sins was grievous unto you, and the burden of them intolerable? If not, you have been only offering to God vain oblations; you never yet prayed in your lives; the Comforter never yet came effectually into your souls: consequently you are not in the faith properly so called; no, you are at present in a state of death and damnation.

For Whitefield, clearly, one can be aware of, and even repent of, particular sins without having a clear understanding of one's spiritual and moral condition and therefore without recognizing the One Path to salvation. That I commit this or that sin is not my problem; what afflicts me, rather, is this inborn, as it were "natural," "perverseness of the heart" that sets my own will at "enmity" with the will of God. As he put it, even more bluntly, in another sermon, "If you have never felt the weight of original sin, do not call yourselves Christians. I am verily persuaded original sin is the greatest burden of a true convert; this ever grieves the regenerate soul, the sanctified soul."

It was Whitefield's experience—and this, I think, should seem reasonable even to those who share none of his theological beliefs—that although this message was consistently offensive to people who held some status in the world (whether the Duchess of Buckingham or Mr. Benjamin Franklin), it could be a message of great comfort to the insulted, the degraded, and the poor. Not all of them, of course. Whitefield was often mocked and heckled by at least a portion of his crowds, and in his journal he makes the inadvertently slightly comical comment that he considered it an honor to be pelted with rotten fruit and "pieces of dead cats" for the sake of the Gospel. (The more dignified and scholarly John Wesley did not like the idea of outdoor evangelism precisely because he preferred not to be subjected to such possibilities, but eventually Whitefield talked him into it and he had some success.) But Whitefield also records in his journal a moving account of his experience preaching to coal miners near Bristol in 1739. The preaching did not go well at first—very likely there were some dead cats at hand—but gradually more and more of the miners came to hear his messages. "Having no righteousness of their own to renounce, they were glad to hear of a Jesus who was a friend to publicans, and came not to call the righteous, but sinners to repentance. The first discovery of their being affected, was to see the white gutters made by their tears, which plentifully ran down their black cheeks, as they came out of their coal pits."

Having no righteousness of their own to renounce—this is the heart of the matter, and a thought deeply consistent with the Catholic Rosenstock-Huessy's celebration of the Feast of All Souls as the "universal democracy" of sinners under judgment. These coal miners, who knew that they were not thought worthy of education, the vote, or perhaps even admission to the local Anglican church, heard from Whitefield that their condition was truly dire—but no more dire than his own or that of the local lord or the owners of the coal pits.

One of the great hymns of later (nineteenth-century) evangelicalism is Charlotte Elliott's "Just as I Am":

> *Just as I am, without one plea,*
> *But that Thy blood was shed for me,*
> *And that Thou bidst me come to Thee,*
> *O Lamb of God, I come, I come.*

This was the word of comfort that Whitefield brought to the miners: that God loves them just as they are and asks for nothing more than their repentant hearts, which is what he asks of everyone, even the Duchess of Buckingham. Really, it's no wonder they wept.

ANOTHER OF THE FRIENDS Whitefield made in America was a near contemporary of Franklin's, and like him a native New Englander, but in other respects about as different a personality as one could imagine. His name was Jonathan Edwards, and he was, among other things, the most powerful articulator of the Augustinian doctrine of original sin that America has ever produced or is ever likely to produce. Known today primarily for the overanthologized sermon "Sinners in the Hands of an Angry God," Edwards was certainly the leading American intellectual of his day and, arguably, as great and comprehensive a mind as this country has ever produced. And there has never been a more forceful defender of Calvinism, not even John Calvin himself.

Yet Edwards was also in many ways a man of the Enlightenment. In an age in which—among the intellectual elite anyway—the greatest commendation one could give to an idea was to affirm that it comported with reason, with "the common sense of humanity," it may seem remarkable to us that many conservative Christians used precisely the same language. Yet they did, and could do so even when complaining about the overuse of the terminology. "One's ears are so dinned with reason," wrote an English Presbyterian minister named John Barker in 1750, "the great law of reason, and the eternal law of reason, that it is enough to put one out of conceit with the chief excellency of our nature, because it is idolized and even deified." Note that even in his complaint Barker does not question that rationality *is* "the chief excellency of our nature"; and it is even more noteworthy that he was talking about what he heard from the pulpits of Dissenting chapels, not Latitudinarian Anglican churches.

Gertrude Himmelfarb, in her recent book *The Roads to Modernity: The British, French, and American Enlightenments*, is just one of many scholars to point out how indebted Whitefield's colleague John Wesley was to the then current emphasis on reason and common sense. For instance, in a debate about original sin with the Presbyterian preacher and theological controversialist John Taylor of Norwich, here is how Wesley responded to Taylor's claim that death is not a punishment for sin, but rather a gift from God: "To talk, therefore, of death's being a benefit, an original benefit, and that to all mankind, is to talk against the common sense and experience of the whole world."

So too with Edwards. When responding to theologians who had claimed that the Calvinist emphasis on the bondage of the sinful will, the inability of a person carrying the burden of Adam's sin to make a free choice, was not rational, Edwards calmly wrote that although "such doctrines, . . . in one age and another, through the blindness of men's minds, and strong prejudices of their hearts, are rejected, as most absurd and unreasonable, by the wise and great of the world," nevertheless, "when . . . most carefully and strictly examined," such doctrines prove to be "exactly agreeable to the most demonstrable, certain, and natural dictates of reason." (Edwards's vast treatise, *The Great Christian Doctrine of Original Sin Defended*, was in fact prompted by the very same John Taylor of Norwich whose views had agitated Wesley.) As George Marsden points out in his magisterial biography of Edwards, he may have devoted much of his career to defending ancient and seemingly outworn teachings, but he did so in the most contemporary idiom available to him. If Edwards shows nothing else, he shows that the doctrine of original sin is not bound to its late Roman origins and medieval development; it is possible, as Marsden puts it, to create a "post-Newtonian statement of classic Augustinian themes."

Post-Newtonian? Yes. Edwards is the first Christian thinker to adapt the explanation and defense of original sin to an intellectual context that celebrates "mechanical philosophy" and sees knowledge as most secure when it is supported by careful and repeated empirical observation. In a wonderful passage near the beginning of *The Great Christian Doctrine* Edwards—that notably strict and puritanical man—writes about throwing loaded dice: "A stated preponderation in the cause or occasion is argued only by a stated prevalence of the effect. If a die be once thrown, and it falls on a particular side, we do not argue from hence, that that side is the heaviest; but if it be thrown without skill or care, many thousands or millions of times, and it constantly falls on the same side, we have not the least doubt in our minds, but that there is something of propensity in the case, by superior weight of that side, or in some other respect." If your opponent in a dice game rolled double sixes every time, you'd be suspicious, wouldn't you? You would recognize, through careful observation, a meaningful pattern. So, then, "In the case we are upon, human nature, as existing in such an immense diversity of persons and circumstances, and never failing in any one instance of coming to that issue—that sinfulness, which implies extreme misery and eternal ruin—is as the die often cast."

Moreover, Edwards continues, such a recurring tendency tells us something not just about individual members of a given set, but about the whole set: "Thus, if there be a succession of trees of the same sort, proceeding one from another, from the beginning of the world, growing in all countries, soils, and climates, all bearing ill fruit; it as much proves the nature and tendency of the kind, as if it were only one individual tree, that had remained from the beginning of the world, often transplanted into different soils, and had continued to bear only bad fruit." Likewise, "if there were a particular family, which, from generation to generation, and through every remove to innumerable different countries, and places of abode, all died of a consumption, or all run distracted, or all murdered themselves," that would clearly constitute "evidence of the tendency of something in the nature or constitution of that race."

For Edwards, a careful post-Newtonian observer could scarcely deny the universality of human sinfulness: "Thus a propensity, attending the present nature or natural state of mankind, eternally to ruin themselves by sin, may certainly be inferred from apparent and acknowledged fact." What remains—and this is the chief task of his long book—is to argue that "the great Christian doctrine of original sin" is the best explanation for this "apparent and acknowledged fact" of human "ruin." In pursuing this course he tries very hard to rely on empirical demonstration as much as is possible, though this runs against his theological and philosophical grain, as he sometimes ruefully admits. At one point he's tempted to show why it must be the case that our sins outweigh, in God's eyes, any possible merit we might claim, but restrains himself, saying, "I shall omit a particular consideration of the evidence of this matter from the nature of things, as I study brevity, and lest any should cry out, metaphysics! as the manner of some is, when any argument is handled against a tenet they are fond of, with a close and exact consideration of the nature of things." There is far more humor in Edwards than new readers expect; I especially like his habit, throughout the treatise on original sin, of referring to John Taylor as "Dr. T."

To be sure, Edwards does not wholly shun rational debate. For instance, Dr. T., like Pelagius before him, insists that it would be unjust of God to bring us into this world in a condition of incompetence to do his will and obey his law. This would be to say that God is in effect the author of evil. But, also like Pelagius, Dr. T. acknowledges that all do in fact sin and therefore must account for why that should be, if we have no inborn propensity to do so. He therefore attributes our sad condition to environmental factors: the "pollution" of the world in which we live, which places temptation before us constantly. But Edwards jumps on this notion with both feet, pointing out that this doesn't at all get God off the hook: "Here may not I also cry out, on as good grounds as Dr. T.—Who placed the soul here in this world? And if the world be polluted, or so constituted as naturally and infallibly to pollute the soul with sin, who is the cause of this pollution? And, who created the world?"

Moreover, Edwards points out, those who wish to say that we sin not because of an inborn propensity, but because we see sin all around us, are simply "accounting for the thing by the thing itself, . . . accounting for the corruption of the world by the corruption of the world. For, that bad examples are general all over the world to be followed by others, and have been so from the beginning, is only an instance, or rather a description, of that corruption of the world which is to be accounted for."

Whether using (supposedly) empirical and historical evidence—neither Edwards nor Dr. T. ever doubts that the Bible offers an accurate historical record—or employing strictly rational and logical arguments, Edwards devotes more time to refuting his opponents' views than to making a positive case for the doctrine of original sin. Moreover, it is rather curious that he devotes so much time and effort to supporting the claim that human sinfulness is universal, given that this is something on which he and Dr. T. agree (as did Augustine and Pelagius before them). This is largely because the very specific claim that "all sinned in Adam" is not one obviously susceptible of either empirical or rational demonstration; it depends, rather, simply and straightforwardly on the biblical account. Yet there is a significant and rather disturbing section of Edwards's treatise in which he tries to support the doctrine through something other than an appeal to Paul's authority. His argument depends on certain events in the biblical narrative, events occurring long after Adam; and as has often been the case in the history of debates about original sin, Edwards's argument focuses on a particular subset of humanity: children.

Like Wesley, Edwards finds incredible Dr. T.'s assertion that death is a benefit rather than a punishment, and absurd Dr. T.'s claim that the curse God laid upon those who would eat of the tree of the knowledge of good and evil—"in the day that you eat from it, you shall surely die"—applied only to Adam and Eve, not to their posterity. All of us (with the curious possible exceptions of Enoch and Elijah) do in fact die, and Edwards is able to quote dozens of biblical verses showing clearly that death is a fearful, terrible thing, the worst of all afflictions, and the single universally applied punishment for sin. Why, then, do infants die? In those days they did in almost every family. It can only be because they share in the curse of Adam, though they have not yet exerted their own individual wills in anything.

Furthermore, continues Edwards—and this is grasping the nettle indeed—look (if you dare) upon those passages in Scripture in which God slew, or caused to be slain, the enemies of Israel. "When God executed vengeance on the ancient inhabitants of Canaan, he not only did not spare their cities and families for the sake of their infants, nor took care that they should not be involved in the destruction; but he often repeated his express commands, that their infants should not be spared, but should be utterly destroyed, without any pity." (This from the story of the conquest of Jericho, in the book of Joshua: "Then they devoted all in the city to destruction, both men and women, young and old, oxen, sheep, and donkeys, with the edge of the sword.") "And when God executed his wrath on the Egyptians, by slaying their first-born—though the children of Israel, who were most of them wicked men, as was before shown, were wonderfully spared by the destroying angel, yet—the Egyptian infants were not spared. They not only were not rescued by the angel, and no miracle wrought to save them (as was observed in the case of the infants of Sodom), but the angel destroyed them by his own immediate hand, and a miracle was wrought to kill them."

Edwards is not content with these examples. He points out that Moses was commanded to destroy all the Midianites, including their children (Num. 31); the Lord likewise ordered Saul to kill all the children and infants of the Amalekites (1 Sam. 15). Could he have done so, had they not been as blood-guilty as the rest of us? Even the children of his own people, Israel, were not to be spared, once the Israelites fell into idolatry. From the book of the prophet Ezekiel:

Now the glory of the God of Israel had gone up from the cherub on which it rested to the threshold of the house. And he called to the man clothed in linen, who had the writing case at his waist. And the Lord said to him, "Pass through the city, through Jerusalem, and put a mark on the foreheads of the men who sigh and groan over all the abominations that are committed in it." And to the others he said in my hearing, "Pass through the city after him, and strike. Your eye shall not spare, and you shall show no pity. Kill old men outright, young men and maidens, little children and women, but touch no one on whom is the mark. And begin at my sanctuary." So they began with the elders who were before the house. Then he said to them, "Defile the house, and fill the courts with the slain. Go out." So they went out and struck in the city.

And while they were striking, and I was left alone, I fell upon my face, and cried, "Ah, Lord God! Will you destroy all the remnant of Israel in the outpouring of your wrath on Jerusalem?"

Then he said to me, "The guilt of the house of Israel and Judah is exceedingly great. The land is full of blood, and the city full of injustice. For they say, 'The Lord has forsaken the land, and the Lord does not see.' As for me, my eye will not spare, nor will I have pity; I will bring their deeds upon their heads."

And behold, the man clothed in linen, with the writing case at his waist, brought back word, saying, "I have done as you commanded me." (9:3–11)

Here endeth the lesson.

"AS INNOCENT AS CHILDREN seem to be to us," wrote Edwards, "if they are out of Christ, they are not so in God's sight, but are young vipers, and infinitely more hateful than vipers." "There is a Corrupt Nature in thy children," the Puritan divine and historian Cotton Mather affirmed, half a century before Edwards, "which is a Fountain of all Wickedness and Confusion." He claimed that both the Jews and the great classical authorities knew this as well as he did. "Will not you that are Christians, then show your Christianity, by Sensibly doing what you can, that your Children may have a Better Nature infused into them?"

Still earlier in that century (the seventeenth), Jesuit missionaries in Canada—not all French Jesuits were Pascal's pampered Parisian lapdogs—had been deeply troubled to learn that the Huron people would not physically punish their children, but rather grew angry when the Jesuits applied the rod. The priests and their coworkers the Ursuline nuns found the Huron parents deficient in understanding and love alike and believed such attitudes to be nearly fatal to pedagogy as well as spirituality. "All the savage tribes of these quarters," one priest wrote, "cannot chastise a child or see one chastised. How much trouble this will give us in carrying out our plans of teaching the young!" They were quick to reward and praise those Huron converts to Catholic Christianity who whipped or even struck and kicked their recalcitrant children, for such behavior revealed a proper and godly intolerance of the sinful nature in the young ones. In any event the priests and nuns thought themselves the true and loving parents of the Huron children under their care. Does not the Bible say, "Whom God loves he chastises"?*

The question of the "nature" exhibited by infants and young children had been central to the debates between Augustine and, especially, Julian; but they had never assumed as central a position in the intellectual life of a whole culture as they came to assume in the eighteenth century. The concerns expressed by Mather and the Jesuits intensified dramatically in the next hundred years, and theologians and other thinkers took up the issue of what children are really like in a much more comprehensive way than Edwards.

Late in his life, in the 1780s, John Wesley preached a curious and revealing sermon, "On the Education of Children." He initiates the substance of his argument with a long quote from his older contemporary, William Law, whose book *A Serious Call to a Devout and Holy Life* (1728) was perhaps the single most significant precursor to Wesleyan spirituality and continued to be influential for another

---

* Clarissa W. Atkinson, from whose fascinating article on these missionaries I learned most of what I know about them, warns us that we should not construct facile and moralistic dichotomies based on such episodes. If the Huron could be shocked by what they felt to be French and Christian brutality in corporally punishing children, the Jesuits and Ursulines were perhaps even more shocked when they learned that the Huron commonly dealt with orphans in their community by killing them.

hundred years or more.* What is most striking about Law is the combination of a deep commitment to life-transforming Christian faith along with a matter-of-fact employment of many of the categories and concerns of the Enlightenment.

For Law education is simply a variety of "physic," or medicine—and, as that marvelous historian the late Roy Porter pointed out in many books, medicine is not only a central practice of eighteenth-century English culture, but also a nearly inexhaustible source of metaphors. "Had we continued perfect as God created the first man," writes Law, "perhaps the perfection of our nature had been a sufficient self-instructer for every one. But as sickness and diseases have created the necessity of medicines and physicians, so the disorders of our rational nature have introduced the necessity of education and tutors." This is the first time in our history that we hear of our propensity to sin as a "disorder of our rational nature," and the first time it is described as a disease, at least in something like the modern sense of that term. (As we have seen, it was often in the early church referred to as a "wound" and sometimes as a "contagion.")

Law continues, with the air of a man stating the obvious: "As the only end of a physician is, to restore nature to its own state, so the only end of education is, to restore our rational nature to its proper state. Education, therefore, is to be considered as reason borrowed as second-hand, which is, as far as it can, to supply the loss of original perfection. And as physic may justly be called the art of restoring health, so education should be considered in no other light, than as the art of recovering to man his rational perfection." But for a Christian, as Law makes clear, this "rational perfection" consists

---

* Samuel Johnson wrote of Law's book: "When at Oxford, I took up Law's Serious Call, expecting to find it a dull book (as such books generally are), and perhaps to laugh at it. But I found Law quite an overmatch for me; and this was the first occasion of my thinking in earnest of religion after I became capable of rational inquiry."

in knowing God—the God of Scripture—and in obeying his commandments. This is more than a little like Sir Philip Sidney's claim that our "erected wit" can help to compensate for our "infected will," though it is interesting that Law does not here speak of the will at all, but rather simply of our rational faculties. But Law more than Sidney emphasizes training in theology and Christian morality as the chief means by which a proper education is to be pursued.

It is from this passage in the *Serious Call* that Wesley begins his account of how Christians are to educate their children. His first question, after citing Law at length, is simply this: "What are the diseases of [the child's] nature? What those spiritual diseases which every one that is born of a woman brings with him into the world?" And he concludes, perhaps surprisingly, that the first of them is atheism.

Let us pause here for a moment to return to Augustine. The African bishop has been much mocked in recent years—centuries?—for his account of childhood in his *Confessions,* and especially for his claim that the inborn sinfulness of infants can be seen in their selfishness, their determination always to have their own way, the wrath they exhibit when they do not get what they want, and so on. And perhaps we, with our deeper knowledge of the development of infants' minds, have good reason to make fun of Augustine on this point. But let's be fair. Does not his account do better justice to the phenomena, as the philosophers might say, than Wordsworthian fluff about the innocence and purity of children? Certainly I have always wondered whether those who talk about "childlike innocence" have had children of their own or even spent much time around them. Augustine's lack of sentimentality on this point can be, if one considers it in a certain light, rather refreshing.

Likewise Wesley's sermon, which cuts nicely through some pious crap about kids. Thus: "After all that has been so plausibly written concerning 'the innate idea of God'; after all that have been said of its being common to all men, in all ages and nations; it does not appear, that man has naturally any more idea of God than any of the beasts of the field; he has no knowledge of God at all; no fear of God at all; neither is God in all his thoughts. Whatever change may afterwards be wrought (whether by the grace of God or by his own reflection, or by education), he is, by nature, a mere Atheist." Any mere awareness of God we possess we have received, as Law puts it, at second hand; far less are we naturally reverent or obedient. Indeed, says Wesley, whatever common sins one can lay to the account of people in general one must also lay to the account of children. They're just like us, or perhaps it is better to say, we're just like them.

And what are the sins to which we are all habitually prone? Wesley thinks the most important are self-will ("Every man is by nature, as it were, his own god"), pride, "love of the world," anger, "deviation from truth," and a tendency "to speak or act contrary to justice." For Wesley, the education of children consists primarily, if not exclusively, in discerning these sins and rooting them out as aggressively as possible. The weeds of sin must be plucked up by the roots before they become too deeply established, ineradicable. He also insists that children should not be allowed to "cry aloud" after they reach the age of one and bluntly affirms that he knows that this can be done: "My own mother had ten children, each of whom had spirit enough; yet not one of them was ever heard to cry aloud after it was a year old." (John Taylor—Edwards's Dr. T.—also addresses the disobedience of children, but is reluctant to attribute it to sin, blaming instead "the animal passions [that are] for some years the governing part of their constitution." This sounds civilized in our ears.)

One must not be unfair to Wesley; he also speaks of the need to inculcate a loving spirit in children, a spirit of gratitude and gentleness. But his primary emphasis is on parents' need "to break the will of your child, to bring his will into subjection to yours, that it may be afterward subject to the will of God." For Wesley—as for Christians throughout history—it is essential to the Christian life that we obey

God, that we conform our wills to his, and the "sin in our members" always resists such conformity. Moreover, it is reasonable to infer that if we do not begin disciplining ourselves at an early age, we will find obedience all the more difficult once we reach adulthood. Indeed, if we grant a few basic assumptions, most of Wesley's model of education can seem quite reasonable, except perhaps for quirks like his strenuous dislike of crying. Too bad for him and for his cause that the book had already been written that would make almost everything he says sound ridiculous to millions of people for centuries to come.

THAT BOOK IS CALLED *Émile,* and it was written by Jean-Jacques Rousseau. At the outset of the second volume of his nearly definitive biography of Rousseau, Maurice Cranston summarizes his subject's first forty years on earth:

> Rousseau's early life was that of a wanderer, an adventurer, the life of a hero of a picaresque novel. Orphaned by the early death of his mother and the defection of his father, he had run away from his native Geneva at the age of sixteen to escape the life of a plebeian engraver's apprentice, and found refuge as a Catholic convert in Savoy. Making his own way in the world as a footman in Turin, a student at a choir school in Annecy, the steward and the lover of a Swiss baroness in Chambéry, the interpreter to a Levantine mountebank, an itinerant musician, a private tutor in the family of Condillac and Mably in Lyons, secretary to the French Ambassador in Venice and research assistant to the Dupins at Chenonceaux, he set out with his great friend and contemporary Denis Diderot to conquer Paris as a writer, and, much to his own surprise, did so almost overnight at the age of thirty-eight with the publication of his *Discourse on the Sciences and Arts.*

It is hard to think of another famous writer or thinker who had reached the age of thirty-eight while showing fewer signs of promise. But when Rousseau finally got his chance, he made the most of it. This first book of his—the *First Discourse,* as it was later called—emerged as Rousseau's entry in a contest sponsored by the Académie de Dijon, whose members wished to see the best essay on a set question: Has the development of the arts and sciences been morally beneficial to humanity? Rousseau later claimed that the answer to the question— No—and the reasons for that answer came to him in a kind of epiphany or revelation; all that remained was for him to transcribe what had been given him. It was instantly clear to Rousseau that the development of the arts and sciences had but corrupted us, alienated us from our original innocent condition, and deprived us of the power to recapture that condition. The essay in which he made these claims not only won the Académie's prize in 1750, but became wildly popular, debated and discussed throughout France but especially in Paris, where the young Genevan exile found himself a celebrated figure.

The book and its key ideas have not always been so well received; in the twentieth century the writer Jules Lemaitre commented that the *First Discourse*'s success was "one of the strongest proofs ever provided of human stupidity." Likewise, when Rousseau developed the same ideas further in his still more famous *Second Discourse*—the *Discourse on the Origins of Inequality*—and sent it with his compliments to that great lion among French philosophers Voltaire, he got in return this coldly sardonic reply: "I have received, Monsieur, your new book against the human race, and I thank you. No one has employed so much intelligence to turn us men into beasts. One starts wanting to walk on all fours after reading your book. However, in more than sixty years I have lost the habit." But there is no doubt that Rousseau's ideas struck an enormously resonant chord in the mind of his whole age; he was soon being read and discussed not just throughout France, but throughout Europe.

Though today Rousseau's most famous book may be *The Social Contract*, with its resonant first sentence—"Man is born free, but everywhere he is in chains"—in his lifetime his most celebrated works were surely his two novels. The first, *Julie, or the New Heloise*, is the tale of two lovers forbidden to marry, who (like the famous medieval lovers Heloise and Abelard) find a higher happiness in a purer love, a union of souls who have risen beyond the need for physical companionship and erotic passion. Upon *Julie's* publication in 1761 Rousseau was deluged with letters from readers who had been emotionally overcome by the story. One of them, a Baron Thiébault, reported that when he finished the book he was "no longer weeping, but crying out, howling like a beast." The second novel is a kind of philosophical tale called *Émile, or on Education*, which appeared in 1762. (Edwards's great treatise on original sin had been published just four years earlier, the same year in which Edwards died from a smallpox inoculation. It is strange to reflect that Edwards was only nine years older than Rousseau.) And *Émile* deserves some significant attention from us.

Near the end of his life Rousseau said of *Émile*, "This book . . . is simply a treatise on the natural goodness of man, intended to show how vice and error are foreign to his constitution, invade it from outside, and imperceptibly alter it." For Rousseau, nothing is more destructive to true education—to the making of fully human persons—that the belief that we are born in corruption. Near the beginning of Book II of *Émile*, as he is beginning to discuss the first steps in the education of a child, he states his key conviction firmly: "Let us set down as an incontestable maxim that the first movements of nature are always right; there is no original perversity in the human heart. There is not a single vice to be found in it of which it cannot be said how and whence it entered."

In making the rejection of the Christian doctrine of original sin a kind of first principle, Rousseau was simply announcing his agreement with almost all of the leading figures of the Enlightenment—of all the various Enlightenments, whether French, English, Scottish, or German. As the German philosopher Ernst Cassirer once noted: "The concept of original sin is the common opponent against which all the different trends of the philosophy of the Enlightenment join forces. In this struggle Hume is on the side of English deism, and Rousseau of Voltaire; the unity of the goal seems for a time to outweigh all differences as to the means of attaining it." Of course, this rejection of the Augustinian position immediately created a puzzle of its own. If sinfulness is not innate, why is it so (apparently) universal? As Cassirer also points out, this was the challenge that Pascal had presented to unbelievers in his *Pensées*, and Pascal was a figure much reckoned with in the eighteenth century, especially in France. Voltaire calls him the "sublime misanthrope" and contests his low estimation of human nature from the beginning of his career to the end, though never very successfully and certainly not consistently.*

But it was Rousseau rather than Voltaire who saw a way to answer Pascal's challenge—or so thought no less a personage than Immanuel Kant, though he did not agree with Rousseau's picture in all its details. But he admired its ingenuity, its pathbreaking innovativeness, and thought that Rousseau's achievement was worthy to be compared with Newton's discoveries in physics. The key to Rousseau's argument in *Émile*, Kant believed, was the distinction he makes early

---

* Though never precisely an optimist in the technical sense, Voltaire did believe early in his career that the world and humanity are "what they should be," a view that he no longer found tenable after the great Lisbon earthquake of 1755, in which thirty thousand people died in space of a few minutes. The philosopher Rebecca Neiman, writing about the mature Voltaire, points out that "It is striking that the one Christian myth to which Voltaire wished to cling was the myth of the Fall. He held the notion of original sin to be a truer reflection of human experience than the optimistic doctrines of [Alexander] Pope or the Socinians."

on between two kinds of self-love, *amour de soi* and *amour-propre*. These are not translatable terms, but when *amour-propre* (a commonplace French term, in Rousseau's time as in ours) is translated, the usual word is "pride" or "vanity." *Amour de soi* simply means "love of self," and Rousseau insists that it "in itself or relative to us is good and useful; and since it has no necessary relation to others, it is in this respect naturally neutral. It becomes good or bad only by the application made of it and the relations given to it."

Amour de soi, then, is simply the instinct that we all have to preserve and care for ourselves. Yes, we come here with *amour de soi* as part of our original equipment, as it were, but there is nothing remotely sinful about it; indeed, we could not survive without it. It is only when *my amour de soi* comes into contact with *your amour de soi* that the troubles begin—and it is for just this reason that the first great principle of Rousseau's pedagogy is isolation: isolation of the child from other people, so that, accompanied only by a tutor who knows how to stay out of the way, the child might learn from nature. As Allan Bloom points out in his translation of *Émile*, Rousseau was very aware of the dark view of human society articulated by Thomas Hobbes a century earlier in his *Leviathan*: that there will always be certain goods or possessions that more than one person will want, and that such scarcity of resources will inevitably produce a "warre of every man against every man." It is precisely to avoid this "warre" that Rousseau isolates the child. Émile will have his willfulness checked and restrained, but by the impersonal hand of nature rather than the imposition of other human wills.

Rousseau is aware, of course, that it is scarcely practical to think of raising all children in such extreme and, we might say, unnatural conditions. He only creates this scenario at all in order to show just how seriously he takes Pascal's claims about the depravity of human beings—though of course he wishes to contest, as vigorously as possible, Pascal's explanation for that depravity. Rousseau himself is a misanthrope, though perhaps not a sublime one. To a claim like that of the early Voltaire, that people and the world as a whole are "as they should be," Rousseau replies, in effect, "Are you *nuts*?" The evidence of our wickedness is thick on the ground, and Rousseau no less than Augustine and his followers sees that the key question we must answer is truly *Unde hoc malum?* Where does such evil come from?

Rousseau answers that it cannot come from the hand of God, whom we know by the innate promptings of our conscience, which for Rousseau are always more reliable than the calculations of reason, to be utterly good. "Everything is good as it leaves the hands of the Author of things," go the first words of *Émile*, "everything degenerates in the hands of man." (Kant's great praise for Rousseau stemmed from his belief that Rousseau comes closer than anyone before to achieving a true theodicy, a justification of the ways of God to men.) Rather, evil comes from the transformation of *amour de soi* into *amour-propre* when our desires come into conflict with the desires of others. Thus the need—in ideal circumstances—for our wills to be disciplined by nature until they are so well trained that the opposition of *human* wills will not endanger our moral equilibrium.

Rousseau believed that because we fail to understand our own nature, and therefore the nature of the problems we face in trying to raise children up to the full stature of humanity, we start making mistakes from the day a child emerges into this world. "A child cries at birth; the first part of his childhood is spent crying. At one time we bustle about, we caress him in order to pacify him; at another, we threaten him, we strike him in order to make him keep quiet. Either we do what pleases him, or we exact from him what pleases us. Either we submit to his whims, or we submit him to ours. No middle ground; he must give orders or receive them. Thus his first ideas are those of domination or servitude." (Rousseau only thinks of the instruction of male children, so in my exposition I will join him in the use of the masculine pronoun.) Such ideas must not be allowed to form; every possible care must be taken that the child never learn to think of relations with others as relations of "domination" and "servitude." And this insight mandates a rather curious role for Emile's faithful and ever present tutor.

I have already noted that one of the tasks of the tutor, as Rousseau conceives the role, is to stay out of the way so that the pupil may become a true disciple of Nature. But it would appear, from the events of *Émile*, that Nature does not always live up to its responsibilities. In fact, Nature often seems indifferent to the education of our children and misses chance after chance to instruct them in wisdom. This means that the tutor must often exercise considerable ingenuity to get child and Nature in proper contact with one another. (Not just the tutor, by the way, must do this. Even the mothers who care for their children until they are turned over to tutors need to do the same, for instance, by gradually, night by night, decreasing the temperature of a small child's bathwater until it is positively icy, which inures the boy to physical discomfort so that, when he experiences it in the future, it will not cause moral or emotional perturbations.) Much of the narrative of *Émile* records the tutor's efforts in this regard.

Those efforts continue when the tutor begins the slow and gradual introduction of Émile to human society. One of the more curious incidents in the book occurs when Émile and his tutor witness, at a pond near their home where a small group of people have gathered, a magician who makes a toy duck pursue a piece of bread in his hand. Émile is entranced, but later, when his tutor reveals to him that this is a trick performed by the use of magnets in the duck and the bread, he is angry at being deceived. He learns the trick himself, so that he can get back at the magician—but the magician is quick to respond with a still more elaborate maneuver that leaves Émile once more baffled and frustrated and, worse, makes him the object of mockery by the crowd. Later the magician visits Émile's house to reveal his contrivance, and the tutor takes the opportunity to explain to Émile how vanity—*amour de soi* fully transformed into *amour-propre*—exposes us to all sorts of "mortifying" experiences.

Here's what's most noteworthy about the scene: the whole sequence of events is stage-managed by the tutor. The magician and the crowd alike are enlisted by the tutor to perform according to a script written by him. It's all a play, a performance for Émile's benefit, but this is never revealed to him. Why? Because that would reveal the tutor's officious interventions, which for Rousseau is strictly impermissible. Why can't that role be revealed? Because if Émile knew that he was being taught, he would rebel against the teaching. The scene of instruction must appear to be accidental, "natural," even if in fact it never is.

Among Rousseau's biographers, Cranston seems to face this troubling tendency more straightforwardly than Damrosch does. The latter writes, in response to the claim that such manipulativeness is a kind of "sadism": "But manipulativeness is the point. Growing up in society, no one can possibly live as a natural man, and the tutor's role is to create artificial situations in which Émile will develop properly without realizing it." But why should this be the tutor's role? Isn't that a rather odd role? Why should the fact that "no one can possibly live as a natural man" in society lead automatically to a pedagogy based on lying?

It's interesting that in this context Damrosch quotes approvingly a little dialogue Rousseau produces early in the book, in which a child is reproved for some action and told that he will be punished, to which the child replies, "I shall fix it so that nothing is known about it."

MASTER: You will be spied on.
CHILD: I shall hide.
MASTER: You will be questioned.
CHILD: I shall lie.

MASTER: You must not lie.

CHILD: Why must I not lie?

MASTER: Because it is bad to do, etc.

"This is the inevitable circle," notes Rousseau sagely. But why need it be a circle? It is perfectly possible for someone to explain to a child why lying is bad, something Rousseau avoids acknowledging by interposing his "etc." Rousseau has worked himself into a strange position. Believing that all human beings are upon their arrival in the world naturally and perfectly innocent, he nevertheless thinks that we must, even in the best of circumstances, undergo lengthy and strenuous moral instruction, and that the most extraordinary care must be taken that we never discover that we are being instructed, lest we rebel and fall into the very depths of sin, which Rousseau and Pascal alike agree is the common fate of human beings.

In Rousseau's model, a child who comes at an ideal age into the care of an ideal tutor who controls seemingly inexhaustible resources for managing that child's education and who can stage-manage everything from a little magic trick to the child's eventual marriage to an ideal young woman—such a child still cannot be taught virtue directly, but must be manipulated into developing along virtuous lines. It seems to me that Rousseau's whole model implicitly admits that our *amour de soi* is, quite "naturally," *amour-propre* after all. One might almost think that we arrive in this world already selfish, rebellious, and corrupt.

And it appears that Rousseau had even less confidence in his pedagogical model than these extremities and inconsistencies suggest. For several years after the publication of *Émile* Rousseau worked, intermittently, on a sequel. In it he explores the life of Émile after he marries Sophie, the perfect wife whom the tutor chose for him and arranged for him to meet—though of course without ever telling his charge that he had played any role in the union at all—and it is not a happy life. The young couple have a child, who dies. They grow disenchanted with each other and become estranged; each has affairs; Sophie becomes pregnant by another man; they part. Émile wanders and is eventually captured by pirates and sold into slavery. At this point Rousseau gave up the tale. In his misery the only benefit Émile receives from his education is his knowledge of cabinetmaking, which his tutor had made him learn so that he never need starve for lack of employable skill. Rousseau called the unfinished book *Émile et Sophie, ou Les Solitaires*—the Solitaries, the Lonely Ones.

IN HER WONDERFUL BOOK *The Lunar Men,* Jenny Uglow tells the story of a group of friends who lived, in the eighteenth and early nineteenth centuries, in the neighborhood of the English city of Birmingham. Among them were the great potter Josiah Wedgewood, the physician-naturalist-poet Erasmus Darwin, the engineer James Watt, and several others. A peripheral member of this group was an enthusiastic and imaginative man named Richard Lovell Edgeworth, who in 1765 decided to raise his three-year-old son, also named Richard, according to the principles articulated in *Émile*. (The book had prompted great and generally admiring conversation among the whole group.) He had the boy go barefoot almost the year round—Rousseau was deeply committed to raising shoeless children—and let him roam wherever he wished, learning such lessons as nature was pleased to teach him without recourse to book learning. "He had all the virtues of a child bred in the hut of a savage," Edgeworth later wrote, "and all the knowledge of things, which could well be acquired by a boy bred in civilised society." By the age of seven the boy was, in his father's estimation, "bold, free, fearless, generous." The proud father even took his son to see, and be seen by, Rousseau; the great man was pleased by young Richard's command of historical knowledge, but discerned in him "a propensity to party prejudice, which will be a great blemish in his character." (It appears that when the boy saw something he found admirable—a horse, a carriage, even "a pair of shoe-buckles"—he declared it to be English.)

In his memoirs, where he recounts this incident, Edgeworth does not record his reaction to Rousseau's stern warnings. But ultimately, to what Uglow calls "Edgeworth's innocent bafflement," unexpected problems arose. The child "was not disposed to *obey*," Edgeworth wrote, plaintively; he showed "too little deference to others" and had "an invincible dislike of control." Several tutors found the boy unmanageable and resigned in frustration. Eventually Edgeworth, with infinite reluctance, gave up on his Rousseauian dreams and sent Richard to a Catholic school in France, where rigorous discipline ruled every minute of every day and disobedient boys were flogged to within an inch of their lives.

Years later the elder Edgeworth berated himself for his foolishness. "I must here acknowledge, with deep regret, not only the error of a theory, which I had adopted at a very early age, when older and wiser persons than myself had been dazzled by the eloquence of Rousseau; but I must also reproach myself with not having, after my arrival in France, paid as much attention to my boy as I had done in England, or as much as was necessary to prevent the formation of those habits, which could never afterwards be eradicated." Richard the younger never took well to schooling of any kind. He became a sailor and eventually immigrated to America, dying in North Carolina at the age of thirty-two.

Though his end was early and sad, one can easily imagine the thoughts that led him across the seas. What better place to shed the burdens of a painful past and start over? Almost like Adam in Eden.

EIGHT

New Worlds

W hen Edgeworth wrote that his young son "had all the virtues of a child bred in the hut of a savage," he was referring to what is now Rousseau's most famous idea, if it can be called an idea—it's more like an image: the noble savage. And having noted that the younger Edgeworth ended his brief career by going to America, we move our story to a new location, where it takes on new levels of complexity and sentences patient readers to ever escalating befuddlement. Perhaps each chapter in this book could be a book in itself, but none of them would make longer books than the two that follow. The tortured story of American history and the doctrine of original sin surely forms the most complex episode of my narrative.

The notion of the "noble savage" now seems welded to the name of Rousseau, but he did not originate either the phrase or the idea— the idea, that is, that certain human beings live (have always lived) in a state of primitive innocence and are not marked by the taint of sin, at least not as the rest of us are marked. Associations gravitate to this core idea like iron shavings encircling a magnet, and not all of them have anything to do with original sin as such: the belief that primitive people know how to live "in harmony with nature," for instance, or that they are fundamentally cooperative (in contrast to our own maniacal competitiveness), or that they remain childlike throughout their simple lives. Savages, children, Americans—they all get mixed together in the rising cult of primitivism in the eighteenth and nineteenth centuries. Sometimes it can even be hard to tell them apart.

It appears that the poet John Dryden, near the end of the seventeenth century, was the first to use the English phrase *noble savage* ("I am as free as Nature first made man / 'Ere the base Laws of Servitude began / When wild in woods the noble Savage ran"); but the *idea* assumed a permanent place in the rhetoric of the Western world a hundred years earlier, with Michel de Montaigne's essay "On Cannibals." There Montaigne, having met some Caribbean Indians who had lately visited France, contests the belief, held (he says) by most of his compatriots, that such people are barbaric and cruel. Noting France's quite recent history of bloody religious war, Montaigne says he can see nothing in the lives of the "savages" to match it; and then, having interviewed one of the visitors, he claims to have discerned little in him other than gentleness, common sense, and a commitment to human equality that (Montaigne implies) made the elaborate hierarchies of the French court seem comparatively silly.*

Montaigne's satirical purpose in "On Cannibals" requires him to insist that his fellow Frenchmen always assume their own habits and

---

* It is noteworthy that when Benjamin Franklin decided to write an essay on American Indians, two hundred years after Montaigne, he swallowed the rhetoric whole. Montaigne had written, "I think there is nothing barbarous and savage in that [Caribbean] nation, from what I have been told, except that each man calls barbarism whatever is not his own practice; for indeed it seems we have no other test of truth and reason than the example and pattern of the opinions and customs of the country we live in." And Franklin began his essay with the same thought, more tersely expressed: "Savages we call them, because their manners differ from ours, which we think the perfection of civility; they think the same of theirs. Perhaps, if we could examine the manners of different nations with impartiality, we should find no people so rude, as to be without any rules of politeness; nor any so polite, as not to have some remains of rudeness."

practices to be civilized and see those of other nations as barbaric. But in fact the French, and most Europeans, had always been susceptible to the idea that somewhere, in a distant and unknown corner of the world, there were people living in peace and harmony in circumstances far superior to those of Europeans. It was this romantic notion that, decades before Montaigne, Thomas More had been satirizing by creating just such a distant and ideal society and christening it Utopia—that is, "Nowhere." Travelers' tales during the European Middle Ages often reported on eastern or southern kingdoms of marvelous wealth and perfect peacefulness. The most famous and compelling of such tales centered on the legendary figure of Prester John, whose Christian kingdom was sometimes placed in Africa, more often in Asia, and on medieval maps nearly always abutted the earthly paradise itself. The gentle governance of Prester John and the shrewd and wise laws he laid down always revealed by contrast the corruption of European rulers and the foolishness of European ways.

So Montaigne's compatriots were perhaps not as parochial as he made them out to be, nor was his language, with its idealizing of far-flung and little-known societies, anything very new. But there *is* something distinctive in Montaigne's suggestion that the excellence of Caribbean society derives at least in part from its simplicity, its lack of political hierarchy and social complexity. This is a trope that begins gathering momentum in the latter sixteenth century. Shakespeare's Lear, for instance, employs a version of it when he and his small entourage, exiled onto the heath, meet the naked madman Poor Tom: "Is man no more than this? Consider him well. Thou owest the worm no silk, the beast no hide, the sheep no wool, the cat no perfume. Ha! here's three on's are sophisticated! Thou art the thing itself: unaccommodated man is no more but such a poor bare, forked animal as thou art. Off, off, you lendings! come unbutton here."

Of course, Lear's notion that by casting off his clothes he can cast off his misery—that by assuming Tom's simple madness he can evade the complex inheritance of his own bad decisions—is tragically mistaken. Shakespeare often in his plays has rich and "civilized" characters seek a simpler life by heading for the forest or the countryside, and this is a fertile source of satirical humor. Yet there remains in Shakespeare a constant recognition that, however naive such flight from civilization might be, it's prompted by an insight that's authentic and reasonable. You can say something similar about Shakespeare's great contemporary Cervantes, whose Don Quixote ends his career as a madman by turning himself from an imaginary knight into an imaginary shepherd—sheep herding being a simpler, more rural, more ancient vocation than knight-errantry.

The city dweller's desire for country simplicity is, of course, as old as cities themselves. The most famous and nuanced depictions of the contrast come from the great Roman poet Horace, but Horace was working in the centuries-old tradition of the Greek poet Theocritus, and some of Theocritus's imagery derives from Homer. So these are old themes, indeed. And yet there is something different happening in the kind of rhetoric that we see in Montaigne's essays, Shakespeare's plays, Cervantes's great novel, and in other writings of that period. There seems to arise a deeper and more widespread longing for the possibility of *going back*, either culturally or personally, to some earlier and more innocent period. Horace is content to move *spatially* away from Rome, to observe it from a critical and ironizing distance, but it is *time* that concerns the figures who emerge in the aftermath of the Renaissance and Reformation. Space plays its part, especially if we can believe that elsewhere in the world there are people who live in innocent harmony, but the core concern is with the past and the question of whether it can be recaptured.

That past can be cultural—as with the Shakespearean characters who try to "go back" to an earlier way of life, carving love poems on trees rather than sweeping a pen across fine paper—but it can also be personal. Thus the ecstatic Thomas Traherne, whose celebrations of childhood preceded Rousseau's by a century:

> I was a little stranger, which at my entrance into the world was saluted and surrounded with innumerable joys. My knowledge was divine; I knew by intuition those things which, since my apostasy, I collected again by the highest reason.... The corn was orient and immortal wheat, which never should be reaped nor was ever sown. I thought it had stood from everlasting to everlasting.... The Men! O what venerable and reverend creatures did the aged seem! Immortal Cherubims! And young men glittering and sparkling angels, and maids strange seraphic pieces of life and beauty! Boys and girls tumbling in the street were moving jewels: I knew not that they were born or should die. But all things abided eternally as they were in their proper places.

But Traherne then adds: "So that with much ado I was corrupted, and made to learn the dirty devices of this world. Which now I unlearn, and become, as it were, a little child again that I may enter into the Kingdom of God." *Which now I unlearn.* Traherne seems to need no more than his own memory and maybe the example of children around him to "unlearn" those "dirty devices" and reclaim his original innocence—for it is clear that he sees no taint of original sin darkening the splendor of his early days.

Perhaps this task would be easier, though, if we could hold before our eyes the examples of other innocent adults: those who had somehow undone their early corruption or (better still) lived in an environment that taught them no "dirty devices." If all we see around us are other corrupted people, and if the daily practices of our world are deceitful and cruel, and if we are drawn every day into the web of this wicked world—and yet we do *not* believe that anything in human nature makes such a web inevitable—why, then, we may well want to find somewhere to start over, a place where we can with conscious care and sober meditation on the dangers we know so well build a society without dirt or devices. We may want to go to America. And it is further possible that in America we can find people who are already living in the way we want to live; perhaps the savages of that vast and little-known continent are themselves noble and can teach us nobility.

These possibilities had their influence even upon the most unlikely people. It is curious to note that Jonathan Edwards wrote his great treatise on original sin while living among and preaching to the Housatonic Indians of western Massachusetts—and yet, as George Marsden points out, the sermons Edwards preached there placed far less emphasis on original sin or on human sinfulness in general than the sermons he was accustomed to preach to his fellow English. Now, to be sure, this was *not* because Edwards believed the Indians to be without original sin, but the alteration of his usual practice is noteworthy all the same. Marsden suggests that Edwards was influenced in this matter by the example of his friend David Brainerd, a missionary to the Indians who a few years earlier had died in Edwards's house, of tuberculosis, at the age of twenty-nine. Though Brainerd was himself deeply committed to the doctrine of original sin and was endlessly and perhaps pathologically conscious of his own corruption—"Oh my meanness, folly, ignorance, and inward pollution!" he would cry in his journal, when he wasn't calling himself a "beast" or a "dead dog"—he claimed that the Indians were most moved by messages of God's love and grace, God's constant affection and concern for the people he had made. And the biography that Edwards wrote of Brainerd (which consists largely of extracts from Brainerd's journal) does reveal that as time went on Brainerd was more and more likely to preach on texts of comfort and exhortation.

The Indians' response to Brainerd's preaching does not indicate sinlessness, but it could certainly be thought to indicate—Brainerd certainly thought it did—an ingenuousness, an openness, one might say a childlikeness, which set the Indians apart from their hard-hearted, cold-eyed European brothers. (After all, Brainerd had considerably less success among the other group he focused his preaching on: Irish immigrants.) A set of traits allegedly shared by children and savages—simplicity, naïveté, guilelessness—seem, to many modern Western eyes, closely allied with other traits—moral innocence and purity—that cast some doubt on the doctrine of original sin. A distinctively modern picture of childhood, which we sketched in the previous chapter, gets progressively entangled with ideas about "primitive" peoples; the Rousseauian cult of childhood and the cult of primitivism arise in the same cultural context and at the same point in history.*

Let's recall those Jesuit missionaries to the Huron we saw, briefly, in the previous chapter. They believed the Huron to be insufficiently

---

* These twin cults find their point of union in a curious recurring character in European history, the "wild child," whose history has recently been written by Adriana S. Benzaquén in her remarkable book *Encounters with Wild Children*. Benzaquén gives us the chilling words of the eighteenth-century philosopher Montesquieu, who wrote: "A prince could do a beautiful experiment. Raise three or four children like animals, with goats or with deaf-mute nurses. They would make a language for themselves. Examine this language. See nature in itself, and freed from the prejudices of education; learn from them, after they are instructed, what they had thought; exercise their mind by giving them all the things necessary to invent; finally, write the history of the experiment." Of course anyone who tried this experiment would discover that we cannot "make a language for ourselves"; alas, some did make this discovery. Others who but found, rather than attempting to create, wild children were continually frustrated when the children failed to meet Rousseauian expectations or, worse yet, ceased to be wild. Benzaquén quotes Harlan Lane—a psychologist and linguist from Northeastern University who received a MacArthur Foundation grant in 1991—complaining about the treatment of a boy known as John of Burundi, who was believed to have been raised by apes in the jungle: "All this teaching the boy is well and good, but it is obliterating the traces of life in the wild and is destroying his value as a scientific discovery."

aware of their children's innate sinfulness and therefore reluctant to address sinful tendencies appropriately, with physical punishment. But what about the adult Huron themselves? How did the missionaries perceive *them*? It turns out that among Jesuit missionaries to the New World there was no clear agreement on such matters. This should not be surprising. We have already seen within French Catholicism the tension between the relatively easy-going attitude toward innate wickedness taken by Parisian Jesuits and the harsh Augustinianism of Pascal and the Jansenists of Port-Royal. In a fascinating article, "Augustine and the Amerindian in Seventeenth-Century New France," the historian Peter Goddard explores some of these disputes within the Jesuit movement.

The Jesuits of the Spanish New World had followed Aquinas's theology back to Aristotle and from Aristotle had derived an anthropology for the native peoples that sounds a lot like Montaigne's: the Indians were naturally good, not (yet) subject to the corruptions of European civilization. As Anthony Pagden points out in his 1986 book *The Fall of Natural Man,* if the very first Spanish Catholic impression of the Amerindians had been that they were "nature's slaves," soon that impression was converted; the natives became "nature's children." But among the French Jesuits who worked in or studied New France (Canada) the Augustinian picture was more common—but still not without some trace of the more optimistic and positive view.

It was a contemporary of Pascal, a Jesuit missionary and theologian named Jean Rigoleuc, who seems to have developed the most explicit, systematic, and nuanced account of the state of the "savage" in relation to Christian truth. (It's noteworthy that Rigoleuc never evangelized outside France. He spent much of his life in Brittany, preaching the Gospel to the wild Celtic Bretons, who in the eyes of Parisians were scarcely less *sauvage* than the natives of New France. But his account bears a striking resemblance to the practices of thoughtful Protestant frontier missionaries like Edwards and Brainerd.) For

Rigoleuc there were three "ways" or "manners" (*moyens*) of life that people followed as they navigated through the world. The ideal one, the path established by the Catholic Church, he calls the "way of grace." Those who follow this path practice a strict asceticism; they mortify the flesh, they annihilate their own will and understanding, so that the will of God may fill them.

But others—far too many—follow the "way of sense and passion." This path is characterized by rampaging and utterly undisciplined desires, self-love (our old friend *amour-propre*), irresolution, aversion to one's duties, outright revolts against God's gracious offers of help, and so on. Rigoleuc makes quite a list, a far longer one than he makes when describing the way of grace. But these are all familiar faults; together they comprise the stock-in-trade of the denunciatory sermon and the satire of a Molière (or a Montaigne).

One might think that these two paths pretty much sum up the options for human beings, but Rigoleuc adds a third, which he places (as it were) *between* the way of passion and the way of grace. This third path he calls the "way of nature," and he has a particular interest in anatomizing it; he lists twenty-three associated traits. The person following the way of nature is certainly in spiritual danger. He or she is prone to sensuality, undue sensitivity to the opinions of others, a kind of overly conservative attachment to familiar thoughts and practices, impatience with the faults of others, a tendency to hold illusory views of his or her own spiritual state, and so on. But it should be obvious that these traits are not nearly as damning as those comprising the way of passion; there is a certain gentleness to Rigoleuc's diagnosis, especially in contrast to the evisceration he performed on that other group of sinners. Rigoleuc is even careful to note that those who follow nature's way desire spiritual goods and gifts, though in an immature and ultimately unhealthy way; but nothing of the kind could be said for the passionate. What accounts for the difference? The most important distinction is that those who follow the way of nature are untaught, ignorant, suffering from a lack of spiritual instruction—very like children. They err, but their erring is less culpable that the rebellious sensuality of the passionate.

Rigoleuc's tripartite typology was to provide, for a century or more, an influential (and quite helpful) model for Catholic missionaries to New France. It struck a constructive compromise between those who found the savages utterly repugnant and those who idealized their native innocence. It enabled missionaries to see that they had real work to do—these people were afflicted, as we are, by inherent sinfulness; they needed to be cured of their ills and delivered from their sad condition—but it also encouraged those missionaries to be gentle, compassionate, and tolerant in their treatment of their charges. "They know not what they do." Moreover, it provided grounds for *hope.* Those deeply corrupt sensualists, those rebels against grace, who follow the way of passion seem to have alienated themselves so thoroughly from the Gospel that it is hard to imagine how they might ever be restored to grace, but these "nature's children" need only instruction. They already desire spiritual things; those desires need only be trained and corrected.

Of course, this is a thoroughly patronizing and paternalistic model based on cultural universals, which lumps every member of a given society into a single category. The model does not, and cannot, deny that there will be at least some people in any given society where Christianity is known who follow the way of passion and others who follow the way of grace, but it has the tendency to see every Indian, every native, every savage as a representative of the party of nature. These flaws are evident to us now. But in the context of the centuries in which Rigoleuc's typology reigned, it provided a powerful way to acknowledge the reality of original sin while acknowledging the virtues that members of the missionaries' target audiences exhibited. Guided by Rigoleuc, the missionaries could see their charges as wicked—but not very.

· · · ·

IN 1809, WHEN HE WAS thirty-seven, the poet Samuel Taylor Coleridge paused to recall a youthful dream, a plan he had hatched fifteen years earlier to immigrate to America and start there a new society governed by his own homemade intellectual system, which he called Pantisocracy. He wrote:

> What I dared not expect from constitutions of Government and whole Nations, I hoped from Religion and a small Company of chosen Individuals, and formed a plan, as harmless as it was extravagant, of trying the experiment of human Perfectibility on the banks of the Susquehannah; where our little society, in its second generation, was to have combined the innocence of the patriarchal Age with the knowledge and genuine refinements of European culture; and where I had dreamt of beholding, in the sober evening of my life, the Cottages of Independence in the undivided Dale of Industry.

Why should innocence be left only to the savage? Why shouldn't disenchanted Europeans get into the act? It was merely a matter, thought young Coleridge, of organizing society properly. "The leading idea of Pantisocracy," he wrote in a letter of 1794, "is to make men *necessarily* virtuous by removing all Motives to Evil—all possible Temptations. . . . It is each individual's *duty* to be just, *because* it is in his *Interest*. To perceive this and assent to it as an abstract proposition—is easy—but it requires the most wakeful attentions of the most reflective minds at all moments to bring it into practice." Though Coleridge's mind was most certainly reflective and his attentions utterly wakeful, it does not appear to have occurred to him to ask whether what is in our *Interest* is therefore in our *Power*. He assumes it; and this assumption constitutes the first axiom of Pantisocracy.

It is worth noting also the dark shadow that inevitably accompanies utopian plans, which we can now see, two hundred and more years later, after the failure of so many of them: the idea of *necessary* virtue, of virtue that we *must* exhibit because no other choice is thinkable.

Coleridge's friends, all of whom he tried to enlist in his great project, were not unanimous in their assessments of it. His fellow poet Robert Southey was as ardent and evangelistic as Coleridge himself and really the cocreator of Pantisocracy; but another friend, the sober Tom Poole, owner of a tannery in the town of Nether Stowey in Somerset, had his doubts. For one thing, he noted, Coleridge had picked out a spot for relocation that none of them had ever seen or knew anything about: "I think a man would do well first to see the country and his future hopes, before he removes his [family] or any large part of his property, there." Moreover, Poole was cognizant of a phenomenon I like to call the Satanic Recognition, after Milton's Satan, who is allowed to escape from his infernal exile only to discover, "Which way I fly is Hell; myself am Hell"—or, in the ancient lament of the tourist, "Wherever you go, there you are." Poole agreed that if Coleridge and Southey succeeded in their plan, they would indeed "realise the age of reason; but however perfectible human nature may be, I fear it is not yet perfect enough to exist long under the regulations of such a system, particularly when the Executors of the plan are taken from a society in a high degree civilized and corrupted."

Some shrewd wisdom is contained in Poole's comment. He knows that the Pantisocratic ideal—the word means "government by all, equally"—could only be "realised" if it was imposed by means of law and regulation, and of course it is human nature to chafe against such restraints. Coleridge wished all property of the colony to be shared equally and was inclined to seek a similar freedom in sexual relationships; Poole wasn't so sure either of these schemes would make people happy. Moreover, those promulgating and enforcing the laws would themselves be the product—Poole sounds very Rousseauian here—of a "civilized" and hence "corrupted" society, which would not encourage the objects of their discipline to further efforts toward moral perfection.

The quotation from Coleridge with which I began this section—which, again, was written fifteen years after he first mooted the Pantisocratic plan—acknowledges this difficulty, perhaps in remembrance of Poole's earlier response; it was only in its *second* generation that the colony was to have achieved its goal of combining "the innocence of the patriarchal Age with the knowledge and genuine refinements of European culture." That is, only when the torch had been passed to a younger generation, raised in the nurturing embrace of sound political philosophy, would Pantisocracy come into its own; only then would Coleridge, in the "sober evening" of his life, be able to sit back and contemplate the rich fruits of his efforts. But of course even this dream assumes what Poole questions: the ability of that first generation to pass along wisdom to the youngsters without passing on their own corruption. Poole, lacking Coleridge's imagination and intellectual power, nevertheless could see that Inheritance is not commonly so choosy.

But Coleridge was fired by the example of Joseph Priestley, the great Dissenting clergyman and discoverer of oxygen—who, by the way, had been a member of the Lunar Society, that astonishing group of intellectual adventurers in the city of Birmingham that also included Josiah Wedgwood, Erasmus Darwin, James Watt, and our old friend Richard Lovell Edgeworth. Priestley immigrated to America in 1794, the very year that Coleridge and Southey hatched their scheme. His three sons had emigrated some months earlier, and Priestley hoped that the New World would be more amenable to his radical, egalitarian politics—not quite as anarchistic as the Pantisocratists, but not far from it—than the Old had been. (He died a decade later in Northumberland, Pennsylvania—on the banks of, yes, the Susquehanna.)

Priestley much occupied Coleridge's mind in 1794. At one point, on a walking tour of Wales, he almost started a riot in a pub by proposing a toast to the old radical—the others in the room were ardent monarchists. (Coleridge had earlier pleased them by proposing a toast to the king; apparently they had not heard him add, "May he be the last!") Moreover, while celebrating Priestley's emigration, researching possible purchases of frontier land, and developing the political model for the colony-to-be, Coleridge and Southey received the shocking news that Robespierre, architect of the French Revolution, had been guillotined in Paris. This was a terrible event for the young men. They understood Robespierre to share their democratic and utopian dreams. Southey announced that he would rather have learned that his father was dead. (Coleridge's biographer Richard Holmes dryly notes, "This might have lost some of its impact had anyone realised that Southey's father was already dead.") They almost immediately began to compose a verse drama called *The Fall of Robespierre*. Their hope was for a quick best-seller whose timely publication would garner them the funds necessary to buy land in Pennsylvania and passage on a ship. If Robespierre's fall proved anything, it was that Europe was stony ground for utopian and revolutionary seed. If the better world was to be made, it would be made elsewhere.

There's a curious passage in *The Fall of Robespierre* in which Coleridge seems to be acknowledging that Robespierre didn't have the right answer after all, that he himself was tainted as well. The "Song to Domestic Peace" cries:

> *Tell me, on what holy ground*
> *May Domestic Peace be found?*
> *Halcyon daughter of the skies,*
> *Far on fearful wings she flies,*
> *From the pomp of Scepter'd State*

From the Rebel's noisy hate,
In a cottag'd vale She dwells,
Listening to the Sabbath bells!

(It is fair to say that at the time of this composition Coleridge had not yet found his poetic voice.) If the "Scepter'd State," which republicans like Coleridge loathed, yielded only to the "noisy hate" of a rebel like Robespierre, what progress was that? It was to a distant and rural world that Domestic Peace was forced to fly, where, curiously enough, though government seems absent, there are still churches.

As for Southey: "Should the resolution of others fail," he wrote, "Coleridge and I will go together, and either find repose in an Indian wig-wam—or from an Indian tomahawk." And then he added: "What is the origin of moral evil?" Our old question, *Unde hoc malum?* "Whence arise the various vices and misfortunes that disgrace human nature and destroy human happiness? From individual property." The elimination of individual property would result, necessarily, in the elimination of sin itself.

They never made it, of course. They never sat in a wigwam, nor did they suffer a romantically violent death from the blow of a tomahawk. Coleridge died in 1834 in Highgate, in North London—forty years nearly to the day after the execution of Robespierre—and Southey died in the Lake District in 1843. But many others sharing their hopes made it to those hopeful distant shores. Among them, one who holds particular interest for our story is a contemporary of these poets, a businessman, factory manager, educational reformer, and early proponent of socialism named Robert Owen. History tells of few more curious characters or ones whose story more illuminates the puzzles of human sinfulness—not because Owen himself was especially sinful; on the contrary, he seems to have been in most ways an exceptionally good man. But he expected other people to be good as well, and thereon hangs a tale.

. . .

OWEN WAS BORN in Wales in 1771, a year before Coleridge. His father was a saddler, and his mother came from a farming family; neither of them expected formal schooling to be of much use to their son, so after age ten he had none. When he was eighteen he moved to the great city of Manchester, then the center of the vast British textile industry, and got a job in a cotton mill. Almost immediately Owen and his employers discovered that the young man had a gift for organization and administration that deserved to be called genius. He reorganized the mill in every respect. He found new sources of cotton, altered spinning techniques, and encouraged the mill hands to higher standards of work than they had previously known. By the time he turned twenty-five—when Coleridge and Southey were dreaming of the Susquehanna—he had been made manager of one of the largest milling companies in Manchester, the Chorlton Twist Company (as it came to be known), and a partner in the business.

It was while traveling to Glasgow on behalf of the company that he met a young woman, the daughter of a mill owner named David Dale, whom he determined to marry. As a means to this end he encouraged his fellow partners at Chorlton Twist to purchase Dale's mill. Owen then moved to Scotland, where, in the last days of 1799, he took his new bride to the mill and assumed management of it.

The mill was at New Lanark, a few miles southeast of Glasgow, on the Clyde River. David Dale had opened the mill there about a decade earlier, attracted to the spot because of its proximity to the river's falls, which provided plenty of energy for the mill wheels. Many of the mill's workers, in those early years, were children from the slums and poorhouses of Glasgow and Edinburgh, and although Dale seems to have had genuinely philanthropic intentions in bringing them to New Lanark and was known for his affection for the children, the conditions there were miserable. The hours that cotton-mill employees were expected to work in those days (eighty hours a week or even more), coupled with the noise and dirt of the mill buildings, made employment there something like a last resort, and few of the mill workers gave much care to their jobs. Whole families lived in single filthy rooms in worker housing that Dale had built; drunkenness was rampant. It's hard to see how the children in particular were any better off than they had been in the city slums. They, like the adults with whom they lived, had become little more than savages. Over two thousand workers lived at New Lanark by the time Owen took over; it was the largest mill of its kind of Britain.

Robert Owen set out to transform the mill community utterly, and transform it he did. With a kind of terrifying energy, he swept into New Lanark and began his revolution by building new and clean housing for the workers. He then sought to convince people to care for their new homes by exhortation and the establishment of awards for well-kept homes. He wrote out vast lists of regulations, informing parents that they were responsible for the behavior of their children, exhorting people to take care to prevent anyone from damaging the mill property, and reminding all members of the community that they held a great variety of religious views and therefore should make every effort not to allow sectarian strife to arise: "It is particularly recommended, as a means of uniting the inhabitants of the village into one family, that while each faithfully adheres to the principles which he most approves, at the same time all shall think charitably of their neighbours respecting their religious opinions, and not presumptuously suppose that theirs alone are right."

Of his further changes, it is difficult to say which was the most revolutionary. All of them were brand-new ideas and absolutely appalled his business partners. He established what we would now call a co-op, a store on the mill's premises that stocked the best goods Owen could get his hands on, sold at almost no profit. (One advantage of this store was that it allowed Owen to strictly regulate the sale of alcohol.) He cut the working day of adults from fourteen hours to ten, that of children to less, and he allowed no child under ten to work in the mills at all. Instead, he had schools built and sent the children there; one of his greatest innovations in this regard was an "Infant School" for children as young as one year. He was probably the first employer in Britain to institute sick pay.

Though the expenses involved in such radical policies were great, so too were the results. New Lanark became the best-run, most efficient mill in Britain, and possibly one of the more profitable. (There is some dispute about the profitability of Owen's methods.) But Owen's partners could not reconcile themselves to the expense of the endeavor and thought continually about the even greater profits that could be theirs if Owen's philanthropic excesses could be restrained. But in nothing that he determined to do could Owen be restrained; he never gave an inch to the demands of his partners. He repeatedly pointed out the capitalist method to his apparent madness. For instance, the Infant School allowed the children's mothers to return to mill work much earlier than had been the norm. In the end he failed to convince anyone and simply raised the capital to buy out the partners and become the sole proprietor of New Lanark.

Over the years the mill became a very famous place, and people from all over Europe came to visit it and to seek Owen's wisdom and advice. Gradually, it seems, it occurred to this relatively unlettered man that there was something like a coherent philosophy underlying his innovations, and he determined to make that philosophy known to the world. As he articulated it, it had two chief components: an account of "the human character" and an account of "social systems."

If Owen had ever had any religious belief, he had lost it at an early age, and throughout his adult life he considered religion one of the greatest enemies of human happiness and social well-being. And he did not mean simply to criticize one or another sect, one or another form of Christianity in particular. To be sure, in his early public pronouncements, Owen took care not to state his views bluntly and took refuge in the old notion that the *abuse* of religion, especially in the form of sectarianism, is the problem. In describing the schools at New Lanark, for instance, he states that "to avoid the inconveniences which must ever arise from the introduction of a particular creed into a school, the children are taught to read in such books as inculcate those precepts of the Christian religion, which are common to all denominations." He continues: "A knowledge of truth on the subject of religion would permanently establish the happiness of man; for it is the inconsistencies alone, proceeding from the want of this knowledge, which have created, and still create, a great proportion of the miseries which exist in the world."

But this raises the question of what *is* "truth on the subject of religion," which Owen does not answer directly, though he does say what such truth is *not*: "The ideas of exclusive right and consequent superiority which men have hitherto been taught to attach to the early sentiments and habits in which they have been instructed, are the chief cause of disunion throughout society; such notions are, indeed, in direct opposition to pure and undefiled religion; nor can they ever exist together." In other words, it is the belief that any one religion or set of religious beliefs is superior to any other that violates religious truth; which is just another way of saying that the truth of religion is that no religion is particularly true.

Eventually Owen grew impatient with such circumlocutions and came right out and affirmed that "every religion that has hitherto been" has done its part to transform each of us into "a furious bigot and fanatic, or a miserable hypocrite." In his "Declaration of Mental Independence," which he wrote in 1826 to celebrate the fiftieth anniversary of America's own Declaration, Owen announced that from that day forward humanity was to consider itself liberated from "the trinity of evils responsible for all the world's misery and vice: traditional religion, conventional marriage . . . and private property." And of course it was religion that sustained pernicious beliefs about marriage and property; it was therefore religion that bore the greatest blame for humanity's ills.

An especially egregious aspect of religion, for Owen, was its belief in human sinfulness. In his first major work, *A New View of Society, Or, Essays on the Principle of the Formation of the Human Character, and the Application of the Principle to Practice* (1816), the word *evil* appears dozens of times, but the word *sin* is wholly absent; and even the word *evil* is used consistently to refer to *conditions*. The very notion of sin, Owen believed, is the central perfidy of religion. Religion fails to blame the external conditions of education, economics, and culture, which truly shape our characters, and focuses instead on some putative internal corruption. Were Owen living today, he would surely say that religion "blames the victim."*

In a telling passage from Owen's *New View of Society*—one that describes, in the third person, Owen's experiences when he first took over the management of New Lanark—we can get a clear sense of how Owen talked about "evil" and how he understood his own remedies for it:

> He spent some time in finding out the full extent of the evil against which he had to contend, and in tracing the true causes which had produced and were continuing those effects.

---

* When Owen published the first of these essays, in 1813, he dedicated it to William Wilberforce, the member of Parliament who had done more than anyone else to end his country's involvement in the slave trade. "My dear sir," began Owen's dedication, "In contemplating the public characters of the day, no one among them appears to have more nearly adopted in practice the principles which this Essay develops than yourself." But Wilberforce was a deeply committed evangelical Christian, a fact that may have affected Owen's decision to remove that dedication from the 1816 edition and replace it with something more sweeping: "To the British Public."

He found that all was distrust, disorder, and disunion; and he wished to introduce confidence, regularity, and harmony. He therefore began to bring forward his various expedients to withdraw the unfavourable circumstances by which they had hitherto been surrounded, and to replace them by others calculated to produce a more happy result. He soon discovered that theft was extended through almost all the ramifications of the community, and the receipt of stolen goods through all the country around. To remedy this evil, not one legal punishment was inflicted, not one individual imprisoned, even for an hour; but checks and other regulations of prevention were introduced; a short plain explanation of the immediate benefits they would derive from a different conduct was inculcated by those instructed for the purpose, who had the best powers of reasoning among themselves. They were at the same time instructed how to direct their industry in legal and useful occupations, by which, without danger or disgrace, they could really earn more than they had previously obtained by dishonest practices. Thus the difficulty of committing the crime was increased, the detection afterwards rendered more easy, the habit of honest industry formed, and the pleasure of good conduct experienced.

It all sounds so simple, as Owen explains it. He believed it *was* a simple matter to identify and exterminate the "evils" that afflict humanity. It was merely a matter of education. People needed to be shown what was in the interest of humanity as a whole and that whatever was in humanity's interest was in their own interest as well. But, as Edmund Wilson points out in his brief but brilliant treatment of Owen in his history of socialism, *To the Finland Station,* Owen simply *assumed* that everyone else was as naturally and passionately interested in the well-being of humanity as he was, and nothing that happened to him could shake this assumption. Wilson believes that a crucial moment in Owen's career occurred in 1817, when he attended a conference in France and spoke with a veteran French diplomat who was the presiding secretary of the conference. Owen, with his typical earnest enthusiasm, explained to the secretary that, thanks to various technological and social developments, it was now possible to extend the blessings of good health, good education, and good manners to the whole of society, even to the poorest of the poor. To this the diplomat responded blandly that he knew that perfectly well but, along with all the leaders of Europe, considered it not the harbinger of a blessed age, but rather an immense social problem to be solved: if the poor and dispossessed were actually to gain all these benefits, how could they be distinguished from those who had always been thought their natural superiors? How could the governing classes continue to govern—and (more important) *justify* their governance?

Owen's response to the secretary's candor is telling: "I had discovered that I had a long and arduous task before me, to convince governments and governed of the gross ignorance under which they were contending against each other, in direct opposition to the real interests and true happiness of both." Blunt though the diplomat was in expressing his view of how things should be, Owen simply could not even entertain the *possibility* that the man was just a corrupt old sinner who took pleasure in social inequity because he was the beneficiary of it. For Owen, only "gross ignorance" could make someone say what the secretary said; for Owen, it is simply impossible that, if he were properly educated, the man could fail to see that universal equality of opportunity is in everyone's real interest and creates everyone's true happiness.

As Wilson points out, Owen's imperviousness to the real lesson of his conversation with the secretary had large implications for the course of his life; it made him, for instance, blind to the real import of his genuine and wonderful achievements at New Lanark. Owen "did not see that human beings were so universally imperfect that the prime questions were where to begin and who was to be trusted to do the beginning. . . . It had never occurred to him that he himself was a man of exceptionally high character and that it was he and not the natural goodness of those ill-conditioned parents who had made New Lanark a model community. He did not understand that New Lanark was a machine which he himself had built and which he had to control and keep going."

In the long passage from *A New View of Society* quoted above, Owen announces proudly that when his people went astray he did not imprison or punish them—and he had every right to be proud, in a time when factory owners had the legal right to do both of those things. (Owen was almost unique in his time in absolutely forbidding physical punishment for errant or unproductive workers.) But it's worth asking what Owen means when he says that, instead of conventional punishments, "checks and other regulations of prevention were introduced." What sort of "checks"? In fact, over the years Owen developed incredibly complex schemes for observing and recording the behavior of his employees. The philosopher Jeremy Bentham—whom, by the way, Owen recruited to be an investor in the mill when he bought out his earlier partners—famously imagined the Panopticon, a circular prison with a small room in its center from which a single jailer could keep watch on many inmates. Owen was a kind of one-man mobile Panopticon. For instance, he ordered installed at every workstation in the mill a wooden post with a wooden block attached to it. One side of the block was painted white, the second yellow, the third blue, and the fourth black. Each day the foreman overseeing a given area "graded" his workers accordingly: those who had been docile and hardworking had the white side of their block turned outwards, while those whose work had been satisfactory but not excellent got a yellow mark, and so on. Every day Owen walked through the mill and noted the grades, turning a fierce glare on those whose blocks were blue or black. So strong was his personality and so much respect did he inspire that these glares were usually sufficient to get workers back on the right track, if fear of those glares had not prevented them from misbehaving in the first place. The foreman even recorded workers' marks in a register, a kind of moral ledger, which Owen could consult when he returned from business trips.

Owen was very proud of the success of such innovations. But, writes Wilson, Owen "never realized that he had created this moral universe himself" and was therefore surprised when communities he created on the New Lanark model—but did not oversee himself—never thrived. He was likewise puzzled when he sent out teachers who had worked at the New Lanark schools and had been thoroughly trained in its methods, only to find that they couldn't get similar results elsewhere. Though Owen was by all accounts a tyrant in most of his dealings with others, congenitally incapable of negotiation and cooperation, he was an exceptionally benevolent one; and though convinced that his understanding of social and moral issues was unerringly right—all of his books could have (unironically) borne the title that Leslek Kolakowski (ironically) used for an essay, "My Correct Views on Everything"—he was oddly without personal ego. At least, he lacked the *kind* of ego that would lead him to attribute successes to his personality rather than to his system.

Edmund Wilson is not unique in his assessment of Owen's peculiarities, his odd combination of insight and blindness. A visitor to New Lanark in 1819 judged the man and his project in remarkably similar ways. This visitor expressed the usual admiration for the organization of the place: "It is needless to say anything more of the Mills than that they are perfect in their kind, according to the present state of mechanical science, and that they appeared to be under admirable management; they are thoroughly clean, and so carefully ventilated, that there was no unpleasant smell in any of the apartments. . . . There are stores also from which the people are supplied with all the necessaries of life." But when Owen, who led this tour himself, began to show off a bit, the visitor felt certain doubts creeping in:

Playing on fifes, some 200 children, from four years of age until ten, entered the room and arranged themselves on three sides of it. A man whose official situation I did not comprehend gave the word, which either because of the tone or the dialect I did not understand; and they turned to the right or left, faced about, fell forwards and backwards and stamped at command, performing maneouvres the object of which was not very clear with perfect regularity. I remembered what T. Vardon told me of the cows in Holland. When the cattle are housed, the Dutch in the spirit of cleanliness, prevent them from dirtying their tails by tying them up (to the no small discomfort of the cows) at a certain elevation, to a cross string which extends the whole length of the stalls: and the consequence is that when any one cow wags her tail all the others must wag theirs also. So I could not but think that these puppet-like motions might, with a little ingenuity have been produced by the great water wheel, which is the *primum mobile* of the whole Cotton-Mills. A certain number of the children were then drawn out and sung to the pipe of a music master. They afterwards danced to the piping of the six little pipers. There was too much of all this, but the children seemed to like it. When the exhibition was over, they filed off into the adjoining schoolrooms.

Owen was clearly more pleased by this exhibition than the visitor, who concludes his account of his tour with these dark words:

Owen in reality deceives himself. He is part-owner and sole director of a large establishment, differing more in accidents than in essence from a plantation: the persons on it are white, and are at liberty by law to quit his service, but while they remain in it they are as much under his absolute management as so many Negro slaves. His humour, his vanity, his kindliness of nature (all these have their share) lead him to make these human machines as he calls them (and too literally he believes them to be) as happy as he can, and to make a display of their happiness. And jumps at once to the monstrous conclusion that because he can do this with 2,210 persons, who are totally dependent on him—all mankind might be governed with the same facility.

This visitor, I might add, was an eminent one, which perhaps accounts for the thoroughness of the show and Owen's personal involvement in it. A man of letters whose youth had been occupied by dreams of revolution and emigration, ultimately he had reconciled himself to the British social order sufficiently to be named the Poet Laureate of England. He was Robert Southey.

OWEN RAN NEW LANARK for nearly thirty relatively prosperous and peaceful years. But his inability to re-create its virtues elsewhere, or to get Parliament to pass laws giving more rights to the poor and protecting them from abuse by their social superiors, or to get foreign governments to accept any of his schemes for social betterment, created in him immense frustration and ultimately led him to believe that the "gross ignorance" of Europeans was beyond his power to remedy. Gradually he began to suspect that he could only realize his dreams abroad, in America, where he could with less interference and resistance create and sustain truly ideal communities—which would then by their *example* convince Europeans of truths that rational argument could not move them to consider. By this point, of course, the American frontier had moved well west; it was not Pennsylvania to which Owen turned, but rather Indiana.

This part of Owen's story requires a mention of one Johan Georg Rapp, whose life could easy illustrate many of the themes I have chosen to explore via Owen. Rapp was German, the founder of an esoteric sect devoted to a range of theosophical opinions and the practice of alchemy called the Harmony Society. Though originally Lutheran, Rapp and his followers split with that church, and by the early years of the nineteenth century had fallen into serious disfavor with the government, at which point they purchased a large tract of land in Pennsylvania and moved there. After a decade during which time their land had greatly increased in value, Rapp decided to move the Society to Indiana, where they founded a town and named it Harmony. But for various reasons Rapp and his confederates were unhappy with life on the Midwestern plains and in 1825 decided to sell their land and move back to Pennsylvania. The buyer they found was Robert Owen.

Having acquired the necessary land in the properly free continent, Owen issued his lofty "Declaration of Mental Independence" and appended to it a call for "the industrious and well disposed of all nations" to join him in his great endeavor. And many did answer the call, though perhaps not all of them fit Owen's description. Some shared Owen's hopes and dreams, among them a gifted and energetic young man named Josiah Warren, who would eventually make a memorable name for himself, though not in the place that Owen had rechristened New Harmony. But overall the participants in New Harmony comprised, in the words of Owen's son Robert Dale, "a heterogeneous collection of radicals, enthusiastic devotees to principle, honest latitudinarians, and lazy theorists, with a sprinkling of unprincipled sharpers thrown in."

It seems that Owen discerned just how motley a crew had responded to his wide-open invitation. "Heterogeneous" is a euphemism he used as well in his statements of the time, though he refrained from employing such adjectives as "lazy" or "unprincipled." But his plans for New Harmony remained more than ambitious. He commissioned from a British architect drawings for a vast complex of buildings that looks a little like an expanded New Lanark, a little like a Roman plaza, and a lot like a frontier fort. He even built a kiln and started firing the bricks needed to build the city. But he also determined to make a radical change in the structure of the community, and make it right away. As we have seen, Owen thought private property a great source of human misery; in certain moods he could say that it is *the* fountainhead of such misery. So from the beginning of his dreams for New Harmony he had planned to abolish property ownership and have the people share all their goods, though he knew that it would take a while to accustom people to such a radical idea.

But on the ground in New Harmony, he lost the long view and announced to his sons that he would institute complete sharing of all goods right away. They seem to have received this news with some trepidation and reminded him of his original recognition of the need for patience. He was, however, unmoved. A constitution for New Harmony was written, promulgated, and implemented. And almost immediately all hell broke loose.

The problems were manifold. One of the original partners refused to go along with the scheme, forced Owen to buy him out, and managed the sale in such a way as to cheat Owen out of a fortune in cattle and farm implements. Almost immediately after property officially went into the common pot, an informal black market economy arose. Owen realized, belatedly, that he had not prepared the people well for this transition to a new economic system and so instituted a scheme for "community education," but found that he could not compel attendance. The community's newspaper acknowledged that "a general system of trading speculation prevails" and, with some evident sadness, attributed it to the residents' "want of confidence in the good intentions of each other." No one believed that anyone else was playing fair; everyone feared that the others were using the shared-goods system to enrich themselves. Suspicion, hostility, dishonesty, and greed spiraled out of control. A decade earlier, Owen had described the scene that had confronted him upon his arrival at New Lanark: "He found that all was distrust, disorder, and disunion." In New Harmony—whose very name now must have tasted bitter in his mouth—he had somehow re-created those very conditions he had devoted his life to ameliorating. In utter frustration and despair, Owen parceled the land into many small allotments and sold them all, at a massive loss. The lust for private property had won out. Again.

In the community newspaper of New Harmony, Owen's sons collaborated on an anonymous farewell editorial:

> Our opinion is that Robert Owen ascribed too little influence to the early anti-social circumstances that had surrounded many of the quickly collected inhabitants of New Harmony before their arrival there; and too much to those circumstances which his experience might enable them to create around themselves in future. . . . We are too inexperienced to hazard a judgment on the prudence and management of those who directed its execution; and the only opinion we can express with confidence is of the perseverance with which Robert Owen pursued it at great pecuniary loss to himself. One form of government was first tried; until it appeared that the members were too various in their feelings and too dissimilar in their habits to govern themselves harmoniously as one community. . . . New Harmony, therefore, is not now a community.

It's noteworthy that the Owen sons never question their father's belief in the essential goodness of human nature; what they question (quietly, implicitly) is his belief that the effects of "anti-social circumstances"—poor upbringing—can so quickly be overcome. Because of the power of those "circumstances," New Harmony never made it to that second and presumably uncorrupted generation in which the young Coleridge had placed his hopes, the innocent children grown into innocent adults whose placid yet festive lives were to have been the comfort of his old age.

Owen's old age had few comforts. In 1828 he returned to Britain with nearly all his fortune gone and continued to deliver lectures, write books, and found communities until he ran out of money altogether, at which point he returned to the small Welsh village where he had been born—from which he had set out on one of the more extraordinary careers of his own or any other time—and died.

As for Josiah Warren, the gifted young man who had been one of the most committed and vigorous members of New Harmony, he drew a lesson from the community's failures rather different from that of Owen's sons, or Owen himself, or (for that matter) orthodox Christianity. He thought that the problem lay in Owen's attempt to *impose* his socialist model through legislation and coercion. Warren believed in people's natural innocence, but also in their natural independence and dislike of governance. He therefore became America's first famous anarchist.

NINE

The Confraternity of the Human Type

Southey's comparison of New Lanark to a plantation reminds us that the Owens and Priestleys of the world were not the only immigrants to America. Thousands upon thousands of others came against their will, as slaves, and their enslavement has been called by any number of writers over the years this country's original sin. The notion that slavery is "America's original sin" appears in documents from the American Civil Liberties Union, in an essay by the conservative political commentator Linda Chavez, and in a study guide produced by the social-justice Christians of *Sojourners* magazine. Though these people are unlikely to agree about the policies that necessarily follow from the recognition of this dark fact of American history, they discern a common implication: the rhetoric of American freedom, of this continent as a place to leave behind the corruption of the Old World and start over, is tainted, or poisoned, at its origin by the practice of slavery. Rather, in this new Garden of Eden there seems to have been no prelapsarian period at all, not even the five and a half hours granted our first parents by the book called the *Slavonic Enoch*. Is there a more sobering detail in American history than the fact that the first slaves came to this country, to Jamestown, in 1619?

But how is this conviction that America, even America, has its own original sin related to the Christian doctrine we have been exploring? In one sense, it is not evidently related at all. After all, this is a local, culturally specific manifestation of depravity, whereas the whole point of "the great Christian doctrine of original sin" (as Jonathan Edwards called it) is its universality. In this light Americans are less like the descendants of Adam and Eve than the Locrians we met in Chapter 1, the countrymen of Little Ajax who were doomed to suffer always for the sins of their great ancestor—even if they repudiated the deeds of that ancestor and strived to atone for them.

Yet in another sense our thoughts about America do not drift far from the Augustinian view of humanity, and this is because America (unlike Locris, unlike any other country) was founded as a refuge and later as a nation by people determined to set aside and leave behind the corruption of the Old World. Though many of the first Europeans in America held to a belief in original sin as fiercely as anyone, their very project of "starting over" called that doctrine implicitly into question. And, as we have seen, the gradual decline of that doctrine in European Christianity made increasingly vivid, in the minds of people like Coleridge and Southey and Owen, the possibility of purging corruption once and for all, of "beholding, in the sober evening of [one's] life, the Cottages of Independence in the undivided Dale of Industry."

So the whole American experiment can be seen—and indeed has been seen by many—as a kind of referendum on the doctrine of original sin or a test case for its universal applicability. And it is the preexisting practice of slavery that, depending on your point of view, either makes a true test impossible or abundantly confirms the darkest Augustinian imaginings of our moral condition. Hovering over the whole American experiment, as we saw in the previous chapter, is this one dark cloud: it is an experiment conducted by *human beings,* who, like Satan flying toward earth—"Which way I fly is Hell; myself am Hell"—take their nature with them wherever they go. One of the most chilling moments in all of literature comes near the end of Dostoevsky's *Crime and Punishment,* when the depraved and tormented Svidrigailov blows his brains out, only pausing first to tell a nearby man, "I'm off to foreign lands, brother. . . . To America. . . . If they start asking you, just tell them he went to America."

IN 1834 LANE THEOLOGICAL SEMINARY, in Cincinnati, was just five years old, but it had reached a point of crisis. That such a crisis would eventually come was guaranteed by geography. As a border city, across the Ohio from the great slave-owning state of Kentucky and shaped to a considerable degree by Southern culture, Cincinnati was a deeply divided city. But a group of students at Lane were not content with such division, with a life of half measures, and they created a series of debates with the purpose of forcing the seminary—and, indirectly, the city itself—to confront two vital questions. The first was quite general: "Ought the people of the slaveholding states to abolish slavery immediately?" The second arose from the work of a highly controversial organization, the American Colonization Society, founded in 1816 by one Reverend Robert Finley in order to create an African homeland for American slaves and to raise money to send those slaves to that land, which was to be called Liberia. Thus the question: "Are the doctrines, tendencies, and measures of the American Colonization Society, and the influence of its principal supporters, such as render it worthy of the patronage of the Christian public?"

Heated though the debates about Liberia could be, they did not go to the heart of the matter. Some ardent abolitionists supported the scheme, while others opposed it. Equally ardent proponents of slavery were likewise divided; some feared that the loss of cheap labor would ruin the Southern economy, while others were more afraid of an eventual slave rebellion. The Commonwealth of Virginia set aside money, in the 1850s, to support colonization, but Abraham Lincoln was also an advocate for the organization. So although arguments on the subject could be heated, they did not prod the festering wound of American society the way the Lane seminarians' first question did.

The debates went on for eighteen consecutive nights in February, with enthusiasm for immediate abolition growing along the way, and, in a move that prefigures the campus protests of the Vietnam era, the students began to put pressure on the seminary's president to take a formal and explicit stand for justice. That president was an eminent New England clergyman named Lyman Beecher, who had arrived in Cincinnati less than two years earlier and clearly was not prepared for the heat now applied to him. (His twenty-three-year-old daughter Harriet, who lived with her parents until her marriage to Calvin Stowe in 1836, observed the whole disastrous scene with an intensity and clarity that emerged many years later in her novel *Uncle Tom's Cabin*.) Beecher not only refused to take a straightforward institutional stand on either question; he also refused to allow African-American students to be enrolled at Lane. Such an act would almost certainly have brought the wrath of the proslavery crowd down upon Beecher and Lane, and that wrath would likely not have remained merely verbal.

But for many who were committed to abolition, Beecher's temporizing was unforgivable. A fellow Presbyterian pastor in Cincinnati was so angry that he formally charged Beecher with heresy; Beecher was eventually cleared, though not without considerable anxiety and uncertainty along the way. And within Lane Seminary itself, the conflict spiraled out of Beecher's control. In the summer of 1834, when Beecher had retreated to his native New England for what he surely thought was a well-earned vacation, the businessmen who led the seminary's board of trustees abolished not slavery, but the campus's antislavery organization. By the time Beecher returned Lane was in fragments. Around fifty students and one trustee, Asa Mahan, left Lane and decided to start their own alternative seminary. With little funding and an imperfect sense of mission, they might have simply drifted away and apart, had not an interesting figure appeared in their midst, a man named John Jay Shipherd.

Shipherd, along with his friend, partner, and fellow Presbyterian minister Philo Stewart, was something like a Christian Robert Owen. A year before Lane's great debates, Shipherd and Stewart had come to northern Ohio and acquired land on which they planned to build a town and an institute that would bring the light of Christianity to the frontier. The Oberlin Institute, they called it, after an Alsatian pastor whose work among the poor they admired. They wanted to bring students of any color to their institute to be trained as missionaries, but also to learn to live communally and work for the common good. No student would pay tuition, but each of them would labor—cooking, cleaning, painting, building—to maintain and extend their communal life. If Shipherd and Stewart had chosen to name the place after their aspirations rather than after an exemplar of their values, they might well have called the place New Harmony.

It was Shipherd, it appears, who saw the shattering of Lane Seminary as a potential boon for his fledgling institute. He went to Cincinnati and met with the Lane rebels, as they had come to be called, and assured them that they would be warmly welcomed to his new community, which shared their commitments entirely. To the one rebellious trustee, Asa Mahan, he offered the presidency of the institute. And he encouraged them all with the promise that he would also recruit a powerful and increasingly famous clergyman from New York, Charles Grandison Finney, to join Oberlin's faculty. This was enough for the rebels; they came, and soon thereafter Finney did too. And his arrival made all the difference.

Oberlin and Charles Finney form a nearly perfect illustration of Emerson's famous claim that "Every institution is the lengthened shadow of one man." Almost from the moment he arrived in Ohio he became the public face of the school, even though he did not succeed Mahan as its president for fifteen years. And this is not surprising: he was a powerfully charismatic man, one of the most important figures in nineteenth-century American Christianity. He would become known above all for two things: his passionate commitment to the abolition of slavery and his passionate rejection of the doctrine of original sin. The two, in Finney's mind, went together.

Born in Connecticut to an undevout farming family—he was named after the protagonist of a novel by Samuel Richardson, which would have been a sure sign of frivolity to many Christians of the time—Finney never even owned a Bible until he was in his late twenties. He was tall, good-looking, and a natural leader, but poorly educated, and he struggled for many years to find his way in life; even up to the time of his conversion, in a culture in which most men of his age had been settled in their careers for a decade or more, he was still debating whether to study law. It was the purchase of that Bible and his first attempts to read it that led him to embrace Christianity when he was twenty-nine years old, in 1821. It was an enthusiastic embrace; almost immediately he sought ordination in the Presbyterian Church.

It was a natural decision in some ways. After all, the man who had shepherded Finney through his conversion, George Gale, was a young Princeton graduate who himself had only recently been ordained as a Presbyterian pastor. Princeton was a Presbyterian school long associated with Calvinism—Jonathan Edwards was its most famous, though most briefly serving, president—but American Presbyterians had been for some time divided in their attitudes toward their Calvinist past, and in any case Finney was temperamentally utterly alien to Calvinism. He was, in a classically American sense, an activist, a pragmatist, and a true believer in technique. After having established himself as a successful evangelist, focusing especially on upstate New York, he often insisted with great pride that he had developed all his principles of preaching and theology simply through reading the Bible and thinking about it, without assistance from anyone else. He never went to college and was convinced that no one needed to: what the reader of Scripture needed was persistence, attentiveness, and a power of drawing inferences. Finney considered himself a kind of experimental scientist, a forensic examiner of the biblical text. When he was preparing for ordination, he made Gale (who was sponsoring him) quite anxious with his scoffing at certain traditional Presbyterian doctrines, especially that of original sin, which he considered to be evidently absurd—as he later put it, "subversive of the gospel, and repulsive to the human intelligence."*

Likewise, when he came to articulate his principles of successful evangelism—in his *Lectures on Revivals of Religion,* which he published in 1835, immediately before coming to Oberlin—he roundly asserted that "the connection between the right use of means for a revival and a revival is as philosophically"—we would say "scientifically"—"sure as between the right use of means to raise grain and a crop of wheat. I believe, in fact, it is more certain, and there are fewer instances of failure." As we need scientific agriculture, so we need scientific evangelism; and Finney believed that, through trial-and-error experimentation, that is precisely what he had discovered.

Finney never realized the extent to which his theological views and interpretations of Scripture, far from being the product of pure and unbiased induction, were utterly characteristic of his time and

---

* The notion of original sin has always been repulsive to those Christians with a strongly populist and activist temperament. A couple of generations later William Jennings Bryan—now (wrongly) associated in the popular mind with unreflective fundamentalism—would place it at the head of a list of theological "facts and theories for which we have no use."

place. He had lived for much of his life and began his preaching career in that portion of western New York state that a later historian called the "burned-over district": burned-over, because one wave after another of revivalistic fire had swept through it, producing some of the strangest and yet most characteristic religious movements of nineteenth-century America. It was here that Joseph Smith claimed that, in 1827, he had discovered the gold plates of the Book of Mormon. It was here that a pair of sisters held séances that gave birth to a powerful stream of American spiritualism. The Shakers were powerful here. The Oneida Community, with its idealistic political principles and commitment to group marriage, arose here, as did the Millerites, whose leader, William Miller, predicted that the world would come to an end on October 22, 1844. These were widely divergent groups in some ways, but they all shared a mistrust of inherited faiths and institutional religions, a belief in human perfectibility, and an absolute denial that the past has the power to shackle us unless we allow it that power.

Though Finney was in comparison to such groups quite orthodox in his theology, he shared their zealous tendencies. He was especially eager to preach a message that led to the utter transformation of persons and societies and was almost frantically impatient with any theology that made such transformation seem less likely. John Wesley, whose evangelistic enterprises lay in the background of all these various revivals (which some have called the Second Great Awakening, though the best historians disdain that terminology), managed to preach human perfectibility *and* original sin, but this required considerable theological nuance, something not within Finney's grasp. For him, to acknowledge original sin—to acknowledge the weight or burden of an inherited weakness or perversion or infection—was to provide excuses to people who needed instead to be spurred on to action. He would have warmly seconded Henry David Thoreau's complaint, in his essay "Life Without Principle": "Thus men will lie on their backs, talking about the fall of man, and never make an effort to get up." Finney wanted everyone to get up, change themselves, and fix a corrupt society whose corruption was seen most clearly in its tolerance of slavery.

Finney was a great man and a brave one. He was far ahead of his time in his insistence that slavery was not a matter on which Christians could agree to disagree. Even before he came to Oberlin, when he led churches in New York City, it was his consistent pastoral practice to deny Holy Communion to slaveholders. Only in this way did he stand a chance of convicting such men of the depths of their sin. And Finney was not one to minimize the power of sin in people's lives or the need for genuine and heartfelt repentance; in this respect he resembled Pelagius more than Pascal's Parisian Jesuits. Like Pelagius, he believed that repentance is wholly in the sinner's power and that, once we have repented, we can and should achieve moral blamelessness. Christians, he wrote in his *Lectures*, "should not rest satisfied till they are as perfect as God." Moreover, Finney understood this moral perfection to have social and political implications: "Politics are a part of religion in a country such as this," and "God cannot sustain this free and blessed country, which we love and pray for, unless the church will take right ground." That is, the church's own sins were restraining the health and moral progress of the whole nation; and "slavery is, pre-eminently, the *sin of the church*."

So it was not the reality or the power of sin that Finney rejected, but rather *original* sin, the idea that something necessarily restrains us from the achievement of moral (and therefore social and political) perfection. Such an idea was "subversive of the gospel," because it had the effect, Finney believed, of compromising our efforts to repent or discouraging us from even trying to be perfect. In Finney's theology, God's grace is evident in that he gave us the power to choose, to be perfect if we wish. And now God's waiting to see what we'll do.

. . .

IN OCTOBER OF 1846 an eminent Swiss naturalist named Louis Agassiz came to America. Asa Gray, a professor of botany at Harvard, led Agassiz on a kind of tour of the East Coast's scientific establishments and their leading scientists, in hopes of convincing him that the scientific community in America was sufficiently robust to make it worth his while to remain and take up a chair at Harvard. In this endeavor Gray was successful. Agassiz regretted the paucity of major museums and universities in this country, but the country's enthusiasm for science—evidenced in its willingness to pay him large sums of money for lectures—more than compensated for any deficiencies. One experience, however, shocked him and had a permanent effect on his attitudes toward America and even on some of his core scientific ideas: in Philadelphia, for the first time in his life, he saw black people.

In December of that year he wrote to his mother about the experience:

> All the domestics in my hotel were men of color. I can scarcely express to you the painful impression that I received, especially since the feeling that they inspired in me is contrary to all our ideas about the confraternity of the human type and the unique origin of our species. But truth before all. Nevertheless I experienced pity at the sight of this degraded and degenerate race, and their lot inspired compassion in me in thinking that they are really men. Nonetheless, it is impossible for me to repress the feeling that they are not of the same blood as us. In seeing their black faces with their thick lips and grimacing teeth, the wool on their head, their bent knees, their elongated hands, their large curved nails, and especially the livid color of the palms of their hands, I could not take my eyes off their faces in order to tell them to stay far away. And when they

advanced those hideous hands towards my plate in order to serve me, I wished I were able to depart in order to eat a piece of bread elsewhere, rather than dine with such service. What unhappiness for the white race—to have tied their experience so closely to that of negroes in certain countries! God preserve us from such contact! [I have slightly emended Stephen Jay Gould's translation of Agassiz's French.]

Clearly an agonized and vacillating letter. We may begin to understand some of the vacillation by noting that Agassiz's father was a Protestant pastor in Switzerland—as had been six generations of ancestors before him—and Agassiz's parents had at one point had hopes that he might enter the ministry himself. But he never had the slightest interest in the ministry or in Christian theology. From an early age his passion was biological science, or what he would have called "natural history" and "natural philosophy," and by the time he was fifteen he had, at first secretly, mapped out a career for himself as a naturalist. He had never abandoned religious belief altogether, but it had contracted in his mind until it meant little more than a belief that God is the creator of all. Agassiz is perhaps most famous today as the last major scientist to repudiate Darwin's theory of natural selection, and as such he is often referred to in scientific histories as a "creationist." But his creationism had nothing to do with biblical literalism: it amounted to little more than a resistance, if a profound resistance, to any idea that would make the natural world seem the product of accident.

In this context we can discern a vital subtext in the account he gives his mother: the letter proves to be a kind of confession and a kind of warning. The radical differences he sees between Europeans and Africans have already caused him to doubt whether they can of be the same "type" (*genre*), whether they are all human beings, belonging to a "confraternity"—which means that he is doubting the veracity of the biblical account that all of us descend from our universal mother and father, Adam and Eve. This is one of the most elemental ideas of Christianity, of biblical religion generally, and therefore not something that a Christian might be expected to set aside. But, Agassiz says—and this is the warning—"truth above all." If the biological facts of the case force him to reject the biblical claim that we are all descendants of one pair, then so be it. And indeed this is precisely the conclusion that Agassiz comes to.

Agassiz's reaction to the black servants at his Philadelphia hotel provides us the opportunity to discuss an issue that has been floating just beneath the surface of this narrative for a long time. One of the arguments that I have been keen to make throughout this book is that a belief in original sin serves as a kind of binding agent, a mark of "the confraternity of the human type," an enlistment of us all in what Eugen Rosenstock-Huessy called the "universal democracy of sinners." But why should original sin alone, among core Christian doctrines, have the power to do that? What about that other powerful idea in Genesis, that we are all made in the image of God? Doesn't that serve equally well, or even better, to bind us as members of a single family?

The answer is that it *should* do so, but usually does not. Working against the force of that doctrine is the force of familiarity, of prevalent cultural norms of behavior and even appearance. A genuine commitment to the belief that we are all created equally in the image of God requires a certain *imagination*—imagination that Agassiz, try as he might, could not summon: "It is impossible for me to repress the feeling that they are not of the same blood as us." Instinctive revulsion against the alien will trump doctrinal commitments almost every time. Black people did not *feel* human to him, and this feeling he had no power to resist; eventually (as we shall see) his scientific writings fell into line with his feelings.

By contrast, the doctrine of original sin works *with* the feeling that most of us have, at least some of the time, of being divided against ourselves, falling short of the mark, inexplicably screwing up when we ought to know better. It takes relatively little imagination to look at another person and think that, though that person is not all he or she might be, neither am I. It is true that not everyone can do this: the Duchess of Buckingham couldn't. ("It is monstrous to be told you have a heart as sinful as the common wretches that crawl on the earth.") But in general it is easier for most of us to *condescend,* in the etymological sense of the word—to see ourselves as sharing shortcomings or sufferings with others—than to lift up people whom our culturally formed instincts tell us are decidedly inferior to ourselves. If misery does not always love company, it surely tolerates it quite well, whereas pride demands distinction and hierarchy, and is ultimately willing to pay for those in the coin of isolation. That the doctrine of a common creation in the image of God doesn't do more to help build human community and fellow feeling *could* be read as yet more evidence for the reality of original sin.

AGASSIZ NEVER REALLY GOT over the shock of his first encounter with dark-skinned people, nor was he able to escape his "feeling" that they are fundamentally alien to Europeans. And lacking any discernible interest or belief in human sinfulness (original or otherwise), he had nothing to restrain him from following where those feelings led. Though in 1845, before visiting America, he had written a paper arguing that all human beings shared a common descent, in 1850 he began to publish articles advocating polygeny—the separate creation of the various human races. Writing for a Unitarian magazine called the *Christian Examiner,* he was reluctant to reject the biblical account outright and found that he need not do so. Genesis, he claims, merely describes the creation of *white* people, leaving the creation of

Africans, Asians, and Native Americans shrouded in mystery.* Does polygeny mean that Judaism and Christianity are meant only for Caucasians? Agassiz does not say; he is more concerned to disavow any *political* purpose in writing his article. Knowing that the controversy over slavery was constantly intensifying—in the year that he wrote the article the Fugitive Slave Act was passed, prompting Lyman Beecher's daughter Harriet to write *Uncle Tom's Cabin*—Agassiz insists that such matters are not relevant to the natural philosopher: "Here we have only to do with the [scientific] question of the origin of men; let the politicians, let those who feel themselves called upon to regulate human society, see what they can do with the results."

Stephen Jay Gould, whose account of Agassiz in *The Mismeasure of Man* I am deeply indebted to, points out that in fact Agassiz's article is "advocacy of social policy couched as a dispassionate inquiry into scientific fact" (a strategy that, he goes on to note, "is by no means moribund today"). After all the disavowals, Agassiz goes on to make any number of political judgments and recommendations. We all share the "obligation," he says, "to settle the relative rank among these races," and if that task can at some points be complex, certain

---

* In an article in the immediately previous volume of the *Christian Examiner,* "Geographical Distribution of Animals," he had already staked out this territory: "Thus we maintain that the view of mankind as originating from a single pair, Adam and Eve,—and of the animals and plants as having originated from one common centre, which was at the same time the cradle of humanity,—is neither a Biblical view nor a correct view, nor one agreeing with the results of science, and our profound veneration for the Sacred Scriptures prompts us to pronounce the prevailing view of the origin of man, animals, and plants as a mere human hypothesis, not entitled to more consideration than belongs to most theories framed in the infancy of science. It is not for us,—for we have not the knowledge necessary for undertaking such an investigation,—it is not for us to inquire further into the full meaning of the statements of Moses. But we are satisfied that he never meant to say that all men originated from a single pair, Adam and Eve, nor that the animals had a similar origin from one common centre or from single pairs."

facts are not in doubt; "history speaks for itself" in showing us that the African race exhibits "a peculiar apathy, a peculiar indifference to the advantages afforded by civilized society." And the consequences for social organization that follow from this scientific and historical "fact" are to Agassiz obvious.

Thirteen years later, in the midst of the Civil War, Agassiz wrote a series of letters in which he does not explicitly regret the abolition of slavery, but expresses deep concern that the freeing of the slaves will lead to social disaster. Black people are "in everything unlike the other races," but especially in their intellectual limitations, and "no man has a right to what he is unfit to use." If there is to be no slavery, there must nevertheless be a strict curtailment of civil rights for people of African descent, a confinement of them to careers of physical labor, and, above all, the strictest prohibitions against miscegenation: "How shall we eradicate the stigma of a lower race when its blood has once been allowed to flow freely into that of our children?"

So, though Agassiz may now be remembered as a belated creationist, his greater historical importance is as a progenitor of "scientific racism"—the view that, setting aside any biblical narratives or doctrines that support the unity and common origin of human beings, there is no such thing as the human race; rather, there are several races that, carelessly and unscientifically, have been lumped in a single category. It was the task of science to disentangle the confused strands, to establish clear distinctions among races, to rank them according to intellectual capacity, and to insist that those rankings be reflected in law and public policy. And so the superstitions of biblical literalism would be set aside in the name of scientific progress, which is also, of course, social progress.

FOUR YEARS SEPARATE Agassiz's shocking exposure to black people in Philadelphia from his bold articles in the *Christian Examiner,* but it did not take him that long to go public with his new thinking on the question of human, or rather racial, origins. Earlier I mentioned Agassiz's popular lecture tours, and one place where his arrival was anticipated with special eagerness was Charleston, South Carolina. When Agassiz spoke there, in December of 1847, the whole intellectual community of the city had been debating for some time the monogeny/polygeny question. In 1844 Josiah Clarke Nott—a physician, South Carolina native, and passionate defender of the traditional ways of the South, including slavery—had published an erudite polygenist tract called *Two Lectures on the Natural History of the Caucasian and Negro Races,* and every educated man in Charleston seems to have been engaged with Nott's argument. By the time Agassiz arrived, a recent article by one of the most famous American scientists, a Philadelphia physician and obsessive collector of human skulls named Samuel George Morton—who also happens to have been Nott's teacher—seemed to answer one of the strongest objections to polygeny. Monogenists wanted to know why, if white people and black people are of different species, they can produce fertile offspring. Morton's answer wouldn't have convinced anyone who was skeptical about polygeny, but Nott and his supporters considered Morton's support a near clincher for their case; if they could just get further support from so obviously disinterested an observer as the great European naturalist Agassiz—whom one excited American scientist had referred to as "this big geologico-everythingo-French-Swiss gun"—they would think the battle had been won.

It is not clear whether any of the Charlestonians knew that, only two years earlier, Agassiz had affirmed monogeny; certainly none of them knew of his shocking experience in his Philadelphia hotel almost exactly a year earlier. But they could not have been more pleased with his clear affirmation that Caucasians and Negroes were distinct species with distinct origins. Agassiz returned to Charleston in 1850 to develop his ideas on the topic further, and on that occasion he shared the podium with Nott. Agassiz's best biographer, Edward Lurie, goes to some lengths to insist that Agassiz did not know that he was playing into the hands of racists, that the intricacies of the race question in America eluded him; but, then, Lurie avoids quoting the portions of the 1846 letter from Agassiz to his mother that reveal most damningly the depths of his revulsion toward black people. Lurie describes Agassiz strolling about a Charleston plantation—its owners hosted him on his visits—as though he were utterly puzzled by what went on there. But it seems more likely that Agassiz understood and, in the main, approved.

As I noted earlier, though Agassiz was committed to a belief in God as the creator of the world and all the living things in it, he had no other theological beliefs that might restrain his polygenist inclinations. Nor did the Charleston intelligentsia who gathered to hear him speak. One might think that in the South as a whole a message like Agassiz's—like Josiah Clarke Nott's—would have been welcomed with great joy, but this was not the case. In a part of the country that was as committed to biblical authority then as it is now, Agassiz's rather cavalier reinterpretation of Genesis did not go down easily. It is true that "scientific racism" gave a uniquely powerful warrant to the institution of slavery. By demonstrating that Negroes were members of a separate and decidedly inferior race, often going so far as to claim that they belonged to a wholly different species, the polygenists were able to describe slavery as an institution little different from the use of domesticated working animals. But most Southern Christian leaders, defenders of slavery though they were, thought the polygenist defense far too costly. If they were to defend slavery, they would do so on different terms.

In recent years the historian Eugene Genovese, sometimes working with his wife, the late Elizabeth Fox-Genovese, has done a great deal to illuminate the intellectual culture of antebellum Southern Christianity. Christian pastors and theologians across the South spent the decades preceding the Civil War developing a strange political theology that envisioned a slave-based, hierarchical, aristocratic, agricultural society as the divinely ordained and biblically warranted form of political order—but they did *not* claim that Southern culture as it then existed lived up to God's standards. Rather, many Southern divines shouted out jeremiads denouncing the cruelty and corruption of most slave owners and predicted that, unless they repented and began treating their slaves as fellow human beings—more, as brothers in Christ—God would pronounce a great judgment on the South and would bring down its pride in ruins. These pastors further denounced the laws passed in several Southern states in the antebellum decades that forbade slaves from learning to read and in many cases recommended that Christians disobey those laws, for slaves were in the same condition of sin—universal, original sin, inherited from Adam—as white people and were therefore under God's curse. How, then, could any Christian justify denying them access to the Book, which revealed to them both their condition and the remedy for it?*

---

* Of course there was a great deal of culturally self-serving and self-justifying blindness in these arguments. Presumably most of these Southern divines, while insisting that the black man is the white man's brother, would also have echoed Albert Schweitzer's notorious remark that the black man is the *younger* brother. No one today can miss the absurdity of a claim like the one famously made by my fellow Alabamian Frederick A. Ross, in his influential *Slavery Ordained of God,* that slavery is a positive good for black people. Abraham Lincoln read the book and quite rightly wrote in the margin, "Nonsense! Wolves devouring lambs, not because it is good for their own greedy maws, but because it is good for the lambs!!!" Yet even Ross denied that there was any racial justification for slavery and at the outset of his book roundly insisted, "Let the Southern Christian—nay the Southern man of every grade—comprehend that *God never intended the relation of master and slave to be perpetual.*" The point is not that the Christian proslavery arguments are anything but loathsome; they are not; the point is that "scientific racism" is perhaps even worse.

When a man as prominent as Stephen Douglas rose to defend slavery on grounds like those of the scientific racists—"I positively deny that he [the Negro] is my brother or any kin to me whatever," he proclaimed in 1858, in one of his debates with Abraham Lincoln—many Christian leaders in the South repudiated him fiercely. One of the greatest of them, the Presbyterian James Henley Thornwell, insisted that "No Christian man . . . can give any countenance to speculations which trace the Negro to any other parent but Adam." And, to make the point more forcefully, Thornwell insisted that "the instinctive impulses of our nature, combined with the plainest declarations of the Word of God, lead us to recognize in [the Negro's] form and lineaments, in his moral and religious and intellectual nature, the same humanity in which we glory as the image of God. We are not ashamed to call him our *brother*." Black people share with white people a common creation in the image of God *and* a common corruption inherited from Adam; and in this double sharing lies the truest fellowship, the profoundest brotherhood.

To complete the roster of ironies with which this section of my story is replete, I pause to note that Thornwell offered this specifically Christian, specifically biblical account of the common humanity of black and white people in Charleston, South Carolina, in 1850—that is, in the same city and during the same year that Louis Agassiz stood with Josiah Clarke Nott and threw all the authority of modern science behind the denial that the black man is the white man's brother or any kin to him whatever.

THERE IS, IT SHOULD BE NOTED, a biblical case for polygeny, which some supporters of slavery had frequent recourse to. In Genesis, after Cain has murdered his brother, Abel, God curses him: "You shall be a fugitive and a wanderer on the earth." But on hearing this, "Cain said to the Lord, 'My punishment is greater than I can bear. Behold, you have driven me today away from the ground, and from your face I shall be hidden. I shall be a fugitive and a wanderer on the earth, and whoever finds me will kill me.' Then the Lord said to him, 'Not so! If anyone kills Cain, vengeance shall be taken on him sevenfold.' And the Lord put a mark on Cain, lest any who found him should attack him." But who could attack him if he and his parents are the only people alive? There must have been a separate creation of other peoples, especially since, once Cain departs, he settles "in the land of Nod, east of Eden," and finds a wife there.

Defenders of slavery have of course sometimes used this passage also to make a tortured argument that black people are the children of Cain, that black skin is the "mark" that God placed upon Cain, and so forth. But since the passage does not say that any of Cain's children bore the same mark—they were not Abel's murderers—and says quite clearly that the purpose of the mark is to ensure that people leave Cain alone, this cannot be taken as serious biblical exegesis. The biblical case for polygeny, however, is more substantive, at least if you confine yourself to Genesis 4 and do not take Paul into account.

It should also be noted that this argument-by-ancestry can be played by more than one party. Another common case for slavery built on biblical genealogy involves Ham, the son of Noah, who sees his father's shameful "nakedness." When Noah learns of this, after recovering from his drunkenness, he curses not Ham, but Ham's son, Canaan: "Cursed be Canaan; a servant of servants shall he be to his brothers." If you can claim that Africans are the descendants of Ham—and defenders of slavery spared no ingenuity in doing so— then you win. To this common argument James Baldwin replies, in *The Fire Next Time:* "In the same way that we, for white people, were the descendants of Ham, and were cursed forever, white people were, for us, the descendants of Cain."

. . .

IT IS PERHAPS JUST AS WELL that Thornwell and his like were not more successful in their efforts to arouse the Christian consciences of the slave owners and to bring them to repentance. A more humane form of chattel slavery would have remained chattel slavery nonetheless, and a gentler system, arousing less public indignation, may well have lasted much longer. But these Christian leaders deserve at least some measure of our sympathy and respect; they made arguments for the "confraternity," as Agassiz put it, of human beings that put them at great personal risk and caught them between the twin hammers of a viciously greedy slave-owning class and a cadre of modern, enlightened, "scientific" racists. And their example reveals to us yet another facet of the doctrine of original sin, yet another example of its having social and political implications that seem on the face of things unlikely. Charles Finney saw the doctrine as a brake on social transformation, a built-in excuse for a depraved national status quo, a way to deflect claims for what *should* be changed by appealing to what *cannot* be changed, what is simply not within our power to alter. And no doubt there is some truth to this. But original sin was also, in the American South at least, a brake of a different kind: a restraint on those who wished to see black people as utterly alien, as having nothing to do with the rest of us.

Kinship is powerful. To identify someone as kin is to grant that person a claim upon us. Such a claim can be denied; its implications can be set aside, its implicit prohibitions ignored. People often abuse their kin, but not as often as they abuse strangers. We recognize obligations to brothers that we deny to others. This is the central theme of two of Shakespeare's plays, *Othello* and *The Merchant of Venice*—the two set in early modern Europe's least kin-based society, its mercantile capital. And even there, though we may *use* others for our own purposes, to *abuse* them utterly we first take the time and trouble to deny any kinship to them. Othello is but a Moor; Shylock but a Jew. They learn that they cannot effectively appeal to a human confraternity. Shylock's

"Hath not a Jew eyes?" speech may have some purchase upon modern viewers of the play, but none upon those whom in that fictional world listen indifferently to it.

I have higher hopes for Portia's plea for a mercy based on our common sinfulness, the Adamic burden we all share: "In the course of justice none of us / Should see salvation." But Shylock himself repudiates such a claim; and, when the tables have turned and he is the one under judgment, we hear no more of Portia's eloquence on this subject. Speaking only for myself, I would like to think that the idea of a common fatherhood in Adam and a weakness or infection or perversion of the will inherited by all from him would be powerful enough to deflect the cruel from their determinations. But it is not. Yet it can at times slow the heating of rage and vengeance, force the persecutor or abuser to pause for a moment, if only to grope for some plausible self-justification. When belief in the "universal human frailty" that Plato's Athenian invokes has been swept aside, the path to unbridled cruelty and the absolute lust for destruction is perfectly, terrifyingly clear.

TEN

The Two-Headed Calf

In the spring of 1936 Rebecca West visited Yugoslavia for the first time, sent on a lecture tour by the British Council. She was rather at loose ends as a writer. She had recently finished a novel, *The Thinking Reed*, which was about to appear to largely rapturous reviews, but thought that her next book would be political, based on reportage. Like many attentive people in that time, she saw that Europe was creeping, evidently helplessly, toward another war, and she wished to write something that could serve as diagnosis and as warning. A few months earlier the council had sent her to Finland, and that country's placement at a juncture between East and West seemed to make it a plausible subject—really, more like a pretext—for the reflections that had been stirring in her mind. But almost from the moment she arrived in Yugoslavia she saw that it provided a *better* pretext, a "more picturesque and convenient example of the political thesis I wanted to expound."

But this confident appropriation of a country for the purposes of political "example" did not last long. West was captivated by the complexity of the land's history and its cultural tensions and threw herself into a frenzy of reading and research. Her original idea for a long essay or "snap book" began to expand in her mind until it lost all recognizable shape and she could not control it or predict its development. In the grip of a kind of compulsion, she visited the country again the next year, once more the year after that, and soon thereafter was referring to her project as a "wretched, complicated book that won't interest anybody." Before her vision of the world of the South Slavs had released her, the "essay" had grown into a vast two-volume work of almost half a million words, nearly as long as *War and Peace*, and West was left to ponder why she had chosen "to devote five years of my life, at great financial sacrifice and to the utter exhaustion of my mind and body, to take an inventory of a country down to its last vest-button, in a form insane from any ordinary artistic or commercial point of view."

But really, she knew why. She had sacrificed time, energy, and health because she believed—and she was right to believe—that in the history and culture of Yugoslavia could be found the key that would explain the whole course of European history, and perhaps something ever deeper and broader than that. Perhaps it held the key to the riddle of human evil, to what St. Paul called "the mystery of iniquity." This riddle, this mystery, is above all what *Black Lamb and Grey Falcon* is about.

A few days into that first visit, she wrote in a kind of rapture to her husband, Henry Andrews (known to her as Ric):

> Dearest Ric, I have been [on] the most incredible journey. I went down on Saturday last in a packed train the 10 hour journey to Skoplje, with this poet who is also Chief of the Press Bureau—half Polish Jew, half Serb, the son of a famous surgeon, the most extraordinary person.... I [went that] night to the Easter ceremony—you know, candles and three processions round the church. I was very tired, but extremely interested—it was so like Augustine.

Immediately before writing *The Thinking Reed*, in 1933, West had produced a biography of Augustine—thus the reference. Of all her books it is the most unexpected and least characteristic; the ancient bishop's world was surely far distant from the concerns that prompted her fiction, her feminism, her political journalism. Though she later claimed that she had read Augustine for the first time when she was fourteen years old, it is not likely that she found the African any more congenial than Julian of Eclanum had. Born and (mostly) raised in Scotland, she knew well the Calvinists who claimed to be Augustine's heirs; and at the age of nineteen (!), writing for an early feminist publication called *The Freewoman*, West had confidently asserted that it is "impossible to argue with a person who holds the doctrine of original sin."

But twenty years later, having seen one world war past and another on the way, and having known in her own life many kinds of struggle and misery, West was no longer so confident in her dismissal of Augustine's most famous idea. In *Black Lamb and Grey Falcon*, a book over which Augustine hovers as an ambiguous ghostly patron, though he would seem to have nothing to do with the story, West admits, "I had . . . written a life of St. Augustine to find out why every phrase I read of his sounds in my ears like the sentence of my doom and the doom of my age."

FEW SIGNIFICANT INTELLECTUALS in the previous century could have so acknowledged Augustine's prescience. In a story quite familiar to most of us, the nineteenth century was an age whose dreams of human progress—moral, spiritual, technological—almost banished the idea of original sin from the scene. Although the collapse of the French Revolution into tyranny and brutality gave a profound shock to those who believed that corrupt societies could be immediately transformed into virtuous ones, opposition to the revolution was rarely couched in terms of innate and universal sinfulness. Early conservatives like Edmund Burke accused the revolutionaries of arrogance not because arrogance is simply the human portion, but rather because those particular persons had rejected "the wisdom of the ancestors." Burke's political admonitions continually emphasize the danger of uncontrolled passions, the limited supply of knowledge that any one person (or small group of people) has, the need to accept the social place assigned us by providence, and the chastising power of nemesis against those who fail to accept that place. None of these ideas is inconsistent with a belief in original sin, but none of them requires it—they all would have been perfectly familiar to any educated Athenian in the fourth century B.C.E. There is much wisdom in Burke, I think, but it is largely if not exclusively pagan wisdom.*

In any event, the defeat of Napoleon, some twenty years after the revolution, inaugurated a century in which European wars were brief and relatively localized and in which, with some exceptions (especially in the year 1848), the spirit of revolution was replaced by that of meliorism—steady and gradual improvement. By the end of the century, revolutionaries had little to show for their efforts, but reformers could look with some complacency upon their achievements. In England, for example, the Reform Bills corrected ancient corruptions in the voting system, the slave trade was definitively ended, fuller civil rights were extended to Roman Catholics, the rights of women to hold property were greatly increased, and (by the end of the century anyway) vast improvements were made in sanitation, from the cleansing of the Thames to the new practice of sterilizing surgical instruments. Similar stories could be told about other European countries, and

---

* A somewhat comparable figure in France, Chateaubriand, does emphasize the reality of original sin in his *Spirit of Christianity,* but only as one of the many doctrines of the Catholic Church worthy of being reembraced by an increasingly secularized Europe. The topic occupies three or four pages in a very large book.

even the horrors of the Civil War in America could be seen, eventually and by some, as necessary to the fuller realization of the promise of the "American experiment." All of these achievements gave energy to the hope that moral and technological progress could continue to march hand in hand into an ever rosier future; and as a popularized version of Darwin's ideas began to make its way into the public consciousness, progress came to be thought not just likely, but inevitable. In fact, the codiscoverer of the principle of natural selection, Alfred Russel Wallace, far more excitable on these and other matters than Darwin, proclaimed that "mankind will [eventually discover] that it was only required of them to develop the capacities of their higher nature, in order to convert this earth, which had so long been the theatre of their unbridled passions, and the scene of unimaginable misery, into as bright a paradise as ever haunted the dreams of seer or poet."*

---

* In his *History of the Idea of Progress* Robert Nisbet makes the fascinating point that the doctrine of progress served to undermine any belief in human unity: "Our stereotypes in Western history teach us to think of the consciousness of medieval man as more parochial than the consciousness of modern man. Perhaps in some ways this is true. But in more important ways it is not. With the diminution of the hold of Christian concepts upon the Western mind—concepts such as the unity of the human race, the chain of being in the universe, and the relative insignificance of both this world and this life in the total scheme of things—Western man became steadily more preoccupied not simply by the things of this world, but, more importantly, with the tiny portion contained in Western Europe. . . . [By the nineteenth century] the spell of the idea of progress—and with it the Eurocentric view of the entire world—had grown to such proportions that little if anything in the world could be considered in its own right. Everything had to be seen through the West and its values." The doctrine of progress was inevitably articulated in such a way that the achievements of the West became the standard of progress by which other cultures were measured and found wanting. An emphasis on progress typically walked hand in hand with the more assertive forms of nationalism and with scientific racism.

Again, this is a story too well known to require extensive rehearsal here. It is enough to say that in the latter part of the nineteenth century the doctrine of original sin—the very notion that some intrinsic primal fault will always thwart or at least compromise our attempts at personal social progress—had never seemed less reasonable.* And yet by the time the following century had followed a third of its course, an agnostic intellectual like Rebecca West could hear Augustine's proclamation of our innate corruption as "the sentence of my doom and the doom of my age." How did this happen?

In trying to understand this development, we should begin by noting that the age of progress had its share of skeptics, but the grounds of their skepticism vary widely. In Russia—to take an example rather distant from the geography we have been traversing—Dostoevsky saw in the rise of secularism an incipient (and ultimately irresistible) nihilism; he believed that the success of such ungodly ideolo-

---

* Of course, throughout the nineteenth century there were Christians of various traditionalist stripes who, as a matter of course, continued to defend the doctrine of original sin. Some of these defenders are quite acute. As early as 1832, the then Anglican John Henry Newman gave a lecture at the University of Oxford in which he argued that the excuse-making and defensiveness of Adam and Eve continue to mark our own self-justifications: "The original temptation set before our first parents was that of proving their freedom, by using it without regard to the will of Him who gave it. The original excuse offered by them after sinning was, that they were not really free, that they had acted under a constraining influence, the subtlety of the tempter. They committed sin that they might be independent of their Maker; they defended it on the ground that they were dependent upon Him. And this has been the case ever since; to lead us, first, to exult in our uncontrollable liberty of will and conduct; then, when we have ruined ourselves, to plead that we are the slaves of necessity." And half a century later, in America, the eminent Presbyterian theologian and leader of Princeton Seminary, B. B. Warfield, wrote a book-length introduction to Augustine's anti-Pelagian writings that emphasized Augustine's (and Paul's) psychological acuity. But however powerful these voices, they were heard almost exclusively by their fellow Christians; they had little power to shape the larger cultural conversation about human nature and behavior.

gies would ultimately abort and then reverse the course of progress, ushering in a new age of previously unimagined evil. But Dostoevsky does not see vulnerability to these ideas as something universal and intrinsic to humanity, but rather as a function of literally *demonic* oppression or possession to which some people make themselves prone because of their ideas, their beliefs. (As one character in *Demons* says to another, "I only know it was not you who ate the idea, it was the idea that ate you.") In Dostoevsky we see a hyperawareness of the horrible power of human sinfulness, or at least the human *capacity* for sin, that never touches, as far as I can tell, on the idea of original sin, but rather focuses on *particular* thoughts and acts that open one to possession by evil spirits.

Or let us consider a very different figure: William James. In the Gifford Lectures he gave in the first year of the twentieth century, later to be published as *The Varieties of Religious Experience,* he considers two very broad categories of religious persons, those who follow "the religion of healthy-mindedness" and those whom he calls the "sick souls," the "children of wrath," who in their terror at their own dark places crave a "second birth." The terms he chooses are, or seem, highly prejudicial, yet he acknowledges that the sick souls discern truths that the healthy-minded know not and even agrees that "the completest religions . . . seem to be those in which the pessimistic elements are best developed." Coming at the end of the most optimistic and progressive of centuries, and from an American no less, this would seem to be a telling admission.

Yet there is something odd about the way that James develops this theme. "The lunatic's visions of horror are all drawn from the material of daily fact," he writes. "Our civilization is founded on the shambles, and every individual existence goes out in a lonely spasm of helpless agony. If you protest, my friend, wait till you arrive there yourself!" But in illustrating the legitimacy of the sick soul's perception of evil, James takes his examples only from the realm of nature:

"Here on our very hearths and in our gardens the infernal cat plays with the panting mouse, or holds the hot bird fluttering in her jaws. Crocodiles and rattlesnakes and pythons are at this moment vessels of life as real as we are;... and whenever they or other wild beasts clutch their living prey, the deadly horror which an agitated melancholiac feels is the literally right reaction on the situation."

Well, I suppose one could see it that way, though it is worth noting that for many Christians in the centuries preceding James, predation was seen as a consequence of Adam and Eve's Fall and therefore as a wound that human sin inflicts on the whole of creation. (The historian Keith Thomas cites a seventeenth-century English gentleman who condemned his brother's love of cockfighting in just these terms: "You make that a cause of your jollity and merriment which should be a cause of your grief and godly sorrow, for you take delight in the enmity and cruelty of the creatures, which was laid upon them for the sin of man.") What's especially curious about James's endorsement of the sick soul's melancholy discernment is that it completely ignores the fact of *human* evil, dark deeds done by *us*. James was nineteen when the Civil War broke out, knew many soldiers himself, and frequently reproached himself for his failure to enlist in the Union cause; this presentation of evil as a natural phenomenon rather than as the acts of men suggests a similar evasive discomfort. After all, he calls those who are aware of evil "sick souls" and "children of wrath" not because they see evil *around* them, but because they sense it *within;* they crave the "second birth" because they know that they themselves are mired in evil and cruelty. How strange that James's very terminology indicates that he knows this, while he refuses to discuss it. After but two paragraphs about cats and crocodiles, he concludes his chapter with these reassuring words: "Fortunately from now onward we shall have to deal with more cheerful subjects than those we have recently been dwelling on."

. . .

IT IS A COMMONPLACE of intellectual history that these evasions and half measures, these sidelong acknowledgments of the pervasive human capacity for evil, were brought to a sudden end by the eruption of the Great War in 1914. A famous poem commemorates this abrupt transition in the history of the West, Philip Larkin's "MC-MXIV," prompted by a photograph of men waiting in line to enlist in the British army. The poem concludes with this stanza:

> *Never such innocence,*
> *Never before or since,*
> *As changed itself to past*
> *Without a word—the men*
> *Leaving the gardens tidy,*
> *The thousands of marriages*
> *Lasting a little while longer:*
> *Never such innocence again.*

This thought echoes in almost every book about the Great War and its aftermath. The estimable military historian John Keegan, to take but one example, affirms that the Great War "destroyed the benevolent and optimistic culture of the European continent." It is a powerful thought, but it is not precisely true.

Robert Nisbet, in his *History of the Idea of Progress,* insists to the contrary that "World War I, with all its unprecedented slaughter, devastation, and disintegrative effect upon the political and moral fabric of Europe, actually seems to have strengthened Western faith in the idea" of inevitable human moral progress. This also may be rather too strong a claim—the examples Nisbet goes on to cite suggest that meliorism continued its triumphal march primarily in America. But Nisbet's evidence clearly indicates that Victorian "innocence" did not immediately "change itself to past," but rather declined, the rate of decline increasing as, in the 1930s, it became increasingly clear to everyone that the Treaty of Versailles had solved nothing, and that the very same animosities that had set off the "war to end war" were undiminished and would sooner or later ignite again. Thus, at the outbreak of the new war in September 1939, C. S. Lewis—who had served in the trenches in the Great War until wounded by an exploding British shell that had fallen short of its target—wrote with poignant resignation, "If it's got to be, it's got to be. But the flesh is weak and selfish and I think death would be much better than to live through another war." And: "What makes it worse is the ghostly feeling that it has all happened before—that one fell asleep during the last war and had a delightful dream and has now waked up again."

It is this just oppressive sense of nightmare that underlies West's *Black Lamb and Grey Falcon*—that prompted the very travels from which the book emerged—just as, at precisely the same time, it was prompting Eugen Rosenstock-Huessy, newly arrived in America, to write his *Out of Revolution*. In fact, the two books, though utterly different in explicit subject matter, are remarkably similar in theme. Each tries to make sense of a European culture that seemed to be breaking into anarchic fragments; each tries to understand whether the events of the 1930s constituted a departure from the main course of European history or the shockingly tragic fulfillment of that course. But as powerful as Rosenstock-Huessy's book is, in its eccentric way, it stops short of West's inquiry. Only West takes her quest into the most obscure recesses of the human heart; only West gets beyond the history of any one part of the world.

So let us return to her narrative. It begins in Croatia, which is where it had to begin, no matter where West had actually entered Yugoslavia. Croatia is the part of Yugoslavia that is historically connected to the West and that therefore, in the typology that sustains much of West's story, is impure and corrupt. Early on she mentions with scorn the "Croat devotion to the Habsburgs"; a little later her charismatic guide, a half-Jewish Serbian poet she calls Constantine, says that the Croats have been "possessed by the West," a possession West says "had meant nothing but corruption." By the time she gets into Serbia itself, she has come to the conclusion that the key division is religious: what matters most is that the Croats are Catholic and the Serbs Orthodox, because "the difference between the Roman Catholic and the Orthodox Churches is so great that it transcended racial or linguistic unity." And what precisely makes this chasm so great? At almost the midpoint of the book West makes her distinctions explicit:

> The problem [of Yugoslavia] was enormously intricate. It sprang from the inclusion in the same state of two kinds of Slavs: Slavs who were the inheritors of the Byzantine tradition of culture and the primitive Christianity of the Orthodox Church, and had been informed with the tragic conception of life by the defeat of Kossovo [by the Ottoman Turks in 1389] and the ensuing five hundred years of slavery; and Slavs who had been incorporated in the Western bourgeois system by Austrian influence and were spiritually governed by the Roman Catholic Church, which owes its tone to a Renaissance unknown to the other Slavs, and were experienced in discomfort but not in tragedy.

So the key terms on the one side are *tradition, primitive, tragic,* and on the other *Western, bourgeois, Renaissance.* Once West puts the matter so bluntly, we see that this is a rather familiar set of oppositions; it adds up to something rather different from the "noble savage" motif, but related to it. The appeal of the noble savage is that his life is minimally cultural, almost wholly natural; the appeal of the Serbs to West is that they are the heirs of an ancient culture—rich, complex, sophisticated, nuanced, responsive to the whole of human life, including its most tragic elements. She sees this most powerfully in the services of the Orthodox Church, and several key scenes in the book take place in churches.

One of the most memorable of these occurs in Ohrid, in Macedonia, a place West sees as lying near the heart of the ancient Slavic world she loves. During a Mass presided over by one Bishop Nikolai—"the most remarkable human being I have ever met, not because he was wise or good, for I have still no idea to what degree he is either, but because he was the supreme magician"—West suddenly discerns the essential nature of the central Christian mystery, that of the Eucharistic feast. The Orthodox Church in this part of the world, she muses, had long been weak, enslaved even, its priests and ministers often corrupt, its ordinary believers subjected to Turkish tyranny, and all of them poor and dispossessed; but this simply meant that the worship of such people was "clear of the superficial ethical prescription, inspired by a superstitious regard for prosperity, which makes Western religion so often a set of by-laws tinged emotionally with smugness." Lacking even the possibility of such comforts,

the [Orthodox] Church had therefore to concentrate on the Mass, on reiterations of the first meaning of Christianity. It had to repeat over and over again that goodness is adorable and that there is an evil part in man which hates it, that there was once a poor man born of a poor woman who was perfectly good and was therefore murdered by evil men, and in his defeat was victorious, since it is far better to be crucified than to crucify, while his murderers were conquered beyond the imagination of conquerors; and that this did not happen once and far away, but is repeated every day in all hearts.

So the Orthodox Church, in its central rite, enacts "the tragic conception of life" by acknowledging the dividedness of "all hearts," the "evil part in man"—in all human beings—that hates goodness. This is a wisdom that reaches back beyond the superficial moralism and optimism that characterize "Western religion." It is a wisdom that once the whole Christian world knew—again, West told her husband that her first Orthodox Easter, in Skoplje, just a hundred miles from Ohrid, reminded her of Augustine—but now only a small part of it retains that knowledge.

And for West the heart of the matter is that insight into our universal corruption, an insight confirmed for her a couple of days later, in the small town of Struga, where Bishop Nikolai performs his magic for another congregation, while West and her husband visit a curious little "biological museum" that contains, among other things, a stuffed two-headed calf in a glass case, an animal "strangely lovely in form," so that "it was a shock to find that of the two heads which branched like candelabra one was lovely, but one was hideous, like that other seen in a distorting glass." The museum's custodian affirms that the calf lived for two days "and should be alive today had it not been for its nature." West's husband expresses puzzlement at this statement, and the custodian explains that when they fed milk to the calf through its beautiful head, its ugly head spit the milk out, so no food got into its stomach, and it died. This account prompts West to meditation:

> To have two heads, one that looks to the right and another that
> looks to the left, one that is carved by grace and another that
> is not, the one that wishes to live and the other that does not;
> this was an experience not wholly unknown to human beings.
> As we pressed our faces against the case, peering through the
> green dusk, our reflections were superimposed on the calf,
> and it would not have been surprising if it had moved nearer
> the glass to see us better.

The whole history of Yugoslavia, West comes to think, is the story of a two-headed calf, and maybe the whole of human history. In

1914—in a conflict that began, of course, in Yugoslavia, with the assassination of Archduke Franz Ferdinand in Sarajevo—the ugly head spat out the life-giving milk, after a century in which it had appeared that the beautiful head would be able to take in nourishment; and now, twenty years later, it was clear that once more the ugly head was about to have its hateful way. The Orthodox Church understood this fact of our nature; Bishop Nikolai knew how to enact it in magical rites of extraordinary power to explain and to comfort.

The confirmation of Bishop Nikolai's magic in the vision of the two-headed calf might have been enough to make someone convert to Christianity. After all, it was something very like this insight that brought a Soviet prisoner named Aleksandr Solzhenitsyn to the Orthodox faith. In *The Gulag Archipelago* Solzhenitsyn describes the terrible (and yet ultimately, for him, life-giving) experience of watching one of the prison guards who habitually mistreated the prisoners and slowly coming to realize that, given the same power in the same circumstances, he himself would surely have behaved with equal cruelty. "In the intoxication of youthful successes" he had believed himself "infallible"; it was the Gulag that taught him that he was "a murderer, and an oppressor." It was the Gulag that taught him that everyone has the capacity to become a Stalin and that therefore "the line separating good and evil passes not through states, nor between classes, nor between political parties either—but right through every human heart." In other words, each and every one of us is a divided self, a two-headed calf. His "bent back ... nearly broke beneath the load" of this knowledge, but in the end it led him into the arms of the Orthodox Church, which alone knew the meaning of this dividedness and its remedy.

Given what she says about her experience in the church at Ohrid, West might have become such a convert. Yet she did not, and the reasons are worth exploring. The key may be found in the midst of her ecstatic account of Bishop Nikolai's Mass, in these specific words: "In his defeat [Jesus] was victorious, since it is far better to be crucified than to crucify." Yes, but (West comes to ask) are those the only choices? Is it not true that to crucify and to accept crucifixion are alike manifestations of the love of death? Are not both acts of the calf's ugly head, merely two different ways of rejecting the life-giving milk?

Reservations about her love of the Serbs dot the whole book, but for several hundred pages are kept at arm's length: "I felt a sudden abatement of my infatuation with Yugoslavia," she writes at one point, but then a handsome young peasant enters the café where she sits, and he holds a tiny black lamb under his coat, and suddenly it is beautiful again. But in the latter stages of her book, West's idealization of the ancient Serbian-Byzantine-Orthodox culture crumbles into dust, and this crumbling has a complex twofold cause. First, she visits a place called the Sheep's Field in Macedonia, where these people whose "preference for the agreeable over the disagreeable" she loves meet at an ancient stone to sacrifice animals, in hopes of making women fertile. The stone is smeared with blood, the stench overwhelms, and West is staggered by the sheer perversity of believing—as people had for untold centuries come to this stone believing—that with such pointless death life can somehow be purchased. "But what they were doing at the rock was abominable." Throughout her travels in Yugoslavia she had deplored the modern and celebrated the ancient; yet here the most ancient of rites, far older, probably, than the Christian Mass, embodies the worst of humanity.

And she thinks, also and above all, of the strange fact that Prince Lazar—who led the Serbs into battle on the plain of Kosovo in 1389—is the greatest hero in Serbian history, not in spite of but *because* he lost that battle. A great poem commemorating the event teaches that the prophet Elijah, in the form of a grey falcon, demanded that he choose between an earthly and a heavenly kingdom, and he chose the latter. To the Serbs this was an act of great courage and piety, since the blood of so many of Lazar's people was therefore on his hands; to West, it is an abysmal revelation:

> "If this be so," I said to myself, "if it be a law that those who are born into the world with a preference for the agreeable over the disagreeable are born also with an impulse towards defeat, then the whole world is a vast Kossovo, an abominable blood-logged plain, where people who love go out to fight people who hate, and betray their cause to their enemies, so that loving is persecuted for immense tracts of history, far longer than its little periods of victory." I began to weep, for the left-wing people among whom I had lived all my life had in their attitude to foreign politics achieved such a betrayal. They were always right, they never imposed their rightness. "If this disposition to be at once Christ and Judas is inborn," I thought, "we might as well die, and the sooner the better, for the defeat is painful after the lovely promise."

And so West comes, at last, after all her experiences and meditations in the land of the South Slavs, to one of the worst positions a person can occupy in thinking of her fellow human beings: an Augustinian anthropology without its accompanying theology. She sees with an absolute clarity our innate dividedness, the immovable and constant presence of an ever vigilant ugly head, always determined to expel nourishment and thereby to reject life and to choose death instead. But the Christian idea that the death of Christ somehow redeems our death wish, transforms it (by a kind of powerful spiritual magic that only the Bishop Nikolais of the world grasp), makes it the entry point to a heavenly kingdom—this idea she cannot accept. And so she cannot and does not become a Christian. She sees with the same absolute clarity a history that makes a mockery of Panglossian optimism, of Rousseauian idealism, of revolutionary aspiration, and of Victorian meliorism as well as of the Christian picture of redemption; but she offers no alternative.

The last pages of the book drift away in a haze. She meets people who do good things and people who do bad things, but the narrative force has dissipated in the dank stench of the Sheep's Field and on the blood-soaked plain of Kosovo. Her travels end with the news that Mussolini has invaded Albania, just across beautiful Lake Ohrid; and a lengthy epilogue describes the explosion of full world war, emphasizing the bravery with which the Yugoslavs fought against the Nazi armies before being crushed, just as they had fought many centuries earlier when the Turks came and the grey falcon spoke his counsel to Prince Lazar.

The Ottomans beheaded Lazar, but his body was recovered and kept as a kind of sacred relic by the Serbs. When West came to Yugoslavia the body lay in royal state in the Vrdnik monastery on the mountain called Frushka Gora; she touched his blackened and dessicated hand.

WEST WROTE THAT SHE HEARD in Augustine's voice her doom and the doom of her age. Perhaps the role of the twentieth century in this story is to renew the plausibility of the doctrine of original sin without renewing the general plausibility of the Christian faith, the faith within which that doctrine is articulated and makes sense. A famous book recording several intellectuals' disenchantment with Marxism is called *The God That Failed*. The twentieth century saw the failure of many gods, most if not all of them invented in the two previous centuries precisely in order to replace the Christian deity. But it has not often happened that, when those gods failed, believers in them questioned the wisdom of their ancestors' jettisoning of Christianity. Of the six authors who contributed to *The God That Failed*, only one, Ignazio Silone, had any substantial relationship to Christian belief, and that did not wax or wane in relation to his changing political commitments. But a writer who declined an invitation to contribute to the book, Whittaker Chambers, was one of the more famous Christian converts of his day.

Between 1948 and 1950, Chambers, who for the previous few years had been a leading writer at *Time* magazine, became one of the most talked-about men in America. His testimony to the House Un-American Activities Committee, identifying certain highly placed officials in the American government as Communists and Soviet agents, made him a hero in some circles and a villain of the first order in others. In his biography of Chambers Sam Tanenhaus shows how deeply reluctant Chambers was to offer testimony on this subject, for complex reasons, including fear for his own physical safety and his family's: when Chambers had backed out of his own secret life as a Communist agent, in 1938, he had had very good reason to think that his former handlers would kill him if they got the chance, and he took extraordinary measures to hide his wife and children. He also knew that his testimony would make him highly notorious and knew that this notoriety would mark his children's lives in unpleasant ways. And perhaps there were old friends he did not wish to expose; certainly he was openly contemptuous of the "informer." But whatever reservations he had, once he got to the witness stand—not just before HUAC, but also in the subsequent perjury trials of Alger Hiss, who became the chief target of the government's inquiries—Chambers made quite a show of it. And when all the testifying was over, he decided that he needed to relate the key events of his own political life yet more fully and systematically.

The book that emerged in 1952, *Witness*, was, at 799 pages, several times longer than he had expected it to be. But Chambers found it necessary to describe his life at such length because he thought that what had happened to him was an exemplary tale, even *the* exemplary tale of his age. "It was my fate," he writes at the book's outset, "to be in turn a witness to each of the two great faiths of our time": Christianity and Communism. Chambers saw the choice he had faced—"faith in God or faith in man?"—as a microcosmic version of the choice the whole world was facing. In the aftermath of the two world wars, with political and military power settling into two distinct and utterly opposed camps, locked in what had already been called a "Cold War," the whole world faced what Chambers called "a total crisis—religious, moral, intellectual, social, political, economic. It is popular to call it a crisis of the Western world. It is in fact a crisis of the whole world." And for Chambers nothing could be more imperative than that "the whole world" make the choice he had made, to repudiate the false god of Communism and choose the true God of Christianity.*

The book's foreword, from which I have been quoting, takes the form of a letter to Chambers's children, and it concludes with an apocalyptic vision of the father leading those children to Golgotha, the Place of the Skull, where Jesus was crucified. Chambers tells them: "When you understand what you see [there], you will no longer be children. You will know that life is pain, that each of us hangs always

---

* To this claim Irving Howe, writing in *The Nation,* replied, "If Chambers is right in believing the major bulwark against Stalin to be faith in God, then it is time for men of conviction and courage to take to the hills." But in *The Atlantic Monthly* Rebecca West wrote a glowing review of the book—calling it "so just and so massive in its resuscitation of the past"—shrewdly identifying Chambers as a kind of modern mystic and showing how the mystic's commitment to the power of personal revelation shapes his narrative. This was perhaps something of a quid pro quo, for in 1947 Chambers had written an equally glowing cover story for *Time* on West's book *The Meaning of Treason,* praising her "warmth of heart and incandescence of mind." Not altogether incidentally, two months before the profile of West *Time* had run a cover story—not written by Chambers, but produced under his editorial governance—on an Englishman who had had a dramatic conversion from atheism to Christianity—his name was C. S. Lewis. *Time* was quite the magazine in those days.

on the cross of himself. And when you know that this is true of every man, woman, and child on earth, you will be wise."

The modern conservative movement in American politics, which in many ways coalesced around Chambers and his multiple testimonies, has often taken this as a statement about original sin—has typically assumed that Chambers is warning his children about the evil that dwells inside of them and is encouraging them to see that when they face that evil, they will achieve true wisdom. I think Chambers's emphasis here is rather different. The whole of the foreword, and indeed the whole of *Witness,* is saturated in the language of decisive *choice,* as was much intellectual discourse in that heyday of existentialism, and it seems to me that Chambers is telling his children that ultimately they will have to choose between being the repentant thief who is promised a place in Jesus's kingdom and the unrepentant, defiant thief who mocks the others on their crosses. But of course we only have to make such a choice if the possibility of doing evil is always a living option for us, and that is true of "every man, woman, and child on earth" only if the doctrine of original sin is true. So perhaps Chambers implies the reality of original sin even if he does not state it, but it is implication at most.

During the first Cold War years, even before Chambers's testimony and with increasing forcefulness after it, the emerging congregation of conservatives began to identify original sin as one of its core principles. George Nash writes in his outstanding history of this movement, "The Christianity which [John] Hallowell, [William F.] Buckley, and others defended was not the Christianity of the Social Gospel or liberal Protestantism. It was a Christianity grounded in what was for many neoconservatives the deepest lesson of World War II: the lesson of evil, of original sin." And then Nash goes on to quote a batch of thinkers who insist on this point: John Hallowell, Gertrude Himmelfarb, Richard Weaver, Eliseo Vivas, and so on, every one of them writing in the years immediately following World War II.

In the defining work of that movement, Russell Kirk's *The Conservative Mind* (published just months after *Witness*), we hear: "The saving of civilization is contingent upon the revival of something like the doctrine of original sin." In that sentence Kirk was summarizing the thought of Irving Babbit, but it was his own thought as well, and he believed it to be intrinsic to the very idea of conservatism, beginning with Edmund Burke. From Kirk on through contemporary writers like Jonah Goldberg, it is axiomatic that Burke's conservatism—and thus, all conservatism descending from him—is grounded in a belief in original sin.

The problem with this axiom is that there is no clear evidence for it. I have already suggested that Burke's wisdom, though real, is not discernibly Christian, and as far as I can discover there is not a single reference to original sin in Burke's writings and speeches, except for an entirely metaphorical use of the term to try to explain hostility between Pitt the Younger and Lord Fitzwilliam. (Burke was so prolific that I have read no more than a fraction of his whole body of work, but his most important and influential works seem free from any reference to this principle, which his devoutest followers say is central to him.) Burke thinks that all politicians and statesmen make mistakes, of course—one could scarcely deny that—and he believes that those mistakes stem from faults of character at least as often as they stem from misinformation or faulty judgment; but one need not affirm original sin in order to hold such views. If Burke has a single governing idea, it is surely this famous sentence from his *Reflections on the Revolution in France:* "We are afraid to put men to live and trade each on his own private stock of reason; because we suspect that this stock in each man is small, and that the individuals would do better to avail themselves of the general bank and capital of nations and of ages." In Burke's view, a truly civilized and relatively just society is an extremely difficult thing to build up, because "the nature of man is intricate [and] the objects of society are of the greatest possible complexity"; generations of trial-and-error development by our ancestors will surely have produced a better system than could be improvised on the spur of the moment by a single tyrant or a small band of revolutionaries. Because the work of those generations can be undone so quickly and thoughtlessly by the arrogant few, "the evils of inconstancy and versatility" are "ten thousand times worse than those of obstinacy and the blindest prejudice."

Certainly these ideas rhyme with original sin. If Adam and Eve sinned by pridefully preferring their ways to the ordinances of God the Father, modern revolutionaries sin by pridefully preferring their ideas to those of their cultural forefathers. But there is also a key point of divergence between the biblical account of the first sin and Burke's account of ongoing political sin: our forefathers were not God. They too were subject—were they not?—to sin contracted from Adam, and it is hard to see how, on the Christian account of things, we could suppose that the institutions they built would be free from that contagion. Nor does it make sense to think that those institutions would automatically or necessarily improve over time; someone who believes that Satan is truly the Prince of this world and that we humans are easily enthralled by him might well suspect that our political and social institutions would become *more* corrupt over time. But Burke is what we might call a conditional meliorist: *if* we show proper respect for our ancestors, then our institutions should, through gentle reform, grow more and more perfect.

Furthermore, Burke believes that those with the greatest power in English society are the ones least likely to sin against their fellow human beings. At times he comes perilously close to exempting them from Adam's curse, as in his (it must be said) fawning letter of 1772 to the Duke of Richmond:

Persons of your station of life ought to have long views. You people of great families and hereditary trusts and fortunes, are not like such as I am, who, whatever we may be, by the rapidity of our growth, and even by the fruit we bear, and flatter ourselves that, while we creep on the ground, we belly into melons that are exquisite for size and flavour, yet still are annual plants, that perish without season, and leave no sort of traces behind us. You, if you are what you ought to be, are in my eye the great oaks that shade a country, and perpetuate your benefits from generation to generation.

All that rescues Burke here is the one subjunctive clause "if you are what you ought to be." Twenty-three years later Burke wrote a slashing open letter to the Duke of Bedford indicating quite clearly what he thought of those aristocrats who failed to be what they ought to be; but in general he sees the oaklike continuity of the old aristocratic families as the strongest bulwarks against the ravages of sin in public life. It is not clear how, on any biblical or Christian account, this should be the case.

So the conservatives of the post–World War II period who invoke the explanatory power of original sin *and* the guiding authority of Edmund Burke formed a link that may not hold. And therefore it's worth noting that during the period we have been discussing—the period, roughly, from Rebecca West's first visit to Yugoslavia in 1936 to the publication of *Witness* in 1952—the American thinker most widely known for renewing a commitment to the depths of human sinfulness and the dangers of an "easy conscience" was Reinhold Niebuhr.

In 1948 one journalist summarized Niebuhr's thoughts on these themes:

Under the bland influence of the idea of progress, man, supposing himself more and more to be the measure of all things, achieved a singularly easy conscience and an almost hermetically smug optimism. The idea that man is sinful and needs redemption was subtly changed into the idea that man is by nature good and hence capable of indefinite perfectibility. This perfectibility is being achieved through technology, science, politics, social reform, education. Man is essentially good, says 20th Century liberalism, because he is rational, and his rationality is (if the speaker happens to be a liberal Protestant) divine, or (if he happens to be religiously unattached) at least benign. Thus the reason-defying paradoxes of Christian faith are happily bypassed.

Who was this journalist? Whittaker Chambers, of course, writing in *Time*, which at this point in a period of six months had devoted covers to C. S. Lewis, Rebecca West, and now Niebuhr. Chambers wrote of "the blind impasse of optimistic liberalism" and, in his stentorian newsreelish way, affirmed: "At the open end of that impasse stood a forbidding and impressive figure. To Protestantism's easy conscience and easy optimism that figure was saying, with every muscle of its being: No. His name was Reinhold Niebuhr."

Chambers could celebrate Niebuhr so wholeheartedly because on what Chambers believed to be the one great issue of the day—the choice between Communism and Christianity, "faith in man or faith in God"—their views were identical. In his 1944 book *The Children of Light and the Children of Darkness* Niebuhr summarizes the case for original sin in a style reminiscent of Chambers's own, in a manner that might suit the pulpit better than the lecture hall. A failure to recognize the truth of this doctrine, Niebuhr says, "has robbed bourgeois theory of real wisdom," because this doctrine "emphasizes a fact which every page of human history attests."

Through it one may understand that no matter how wide the perspectives which the human mind may reach, how broad the loyalties which the human imagination may conceive, how universal the community which human statecraft may organize, or how pure the aspirations of the saintliest idealists may be, there is no level of human moral or social achievement in which there is not some corruption of inordinate self-love.

This sober and true view of the human situation was neatly rejected by modern culture.

But though he and Chambers were at one on this point, Niebuhr was a man of the Left and repudiated the free-market affections of the Right almost as fiercely as he repudiated the collectivist fantasies of the Marxists. Chambers himself was scarcely an orthodox conservative on these economic matters, but was willing to make common cause—to the point of joining the staff of Buckley's new magazine *National Review*—with those who shared his sense that the Communist threat had to be resisted above all and at any cost. But there were not many on the Right who praised Niebuhr as Chambers did, precisely because of Niebuhr's suspicions of the market. There are points in *The Children of Light and the Children of Darkness* (and elsewhere) where Niebuhr suggests that Marxism and the market may be equally dangerous to the social order: "Conflicts in the community between varying conceptions of the good and between competing expressions of vitality are of more tragic proportions than was anticipated in the basic philosophy which underlies democratic civilization." That is, both Marxism and free-market conservatism may represent extreme views ("competing expressions of vitality") whose vastly different "conceptions of the good" may be driving our society toward some kind of "tragic" crisis.

Niebuhr believed that the conservatives of his own day misread Adam Smith, the father of their economic philosophy, in some ways and took him too seriously in others. "Smith was highly critical of the budding large-scale enterprise of his day," Niebuhr argues, and would be even more critical of "the vast collective forms of 'free enterprise'" in our own; but even so, he relied too heavily on a "secularized version of providence" in his notorious language of the "invisible hand" that guides human economic choices. For Niebuhr, the free-marketers no less than the Marxists are too placidly hopeful, too confident in human nature. "Perhaps the most remarkable proof of the power of this optimistic creed, which underlies democratic thought, is that Marxism, which is ostensibly a revolt against it, manages to express *the same optimism* in another form" (emphasis mine). The Marxist and the free-marketer alike have easy consciences and utterly fail to see that their own lives and thoughts are marked by "some corruption of inordinate self-love."

"The demonic fury of fascist politics," wrote Niebuhr—and he would have included Soviet totalitarianism in this description—"in which a collective will expresses boundless ambitions and imperial desires . . . represents a melancholy historical refutation of the eighteenth- and nineteenth-century conceptions of a harmless and essentially individual human life." But this demonic fury, Niebuhr makes it clear, refutes Adam Smith's would-be followers just as fiercely as it refutes Marx's revolutionary millennialism. The doctrine of original sin stands in judgment of *every* political system. This happens in part because sinful human individuals lack the will to resist the transformation of all social orders—past, present, and future—into something corrupt: thus even the most dedicated individualist ends up contributing to "free enterprise" as a *system,* as what Niebuhr calls a *collective* form, which then turns about and dominates the persons who made it or allowed it to be made. Even people who in their daily lives do little harm will nevertheless *allow* great harm to be done by their institutions—this is the thesis of the first book Niebuhr wrote after breaking with melioristic liberalism, the book from which I have been quoting, *Moral Man and Immoral Society.*

· · ·

I CONCLUDE THIS CHAPTER with a kind of parable. In 1939 an English philosopher named C. E. M. Joad published a surprisingly light-hearted book called *Guide to Modern Wickedness,* in which he devotes a chapter to assessing the condition of Christianity in England. Joad sees little to encourage him, except, perhaps, for the evident abandonment by many clergymen of some of the more offensive and dubious teachings of the Bible—for instance, the absurd story of the Fall. Surveying what remains, he concludes, "There is little enough here to strain our credulity; there is even less to awaken our enthusiasm." As far as Joad can see, the Church of England (the churches in England) simply evade the key issues of the day. To the Dean of Exeter's vacuous proclamation that "The Bible stands for belief in God and belief in man," Joad replies, "The quotation admirably illustrates the bankruptcy of Christianity in the modern world."

I think one can get from these brief references a sense of Joad's lively style. He was indeed a populist sort of philosopher who wrote mostly for common readers; he was also politically active through most of his adult life, even running for Parliament a time or two. But he became famous just after publishing the *Guide to Modern Wickedness* when he became a regular on a radio program called *The Brains Trust.* Panelists on the extraordinarily popular show answered questions—questions about anything at all, from the most sublime to the most mundane of issues. Other regulars included the political philosopher Isaiah Berlin, the art historian Kenneth Clark, and the eminent biologist Julian Huxley, but Joad was by far the most popular, and he became one of the most familiar voices known to the British public. In the years just after the war there was even talk of a peerage for this dynamic public philosopher. Though *The Brains Trust* prompted a couple of American imitators, Joad's fame did not cross the Atlantic until 1948, when *Time* ran a brief profile of him.

Yes, *Time* again! And within that very same six-month period that saw its celebrations of West, Lewis, and Niebuhr. One senses the invisible hand (as it were) of Whittaker Chambers at work here, because the profile converges on familiar themes. Let's let *Time*'s unnamed writer—could it be Chambers himself? No, the piece is too badly written—take it from here:

> Having returned to the Anglican faith of his childhood, Believer Joad worships regularly at his parish church in Hampstead or at the church near his Hampshire country place. But he has lost none of his saucy skill at dialectic. He explained last week: "When war came, the existence of evil hit me in the face.... Human progress is possible, but so unlikely. People don't know how to conceive it." Wrote Pessimist Joad shortly after the end of the war: "I see now that evil is endemic in man, and that the Christian doctrine of original sin expresses a deep and essential insight, into human nature."
>
> Of his rediscovered faith, Joad says: "It affords me a light to live by in an ever darkening world."

At this point readers may be wondering why, given the enormous and still ongoing popularity of C. S. Lewis—another quick-witted, stylistically gifted English academic who had converted to Christianity and become a popular figure on BBC radio—Joad's name is now virtually unknown. Alas, in the very month that *Time* profiled him Joad was caught riding a train without paying for a ticket, something that, it then emerged, he did all the time. Though his fine was but two pounds, every newspaper in the nation gleefully leaped on the story. "Christian Philosopher Exposed as Fare Dodger" was too good a headline to pass up. No peerage for Joad, and, worse still, he was sacked by the BBC, so he never again had a public platform to share his ideas. The British public never learned in any detail just what Believer Joad found so compelling in the doctrine of original sin.

ELEVEN

In the Genes

In December of 1854 Pope Pius IX issued an apostolic constitution—the sort of document commonly called a "papal bull"—entitled *Ineffabilis Deus*. The bull's chief subject was not the ineffable God of the title, but rather the woman chosen to bear God's son, the Blessed Virgin Mary. "Above all creatures," wrote Pius in his opening paragraph, "did God so love her that truly in her was the Father well pleased with singular delight. Therefore, far above all the angels and all the saints so wondrously did God endow her with the abundance of all heavenly gifts poured from the treasury of his divinity that this mother, ever absolutely free of all stain of sin, all fair and perfect, would possess that fullness of holy innocence and sanctity than which, under God, one cannot even imagine anything greater, and which, outside of God, no mind can succeed in comprehending fully."

The Holy Father was not stating a mere personal opinion in this bull, though he was aware that it was possible for faithful Catholics to be confused about the force and status of his words. The doctrine of papal infallibility would not be promulgated for another sixteen years, and before that could happen there had to be a great deal of wrangling about just which statements by popes carried absolute authority. So at the end of *Ineffabilis Deus* Pius takes care to be very explicit about his expectations:

> We declare, pronounce, and define that the doctrine which holds that the most Blessed Virgin Mary, in the first instance of her conception, by a singular grace and privilege granted by Almighty God, in view of the merits of Jesus Christ, the Savior of the human race, was preserved free from all stain of original sin, is a doctrine revealed by God and therefore to be believed firmly and constantly by all the faithful.

In other words, all Catholics must affirm Mary's Immaculate Conception, and anyone who fails to affirm it falls short of the obedience required of a true son or daughter of the church.

Pius knew that this pronouncement would be controversial, but he was confident that the history of the church, in theology and in practical worship, was clearly on his side—as was the current devotional mood of European Catholics. Just four years after Pius's announcement, in the French town of Lourdes, a miller's daughter named Bernadette Soubirous received a vision in which the Virgin addressed her with these words: "I am the Immaculate Conception." One might think that the pope's words had had great influence, were it not for the fact that Bernadette's vision was a relatively common thing—devotion to the Virgin had reached an exceptional (perhaps an unprecedented) pitch even before Pius had ascended to Peter's throne. In 1830, for instance, in another part of France, a farmer's daughter named Catherine Labouré had her own vision of the Virgin, which she described in such vivid detail that a kind of medallion depicting the scene was cast and widely sold. This "Miraculous Medal," as it was known, was decorated with these words of prayer: "O Mary, conceived without original sin, pray for us who have recourse to thee."

At around the same time Anne Catherine Emmerich, a Westphalian nun, received visions in which she was told not only that Mary's conception was immaculate, but that her mother Anne was herself a virgin, which made Mary's birth doubly miraculous. (This, like many of Emmerich's visions, transgressed the bounds of orthodoxy, which is the primary reason, in spite of great devotion to her utterances by many Catholics, she was not beatified until 2004, by a pope whose love for the Virgin nearly matched that of Pius.) She dictated much of what she saw to a poet named Klemens Brentano, but Brentano did not publish his account of Emmerich's Marian visions until 1852, at which point they became immediately and overwhelmingly popular. It is possible, therefore, that their appearance had some influence on Pius's decision to proceed with his proclamation. After all, in comparison to Emmerich's claims on Mary's behalf, the idea of the Immaculate Conception seems rather modest.

But again, though the nineteenth century was a high-water mark of Marian devotion, the whole history of Catholicism—but especially the work of the church fathers—is dotted with the same idea, a point that *Ineffabilis Deus* takes some pains to emphasize. And it is fascinating to consult those early promoters of the Immaculate Conception and note the *language* they use, for the condition of sinlessness is one that demands metaphorical description.

A feast day celebrating the conception of Mary began in the ninth century, in England, the country that throughout the Middle Ages led the way in attentiveness to the Virgin, but the belief that God had preserved her from sin is much older. In his debates with the Pelagians Augustine had insisted upon Mary's sinlessness, but even by his time the tradition was a familiar one. Hippolytus of Rome, a hundred and fifty years earlier, wrote that Mary was a kind of tabernacle—holding the Eternal Word of God as Israel's tabernacle had held the ark of the covenant—and claimed that as such she was "exempt from defilement and corruption." At about the same time Origen of Alexandria called her "immaculate of the immaculate, most complete sanctity, perfect justice, neither deceived by the persuasion of the serpent, nor infected with his poisonous breathings" (though by Augustine's standards Origen fell scandalously short of the truth when he wrote that at the Crucifixion of her son Mary fell prey to the sin of doubt, thereby failing to sustain her sinlessness throughout her life). Augustine's mentor, Ambrose, said that Mary was "immune" to the "stain of sin." St. Proclus, a patriarch of Constantinople, likewise said that the Virgin was "formed without any stain."

Other Eastern fathers agreed. Listen to the Syrian hermit St. Ephraem:

> Most holy Lady, Mother of God, alone most pure in soul and body, alone exceeding all perfection of purity, . . . alone made in thy entirety the home of all the graces of the Most Holy Spirit, and hence exceeding beyond all compare even the angelic virtues in purity and sanctity of soul and body, . . . my Lady most holy, all-pure, all-immaculate, all-stainless, all-undefiled, all-incorrupt, all-inviolate spotless robe of Him Who clothes Himself with light as with a garment . . . flower unfading, purple woven by God, alone most immaculate.

And the great John of Damascus, often called the last of the fathers, though he did not go quite as far as Anne Catherine Emmerich, nevertheless affirmed that Mary's parents, in the very sexual act that conceived her, "were filled and purified by the Holy Ghost, and freed from sexual concupiscence."

The language is consistent, always emphasizing the contrast between spot and spotlessness (the Latin word *macula* means "spot"), purity and stain or taint. To have what St. Paul called "sin within our members" is to be stained, that is, to be marked by something ugly that cannot be washed away (save by supernatural interference), or—if we think of our souls as liquid rather than solid—contaminated by the presence of some offensive additive that renders us impure. Thus Pius holds firmly to the tradition when in his summary of his bull he says that Mary "was preserved free from all *stain* of original sin."

But it should be noted that although this language may capture rather well the condition of sinfulness, it doesn't do anything to help us understand how we all share in the sin of Adam. That is, it gets the "sin," but not the "original." Some of the fathers also speak of sin as a "wound," which again has limited explanatory power; the metaphor could be read as suggesting that we are the innocent victims of something inexplicably inflicted on us by our first father. So other early Christians, as we have occasionally seen, tried out the language of disease: original sin is a "contagion," an "infection" we have caught from Adam. That's certainly better. Though it still can allow us to think of ourselves as helpless in the face of a ruthless and mindless pandemic, it contains within it the logic of *transmission,* the means by which that disease comes to us and by which we can pass it along to others. But something's not quite right here either: diseases can be transmitted from anyone to anyone—from a child to a parent, from a friend to a friend—whereas original sin, a moral version of time's arrow, follows a single path down through the generations. What we need is a different set of metaphors, a different language—the language of *inheritance.*

IT WOULD NOT HAVE taken long for the text of *Ineffabilis Deus* to make its way to the Abbey of St. Thomas in the town of Brünn in Moravia—now Brno in the Czech Republic—and one wonders what one particular monk thought of it. He had recently (in 1853) returned to the abbey after two years studying science at the University of Vienna and had begun teaching physics in the abbey's middle school. In the year of Pius's bull he began planting peas in the abbey's greenhouse and soon thereafter embarked on an extensive and methodical study of the transmission of certain traits through multiple generations of pea plants. His name was Gregor Mendel.

It is tempting to imagine Mendel reading the promulgation of Mary's preservation from sin and being moved to a profound theologico-scientific meditation on inheritance, a meditation that simultaneously birthed in him new devotion to the Virgin *and* prompted a vision of what would become the science of genetics. After all, he was a faithful monk, was he not? (He was later named abbot of St. Thomas.) And his primary academic interest was in physics, not biology, was it not?

Alas, there's no shred of evidence that Mendel even read Pius's bull, much less that his scientific thought was shaped by it. Throughout his childhood and adolescence he worked as a gardener, so his interest in biology long predated his science teaching and even his calling as a monk. But there is a curious correspondence nonetheless between Mendel's work in genetics and the Immaculate Conception, for the burgeoning science of genetics would provide a whole new vocabulary, a fresh set of metaphors, for describing original sin, and this new language eventually led to a surge of interest in the idea and complex reflections on its possible scientific basis.

I have heard a few village atheists over the years say that early Christians believed the story of Jesus's virgin birth because, being primitive people and all that, they didn't understand how babies are made. This is a silly thing to say simply in light of the biblical story itself—when Joseph finds out that his betrothed is pregnant, he decides to "put her away," an action there would be no reason for him to take if he didn't know how women got pregnant. But it is also more deeply silly because we can find no period of human history when people did not understand where babies come from or notice the resemblances between children and their parents. All human cultures have been equally aware that family resemblances can be seen in animals and plants as well. Augustine regularly responds to Pelagian incredulity about original sin by offering mini-lectures in agriculture: sinners give birth to other sinners, he writes, in the same way that olive trees grow only from olive seeds; but please don't try to argue that the sons of righteous men will also be righteous men. "Therefore, be a man guilty of unbelief, or a perfect believer, he does not in either case beget faithful children, but sinners; in the same way that the seeds, not only of a wild olive, but also of a cultivated one, produce not cultivated olives, but wild ones."*

But though every intelligent person noticed these facts of life, no one could explain them. Not for lack of trying, of course. As far back as Aristotle and Pythagoras there are detailed theories of inheritance, but none of them really make any sense, and even by the time of Darwin the only real progress was the increasingly universal awareness that no progress had been made. In *On the Origin of Species* (1859) Darwin states, soberly and flatly, "The laws governing inheritance are for the most part unknown; no one can say why the same peculiarity in different individuals of the same species, or in different species, is sometimes inherited and sometimes not so; why the child often reverts in certain characteristics to its grandfather or grandmother or more remote ancestor; why a peculiarity is often transmitted from one sex to both sexes, or to one sex alone, more commonly but not

---

* Augustine returns to this metaphor repeatedly, here for instance in his treatise *On Marriage and Concupiscence* (*De nuptiis et concupiscentia*): "It is a wonderful thing, then, how those who have been themselves delivered by grace from the bondage of sin, should still beget those who are tied and bound by the self-same chain, and who require the same process of loosening? Yes; and we admit the wonderful fact. But that the embryo of wild olive trees should latently exist in the germs of true olives, who would deem credible, if it were not proved true by experiment and observation? In the same manner, therefore, as a wild olive grows out of the seed of the wild olive, and from the seed of the true olive springs also nothing but a wild olive, notwithstanding the very great difference there is between the wild olive and the olive; so what is born in the flesh, either of a sinner or of a just man, is in both instances a sinner, notwithstanding the vast distinction which exists between the sinner and the righteous man" (chap. 21).

exclusively to the like sex." *No one can say.* And Darwin does not claim to do anything to remedy this ignorance.

Though Darwin had no way of knowing it, a certain Moravian monk could say, or would soon be able to. This is no place for a lecture in elementary genetics—or perhaps, this is *precisely* the place for such a lecture, were a competent author present—but a little explanation is unavoidable. Mendel worked with pea plants because they self-pollinate and breed true—that is, they pass along their traits consistently, unlike, say, human beings. He spent the first two years of his study simply raising enough peas to make sure that they did indeed breed true: tall plants from tall, short from short, and so on. These features of pea plants made Mendel's experiments far simpler than they would have been, had he chosen any number of other organisms—his first idea had been to raise mice, but this proved messy in more ways than one—and gave him much greater control over those experiments. But even so, the results were immensely complex. It was not at all obvious to him or to anyone else at the time, why, when pea plants reproduced in an uncontrolled environment, some ended up taller than others, why the unripe pods of some were green and others yellow, why the dried seeds of some remained round while others wrinkled up. Such variations just seemed random, a function of the luck of the draw—and yet every botanist and every good farmer knew that you could, with time and effort, breed plants and animals to possess, consistently though not invariably, certain desirable traits in almost any organism.

Mendel had to grow thousands of plants over dozens of generations before he could see with any clarity what the patterns of inheritance were, but eventually those patterns (mathematical ratios, really, like 3:1 and 9:3:3:1) became clear to him. And upon studying them, he came to believe that each pea plant contained deep within itself things—he called them, vaguely, *Anlagen,* a complicated German word that can mean any one of a dozen things but is probably best translated as "factors"—factors that produced certain traits in offspring, but only in certain circumstances. Those ratios I just mentioned describe the conditions under which certain traits turn up in offspring and the frequency with which they do so. Once these basic principles were understood, a new branch of biological science could be born.

As is widely known, the birth was rather delayed. Mendel's ideas went almost unnoticed in his lifetime, and it wasn't until the first decade of the twentieth century that they began to receive widespread attention. In 1905 an English biologist and early advocate of Mendel's ideas, William Bateson, coined the term *gene* to replace Mendel's *Anlage* and decreed that the study of such matters should be called *genetics*. From this point on acceptance of Mendel's discoveries accelerated, and one piece of the biological puzzle after another was added: the understanding that genes are carried on chromosomes, the isolation of a protein called DNA as the carrier of genetic information, the discovery of the double-helical structure of the DNA molecule, and so on. More important for our purposes here—though perhaps not for any others—the *vocabulary* of genetics crept into the public mind. Of course Barry Bonds and Ken Griffey, Jr., are outstanding baseball players—it's in their genes! (The fathers of both men were major-league players.) Ditto with the sons of J. S. Bach, who surely were virtually predestined to be composers and musicians. Some women claim to have a "shopping gene"; some men confess with embarrassment their failure to possess the "sports fan gene." (Go ahead and Google those phrases, just for fun.)

Never mind that each of these ideas is a travesty of genetics, and that even traits we legitimately attribute to our genetic inheritance don't work in this way—there's no "gene for" blue eyes, for instance. The point is that the language of genetics has an extreme metaphorical power, to the point of irresistibility. And that language continues to shape our thinking about much of our behavior, including what some people still call our sins.

FROM THE BEGINNING of modern genetics, certain intellectually bold men—often the same men who advocated scientific racism—saw heredity as a key to social engineering. Such endeavors were well under way before the scientific community knew anything about Mendel's experiments. It is rather chilling to reflect that the English polymath Francis Galton coined the term *eugenics* more than twenty years before Bateson came up with *gene* and *genetics*. Galton was primarily interested in *encouraging* British society's most intelligent and otherwise gifted people to reproduce, and to reproduce more than their inferiors, but it was only a matter of time before Galton's disciples and like-minded people turned their attention to the importance of *discouraging* the "unfit" from reproducing. In 1907 Indiana became the first state (thirty more would follow) to pass a law allowing the involuntary sterilization of certain persons.

What persons? The opening sentences of the Indiana legislature's act are illuminating:

> Whereas, Heredity plays a most important part in the transmission of crime, idiocy and imbecility;
>
> Therefore, *Be it enacted by the general assembly of the State of Indiana,* That on and after the passage of this act it shall be compulsory for each and every institution in the state, entrusted with the care of confirmed criminals, idiots, rapists and imbeciles, to appoint upon its staff, in addition to the regular institutional physician, two (2) skilled surgeons of recognized ability, whose duty it shall be, in conjunction with the chief physician of the institution, to examine the mental and physical condition of such inmates as are recommended by

the institutional physician and board of managers. If, in the judgment of this committee of experts and the board of managers, procreation is inadvisable and there is no probability of improvement of the mental condition of the inmate, it shall be lawful for the surgeons to perform such operation for the prevention of procreation as shall be decided safest and most effective.

The eugenics movement is most infamous today for its insistence on forced sterilization of those deemed mentally inferior by reason of "imbecility" or "idiocy," but here we see that no legal distinction is made between such people and violent criminals. The key assumption underlying such laws was that (to use anachronistic language) there are genes for criminality just as there are genes for mental deficiency.

Though forced sterilization is no longer practiced in this country, research and speculation continue regarding the possible genetic bases for criminality and more generally for violence. Nowadays the conversation often focuses on the limbic system, the so-called old brain and the primitive instincts that seem to be lodged there. Are violent criminals governed by their amygdala, as it fires off its visceral emotional signals to fight or flee? Perhaps the amygdala of criminals is overdeveloped, or perhaps their higher-order brain functions, which in most of us serve to control or counter the synaptic zaps from the old brain, are underdeveloped; but the results would be the same in either case. And if the impulsive and violent traits associated with the limbic system turn out to be highly heritable—that is, far more dependent on genetic inheritance than on environmental factors—then criminals are disturbingly likely to produce criminal offspring.

This would be pretty bad news for you if you have violent parents or even more distant ancestors with a track record of nastiness; but, on the other hand, if you come from peaceable stock you could take a certain comfort in this picture of things (as long as you don't have regular contact with people whose genetic legacy can't match yours). However, the question of heritability isn't settled. If environmental factors play a proportionately larger role in violent behavior than would be indicated by the scenario I just sketched out, then the man with a violent parent or two might not be quite so helpless before his overbearing amygdala, and you or I might not be as immune to an outburst of aggression as we think we are.*

Of course, violence is not the same as sinfulness. Dante, in his *Divine Comedy,* places the fraudulent and deceptive deeper in Hell than the merely violent. Some of the deceivers employed deception in order to do violence, but not all; and for Dante the use of our God-given intellects in order to manipulate other human beings is a kind of betrayal of God—even, perhaps, an attempt to *play* God— whereas thoughtless violence is more like a descent into an animal state. *Forza* (force) is deeply sinful, but not *as* sinful as *Froda* (fraud). People today come closer to holding Dante's view than they think they do. Our fascination with serial murderers, for instance, whether fictional (Hannibal Lecter) or real (John Wayne Gacy), stems from

---

* As I write these words a movie called *Mr. Brooks* has just been released. In it, Kevin Costner plays a serial killer, Earl, who is exhorted to his evil deeds by an (imaginary?) tempter named Marshall. Interestingly, in light of some of our concerns in Chapter 5 of this book, Marshall sits in the back seat of Earl's car and leans forward to whisper tempting thoughts in his ear—but there's no angel over Earl's other shoulder. It's also noteworthy that Marshall is not played by Kevin Costner, but by William Hurt. This makes him seem less like an aspect of Earl than a real tempter or an especially nasty imaginary friend. But the most intriguing moment of all comes when Earl learns that a classmate of his college-age daughter has been murdered and immediately guesses who's responsible. "She has what I have," he moans, conceiving of homicidal mania as a hereditary disease. Alas, it's Marshall to whom he confesses this thought.

our realization that they must think through and carefully plan their acts of violence. But when you ask us to *imagine* sinfulness, it is always violent acts that come to mind—perhaps because they are acts, rather than convolutions of the depraved mind.

A vigorous debate on the violence we inflict on one another has recently been prompted by a new book by Philip Zimbardo called *The Lucifer Effect: Understanding How Good People Turn Evil*. In this book Zimbardo tells, for the first time, the full story of a now famous psychological experiment he designed and conducted in 1971, the Stanford Prison Experiment. The design of the experiment was remarkably simple. At Stanford University, Zimbardo recruited some college students, created a simulated prison in the basement of the building that housed Stanford's psychology department, and randomly divided the students into two groups. Half of them would be prisoners, the other half guards. Those playing the role of prisoners were told to expect some curtailment of what in ordinary life would be their civil rights, along with minimal nourishment and few comforts.

The first day of the experiment proved relatively uneventful, but on the second day tensions between the two groups rose extraordinarily, and the guards began to mistreat the prisoners. Six days into the experiment, which Zimbardo had planned to extend over two weeks, the guards' reign of terror over the prisoners had become so brutal that Zimbardo had to call the whole thing off. (Interestingly, he did so only with great reluctance. Christina Maslach, a fellow psychologist who was also Zimbardo's lover and later his wife, got into shouting matches with him while demanding that he send the students home.) "At the start of this experiment, there were no differences between the two groups," Zimbardo writes, and "less than a week later, there were no similarities between them."

When psychologists debate the question of why some—but only some—people behave violently or otherwise cruelly to others, they often fall into two camps, the dispositionists and the situationists. The terms are self-explanatory: dispositionists believe that certain people are (for whatever reason) disposed toward cruelty, while situationists believe that particular situations produce cruelty. The prison experiment made of Zimbardo a lifelong, deeply committed situationist. *Anyone,* he came to believe, could be placed in conditions that would transform that person into an active perpetrator of cruelty or, at best, a passive accepter of it.

Yet it seems to me that Zimbardo shies away from the implications of his own experiment and his own position. He presents his key question in this way: "What happens when you put good people in an evil place?" And notice his book's subtitle: "Understanding How Good People Turn Evil." But on what grounds does he say that the people were good? Simply because they had not—to his knowledge, which was extremely limited, if not nonexistent—done anything especially foul before being assigned the role of prison guard? Long ago John Milton wrote, "I cannot praise a fugitive and cloistered virtue, unexercised and unbreathed, that never sallies out and sees her adversary, but slinks out of the race where that immortal garland is to be run for, not without dust and heat." But Zimbardo does just that; he is happy to call people "good" who may simply have not had the opportunity to do noticeable evil.

Similarly, when Michael Bywater reviewed the book for the *Times* of London he commented that *evil* is "a word so empty that it should surely have withered away." But doesn't Zimbardo's book suggest just the opposite, that the word is of wider application than most of us (especially Zimbardo) would want to admit? Doesn't it make us wonder whether something is *wrong* with all of us? Whether we are somehow stained, or tainted, or infected with some contagion? Whether we're *all* born with the intrinsic, well, *disposition* to do bad things?

. . .

I DO NOT MEAN to take this line of thought too far. Zimbardo's experiment does not by any means prove original sin; it does not even prove situationism. In fact, elements of the story call situationism seriously into question, especially the varying behavior of the guards. The legal scholar Cass Sunstein, in a thoughtful review of Zimbardo's book, notes:

> Some of the guards did their jobs, but without cruelty, and they did various favors for the prisoners. These identifiably "good guards" were altogether different from others, whose behavior was sadistic. To his credit, Zimbardo acknowledges the diversity of behavior on the part of the guards. In his own words, "some guards have transformed into perpetrators of evil, and other guards have become passive contributors to the evil through their inaction." So dispositions did matter. There is a real difference between the "perpetrators" and the "passive contributors."

Sunstein is right—to a point. What he neglects to note is that this difference, though real, doesn't do a damned thing to rescue the victims of cruelty. Which is why Zimbardo is also right when, in an essay summarizing this part of his book, he says that

> good guards, on the shifts when the worst abuses occurred, never did anything bad to the prisoners, but not once over the whole week did they confront the other guards and say, "What are you doing? We get paid the same money without knocking ourselves out." Or, "Hey, remember those are college students, not prisoners." No good guard ever intervened to stop the activities of the bad guards. No good guard ever arrived a minute late, left a minute early, or publicly complained. In a sense, then, it's the good guard who allowed such abuses to

happen. The situation dictated their inaction, and their inaction facilitated evil.

Sunstein wants to insist that "different people have radically different 'thresholds' that must be met before they will be willing to harm others." Some people "have exceedingly high thresholds, or perhaps their moral convictions operate as an absolute barrier. There is a continuum of thresholds from the sadists to the heroes, or from the devils to the saints." This may be true, but it overlooks the chilling fact that in Zimbardo's experiment there were no heroes; there were no saints.

Sunstein surely knows this, which is perhaps why in his review he speculates that a different mix of people might have led to a different result. This is indeed possible. A similar thought came to the mind of Stanley Milgram, a psychologist at Yale whose experiments on obedience to authority predated the Stanford Prison Experiment by several years and yielded similar results. Milgram wanted to find out how much pain people would inflict on others if told to do so by an apparently competent authority and if prevented from actually *seeing* the infliction of pain. (No one was harmed; actors pretended to be hurt.) His expectation was that "almost all subjects" would refuse to inflict such pain once they could tell that another person was suffering, but as it turned out, just the opposite was true. Milgram and his colleagues were shocked.

When the very first experiments were carried out, Yale undergraduates were used as subjects, and about 60 percent of them were fully obedient. A colleague of mine immediately dismissed these findings as having no relevance to "ordinary" people, asserting that Yale undergraduates are a highly aggressive, competitive bunch who step on each other's necks on the slightest provocation. He assured me that when "ordinary" people were tested, the results would be quite different. As we moved from the pilot studies to the regular experimental series, people drawn from every stratum of New Haven life came to be employed in the experiment: professionals, white collar workers, unemployed persons, and industrial workers. The experimental outcome was the same as we had observed among the students.

Moreover, when the experiments were repeated in Princeton, Munich, Rome, South Africa, and Australia, the level of obedience was invariably somewhat higher than found in the investigation reported in this article. Thus one scientist in Munich found 85 percent of his subjects obedient.

Though Zimbardo never re-created his prison, he knew that Milgram had often repeated his very similar experiments, and he knew that increasing and varying the sample size had not led to any more reassuring results. Perhaps that is why he has turned his attention, as he explains in the latter chapters of *The Lucifer Effect,* to an investigation of what he calls "heroism." Though he himself found no heroes in that makeshift basement prison, he knows that there are occasionally such people. It is not clear how, given the situationist account of things, there *could* be such people; but there are, and Zimbardo wants to help create more of them. With his colleague Zeno Franco he is now pursuing ways of cultivating the "heroic imagination."

In a recent article Franco and Zimbardo claim that "there are several concrete steps we can take to foster" that imagination. For instance, "We can start by remaining mindful, carefully and critically evaluating each situation we encounter so that we don't gloss over an emergency requiring our action." Also, "it is important not to fear interpersonal conflict, and to develop the personal hardiness necessary to stand firm for principles we cherish." And "we must try to transcend anticipating negative consequence associated with some forms of heroism, such as being socially ostracized." These are "concrete steps"? I cannot imagine anything more amorphous. (I am reminded of a cartoon I once saw: a clown stands in front of a TV camera and stares blankly at a cue card that says, "Tell a funny joke.") Verily, it is good to be mindful and transcendently fearless, but how exactly do I manage that? Franco and Zimbardo do not appear to have the first idea how "heroism" or even just plain decency is cultivated or how it can be made strong enough to overcome the temptations to act cruelly or to acquiesce in cruelty. St. Paul wrote of the "mystery of iniquity," but in light of the Stanford Prison Experiment and indeed of most of human history, it would appear that virtue is the greater puzzle.

IN HIS 2002 BOOK *The Blank Slate,* the cognitive scientist Steven Pinker briefly discusses Zimbardo and the Stanford Prison Experiment. He does so in the midst of a chapter that strives to give an evolutionary account of human propensity to violence or, more specifically, violence toward those whom we perceive to be outsiders. As Pinker puts it, "People discern a moral circle that may not include all human beings but only the members of their clan, village, or tribe"—or, in the case of the Stanford prison guards, their temporary occupation. Circumstances and individual dispositions can cause that "circle" to expand or to shrink, and although Pinker places himself firmly on the side of those who wish the circle to be as wide as possible, he also says quite bluntly that there have been, throughout most of human history, sound evolutionary reasons for the circle to be limited in size. "The first step in understanding violence is to set aside our abhorrence of it long enough to examine why it can sometimes pay off in personal or evolutionary terms." And after engaging in that examination, he concludes by insisting that "violence is not a primitive, irrational urge, nor is it a 'pathology' except in the metaphorical sense of a condition that everyone would like to eliminate. Instead, it is a near-inevitable outcome of the dynamic of self-interested, rational social organisms."

Throughout this chapter Pinker repeatedly insists that he does not condone violence, that he repudiates it as thoroughly as the most gentle-hearted among us do, and that the "human nature" that has been produced by evolution gives us reasons to hope that human-against-human violence can be significantly reduced, though not eliminated. But Pinker has no way of elevating his own distaste for violence to anything more than a personal preference, and his hope-fulness about the eventual limiting of violence is really nothing more than guesswork and wishful thinking. It may be that those who keep their moral circles small and act cruelly toward outsiders prove in the long run to be more successful at passing along their genes than the nonviolent. Is it really true, then, to say, as Pinker does, "With violence . . . human nature is the problem, but human nature is also the solution"? On Pinker's own account the only possible answer to that question is: time will tell.

Pinker's frank admission that tendencies toward aggression, espe-cially aggression toward outsiders, is simply part of our genetic legacy has generated much consternation in his readers, and it is interesting to note the language in which they register their protests. The wide-ranging English writer Richard Webster wryly notes that "instead of putting forward a new theory, Pinker ends by reaffirming an old one. Although the register in which he writes is very different from that of John Wesley . . . the underlying gospel which he preaches is in reality little different. . . . For what he too calls upon us to recognise is the bestial nature of mankind and the limitations which go with that bes-tial nature." The economist John Gray uses similar language:

> In an interesting aside, Pinker notes that the view of human
> nature which is emerging from science has more in common
> with that defended by Christian thinkers and by Freud than it

does with theories such as Marx's. This is a point worth further elaboration, because it suggests another curious turn in the history of ideas. Enlightenment thinkers took up the scientific study of human behaviour in the hope of transforming the human condition. The result of scientific inquiry, however, is to vindicate a secular version of the idea of original sin.*

But the American philosopher Jerry Fodor had already beaten those gentlemen to the punch. In reviewing one of Pinker's earlier and similarly themed books, *How the Mind Works,* he had said: "*Prima facie,* the picture of the mind, indeed of human nature in general, that psychological Darwinism suggests is preposterous; a sort of jumped up, down-market version of original sin."

How curious that Pinker's commitment to a purely evolutionary account of human behavior—his "Darwinian fundamentalism," as the late Stephen Jay Gould labeled such a position—immediately called to the minds of three very different thinkers the same connection to an ancient and (in their minds) thoroughly discredited Christian doctrine. Of course, a partial explanation is that these writers all wanted to say the worst things they could think of to say about Pinker, and in their intellectual ecosphere you do that by comparing a person's ideas to Christian belief; but still, the coincidence is intriguing. It is as though,

---

* Gray is not quite right in this claim. Pinker's "aside" comes in a section in which he is emphasizing the "modularity" of the human brain—that is, his belief that the brain is comprised of many different modules, each of which has been selected because it achieves a very specific kind of adaptability, but none of which rules over the others. This "interplay of mental systems can explain how people can entertain revenge fantasies that they never act on, or can commit adultery only in their hearts. *In this way* [emphasis mine] the theory of human nature coming out of the cognitive revolution has more in common with the Judeo-Christian theory of human nature, and with the psychoanalytic theory proposed by Sigmund Freud, than with behaviorism, social constructionism, and other versions of the Blank Slate."

here in the West at least, any attempt to argue that we are "by nature" vulnerable to certain temptations, that certain troubling inclinations are ineradicable in us, calls to mind the dark anthropology of St. Paul and Augustine—an anthropology no reasonable person would *want* to believe in, unless, perhaps, that belief were accompanied by an equally fervent belief in a God of matchless grace.

Pinker's own view is that for a couple of hundred years now the humanities and social sciences have been dominated by a "blank slate" view of human nature, a kind of naive empiricism that sees us born into this world without characteristic traits and therefore wholly susceptible to what we now call the "social construction" of identity. This commitment to a blank slate is accompanied, argues Pinker, by an equally intense commitment to a Rousseauian belief in the "noble savage," that is, in the natural innocence of primitive peoples. As one reviewer of *The Blank Slate,* Simon Blackburn, has pointed out, you can't logically hold both of those positions at the same time, but of course people are invariably illogical and do indeed believe, or claim to believe, in the blank slate *and* the noble savage. Take Philip Zimbardo, for instance, who claims to be a pure situationist—which requires a blank slate—but also calls his experimental subjects "good people" who "turn evil," a Rousseauian formulation if there ever was one.

Pinker thinks that both of these views—along with other, associated ideas—are nonsense, and commitment to them continues to interfere with a real understanding of human nature and an honest engagement with its limitations. Believers in the blank slate and the noble savage are like people peering into a glass case containing a two-headed calf who deny that the calf has two heads, who insist that they see only a beautiful head, perfectly formed. Pinker thinks that only if you acknowledge the existence of the evil head, do you have a chance of getting the nourishing milk past it and into the calf's stomach. Maybe. But that didn't happen with the calf whose preserved body West saw, because the evil head always—always—managed to spit out the milk. The calf was perfectly formed, the custodian said, "and should be alive today had it not been for its nature."

Original Selfishness: Original Sin and Evil in the Light of Evolution is a recent book coauthored by a paleontologist named Daryl Domning and a theologian named Monika Hellwig—both of whom are Roman Catholics and therefore required as a matter of faith to believe that "the Blessed Virgin Mary . . . was preserved free from all stain of original sin." Alas, the Immaculate Conception goes unmentioned in their book. It would have been interesting to learn what they make of it.

Domning and Hellwig set themselves the task of grappling with the very issues that this chapter has, in its own ham-fisted way, been trying to address. They begin—and it is a significant beginning—by flatly rejecting the ideas that there could have been such people as Adam and Eve, that we have first parents whose DNA continues in all of us. From this point they could simply reject the idea of original sin, but they do not want to do that; they believe that it retains a certain explanatory power, and they wish to account for that power in ways they believe to be both scientifically and theologically responsible.

However, the coauthors actually don't agree, especially about the theology. They did not write the book together in the sense that all the words come from both of them; rather, the book consists of chapters by Domning followed by Hellwig's reflections. And the lack of fit between the two is noteworthy.

In his introduction to the whole volume, Domning considers various theological interpretations of the Genesis account of the Fall and of St. Paul's reflections in his letter to the Romans. He notes that a very common one among today's theologians is the "cultural transmission" idea: "Original sin is transmitted culturally, as a necessary result of each individual's birth and acculturation into a sinful human society." Domning doesn't think much of this interpretation. For one thing, it seems to him to contradict both the Bible and the teachings of the church fathers. But more important, it strikes him as an unacceptably shallow model of sin, one that implies that if we but implement the proper social and political strategies sin will go away. But Domning, writing as a scientist more than as a Christian, argues that "sin is rooted much deeper than that, not just in human history, sociology, and psychology, but in the farthest depths of evolutionary time and in the mechanics of the evolutionary process itself." Domning believes that recent scientific explorations of our genetic legacy, of just the kind that Pinker celebrates in *The Blank Slate,* have accentuated both the "truth value" and the "practical relevance" of the doctrine.

But his theological interlocutor is having none of it. Monika Hellwig is a fine representative of a school of modern theology that finds the catastrophism of Paul and Augustine embarrassing at best. "Our contemporary sense of reality does not allow us to adopt" the Pauline or Augustinian or medieval views of original sin, so we must find an alternative. Like many progressive theologians, she takes pains to insist that everyone agrees with her, and as in all such cases what she really means is that she has no interest in those who disagree: "The position was suggested and in the course of time almost universally accepted among theologians and theologically knowledgeable people that what is meant by original sin is grounded in the common observation that that each of us is greatly diminished by what has happened prior to our own decisions and actions." We are all the victims of "the cumulative effect of choices and actions which were less than worthy of human freedom and community. . . . Thus the individual . . . is at the mercy of the heritage of confusion of values."

Now, it should be obvious that Hellwig is here simply restating and reaffirming the "cultural transmission" model that Domning finds inadequate. But more important, this account does little more than translate the doctrine of original sin into the banal observation that bad stuff happens. Hellwig complacently observes that "in this contemporary interpretation the doctrine of original sin appears to be not only defensible but even self-evident." And that is true, in the sense that the "contemporary interpretation" reduces the idea to such inanity that no one could disagree with it. But no one can disagree because the doctrine has been evacuated of any meaning whatsoever. We all *know* that bad stuff happens. What we do not know is *why* it happens, and St. Paul's interpretation is a passionate (if apocalyptic) attempt to offer an explanation. *Unde hoc malum?* Hellwig, like many theologians today, leaves the question not only unanswered, but unasked.

In Homer's *Odyssey,* when Odysseus is telling the tale of his and his crew's dalliances with Calypso and Circe, he twice offers this delightfully self-justifying comment: "As we are men, we could not help consenting." This is Hellwig's position too, as it was Rousseau's. Surrounded as we are by other people who sin, what choice do we have? We are "at the mercy" of a "confusion of values." But again, this is an explanation that explains nothing. As Jonathan Edwards wrote in exasperated response to Dr. T., this is just "accounting for the corruption of the world by the corruption of the world." Again, *why* is sin so pervasive? And why can none of us resist it? We find ourselves back in the basement of Stanford's psychology building without a clue to explain the chaos that reigns among us. We guards were given power without restraint, so we used it. As we are men, we could not help consenting.

AFTERWORD

I'm not sure I should admit this—and if any students of mine are reading, they should skip the next few sentences—but sometimes I write with the television on in the background. Not long ago I was doing so when I heard the chords of a familiar song, "Bad to the Bone," by George Thorogood and the Destroyers. Though I did feel for a split second that God might be indicating his favor toward my book by providing me a soundtrack to work by, I quickly realized that no miracle was involved. I shouldn't have been surprised anyway. The song, in some version or another, has turned up almost everywhere in the quarter century since it came out—especially in movies, from *Terminator II* to (in suitably modified form) *The SpongeBob SquarePants Movie*. (It appears that killer whales are "Bad to the Fin.")

So when I turned my eyes to the screen I naturally discovered it was an ad for a movie: the then upcoming DVD release of *Ghost Rider*, starring Nicholas Cage as Johnny Blaze, a motorcycle stunt rider who has sold his soul to the devil and wants to renegotiate his deal. "Bad to the Bone" seems a perfect song for a man who works as the devil's bounty hunter, tracking down nasty cases and delivering them to the gates of Hell. Seeing Johnny's face turn into a blazing skull—which is what happens to him when evil forces are near—and watching him mount his blazing chopper and go riding off to do his foul duty, you're supposed to think: *That's one bad dude.*

I still remember when I first heard the word *bad* used in this way. When I was a child and a devoted fan of the Atlanta Braves, one of Hank Aaron's teammates referred to him as "Bad Henry." Bad Henry Aaron. I loved that, especially since it called to mind the contrast between Aaron's quiet, mild demeanor and his dangerousness as a hitter. I am too young to remember the fights between Sonny Liston and Muhammad Ali—then known as Cassius Clay—but many times over the years I have seen the clip from Ali's manic interview after that fight in which he screams into the camera, "I'm a baaad man!"

It's pure joyous boasting, of course, the kind of boasting that has a central place in the blues tradition. The music of "Bad to the Bone" and the tone of the lyrics (if not the actual words) mark it as an obvious tribute to—or a rip-off of, depending on your point of view—Muddy Waters's classic "Mannish Boy."

Thorogood:

On the day I was born,
The nurses all gathered 'round
And they gazed in wide wonder,
At the joy they had found.
The head nurse spoke up,
And she said leave this one alone.
She could tell right away,
That I was bad to the bone.

Muddy Waters:

Now when I was a young boy
At the age of five
My mother said I'll be
The greatest man alive.
And now I'm a man,
I'm over twenty-one.

You better believe me, baby,
And I'll say, we can have lots of fun.

Two ways of saying, "Ain't nobody else like me."

How does someone get to be so special—so *absolutely* bad? One way, the old bluesmen tell us, is to do what Johnny Blaze did, make a deal with the devil. Many people who knew the most famous of all Delta blues singers, Robert Johnson, believed that he had sold his soul in order to play the guitar the way he did. As a young man he could hardly play at all, those people said, and then he went away for a while, and when he came back he was playing that guitar like nobody else could. It was a belief that Johnson did nothing to discourage.

Other bluesmen claimed the same power and the same source. Here's what Tommy Johnson (Robert's contemporary in Mississippi, though not related to him) told his brother LaDell:

If you want to learn how to play anything you want to play and learn how to make songs yourself, you take your guitar and you go to where a road crosses that way, where a crossroad is. Get there, be sure to get there just a little 'fore twelve o'clock that night so you know you'll be there. You have your guitar and be playing a piece sitting there by yourself. You have to go by yourself and be sitting there playing a piece. A big black man will walk up there and take your guitar, and he'll tune it. And then he'll play a piece and hand it back to you. That's the way I learned how to play anything I want.

A deal like this doesn't just give you technical proficiency. The one who sells himself to the devil is not only able to play anything he wants, but also is able to tell the devil's story, the story of darkness, sin, and evil. Listen to Robert Johnson songs like "Hellhound on My

Trail" and "If I Had Possession over Judgment Day," and you'll know exactly what I mean.

But here's the key point about this tradition, at least in relation to the story I've told in this book: it's only cool to be bad to the bone if hardly anyone else is. Curious, isn't it, that a man who plays the guitar with extraordinary skill and style would prefer his listeners to think that he had achieved such mastery *not* through years of hard, disciplined work, but rather through a single bold decision, the decision to visit that crossroads and confront that big black man. Anyone can practice until fingertips bleed, but very few indeed possess the innate courage to make that midnight assignation.

The story told in this book is quite different, and in several respects deflating. If we are divided selves, two-headed calves, if we are indeed malleable—in one moral direction anyway—such that circumstances could drag us into a depravity that in our daily lives we cannot even imagine, then being bad to the bone is our *common* lot. There's little comfort in this for the self-proclaimed virtuous *or* the self-proclaimed baaad man. No wonder people resist it. No wonder even the "situationist" Philip Zimbardo gives the very last words of his book to Aleksandr Solzhenitsyn—those famous words about the line between good and evil that passes through every human heart—though he does not pause to consider what Solzhenitsyn himself meant by them.

Solzhenitsyn would not have said that the guards in the Gulag were "good people" who had "turned evil." His view was that the evil *already in them* was *elicited* by the Gulag—and that the same evil in him would have been elicited in much the same way, had he been given their role. Nor would anyone else have been free from temptation, though some would prove less cruel than others. And the deeper problem for situationism is that no one has found a way to bend people the other way; no one has found a "situation" that makes people virtuous, that creates uniformity of kindness, decency, self-giving. Robert Owen tried to create just such a situation in New Harmony, but found that his people fell back into the worst of habits, in large part because none of them trusted the *others* to be fair-dealing. They nearly instantly fell into the very same mutual recriminations that began when Adam and Eve were sewing their first fig leaves. If paradise lasted but five and a half hours, New Harmony didn't better that by much. Zimbardo says he's trying to do discover situations that would bypass these difficulties, situations that would make heroes as reliably as his prison experiment made villains. Good luck.

Several responses could be made to the story I have told in this book. One is simply to reject its premises, to insist on the intrinsic innocence and decency of each human person. As I have tried to suggest, one who holds this position must be content to have no answer at all to the question *Unde hoc malum?* Some people will be so content; and to them I bid a friendly farewell, should any have hung around this long, which seems doubtful.

Among those who acknowledge that all of us, in one way or another, fall well short of what we believe to be good, there are several subcategories. One group, the one to which I belong, is made up of Christians who believe that all human beings have an inclination or propensity to sin. (There are, as we have seen, Christians who do not believe this, whose response to my account would place them in the group I just said good-bye to.) Some of those Christians are in the Augustinian tradition; others, in particular the Eastern Christians I discussed in Chapter 3, would deny that Augustine read Paul correctly, but would agree that all of us sin and that that universal sinfulness has *something* to do with what happened to our first parents.

But there is also that curious group of people, Rebecca West being the most vivid example we have seen, who share the Augustinian anthropology, but who cannot bring themselves to believe in the accompanying theology; and as we have seen, those people live in a dark, dark place. Many who have seen the world in this way (I think particularly of Jonathan Swift) have been driven by it to, or over, the brink of madness—which is where R. D. Laing thinks they should be.

Yet another category includes people who acknowledge the behavior, but decline to make the traditional moral judgment upon it—who say that people are hard-wired for selfishness but that that's good, or that moral categories don't apply, or that our usual moral categories need to be used selectively and judiciously in such matters. I take it that Steven Pinker and the biologist and polemicist Richard Dawkins belong to this camp. They use words like *selfish*—as in Dawkins's notorious coinage of the term *selfish gene*—but they deny the word its usual pejorative meaning. The philosopher Mary Midgley thinks this is confusing to everyone and urges evolutionary psychologists to come up with more precise language. Referring to how Pinker and Dawkins talk about "selfishness," she writes, "Of course the word officially has only a technical meaning. . . . Pinker writes it off as just a casual figure of speech. But so lurid and controversial a term cannot possibly be cleansed of its everyday meaning. People who are clear about what they are saying avoid using such metaphors in the first place."

I think Midgley is right. As I noted earlier, Pinker denounces violence at one point while claiming at another that violent behavior has obviously been highly adaptive. The latter point he believes to be factual, but on what grounds does he denounce, other than an utterly accidental preference? Similarly, Dawkins sternly lectures us in *River Out of Eden:* "Nature is not cruel, only pitilessly indifferent. This is one of the hardest lessons for humans to learn. We cannot admit that things might be neither good nor evil, neither cruel nor kind, but simply callous—indifferent to all suffering, lacking all purpose." Yet he repeatedly, especially in his recent book *The God Delusion*, denounces religion on specifically moral grounds—for instance, its supposed encouragement of sexism, and its promotion of violence, as in the 9/11 bombings—without ever managing to answer the question of why *we* should exhibit traits that the universe as a whole does not and indeed cannot exhibit.

Dawkins attributes "good Samaritan" behavior—sacrificial kindness toward people unrelated to us, people clearly outside our "moral circle"—to "misfirings" of our genetic wiring. That is, we really shouldn't (in purely evolutionary terms) give a rip about the suffering of strangers, but our internal evaluators aren't yet perfect and sometimes return what we might call false positives. Dawkins calls these misfirings "blessed" and "precious," but on his own account of things they are bound to become less and less frequent, as those organisms who don't so misfire outbreed those whose misdirected compassion leads them to, say, die while saving children from an oncoming train or (like Raoul Wallenberg) disappear into the Soviet Gulag after devoting years to saving Jews from the Nazis. A "piteously indifferent" nature doesn't have a soft spot for Raoul Wallenberg, and if Dawkins does, his own philosophy says that he is a dying breed. If Dawkins is right, evolution may never *eliminate* Wallenberg-like "misfirings," but gradually it will reduce their frequency until they are vanishingly rare. So enjoy these "precious" errors while you still can.

In one respect, the Dawkins and Pinker view of "human nature" as such is not all that different from the Rousseauian view, despite Pinker's harsh criticisms of the "noble savage" idea. Rousseau says there's no innate human predicament because human nature is good; Dawkins and Pinker say there's no innate human predicament because human nature is what it is—what natural selection has made it. If "things" are "neither good nor evil, neither cruel nor kind," what meaning could the term "predicament" have?

As far as I can tell, then, you must hold five distinct beliefs in order to affirm the Augustinian anthropology. You must believe that *everyone* behaves in ways that we usually describe as selfish, cruel, arrogant, and so on. You must believe that we are *hard-wired* to behave in those ways and do not do so simply because of the bad examples of others. You must believe that such behavior is properly called *wrong* or *sinful,* whether it's evolutionarily adaptive or not. You must believe that it was not originally in our nature to behave in such a way, but that we have *fallen* from a primal innocence. And you must believe that only *supernatural intervention,* in the form of what Christians call grace, is sufficient to drag us up out of this pit we've dug for ourselves. (If we add to this list a sixth belief, that through the death of Jesus Christ God has provided this intervention, then we have the core of the theology that complements the anthropology. But that hasn't been the concern of this book.)

Once the model is laid out in this way, with these five interlocking and necessary propositions, it may be surprising that *anyone* has ever affirmed it. Yet millions have, and millions more will. Perhaps that's because each of these positions is well warranted by careful observation of human beings.

Well, these are sobering thoughts, indeed, and we should take them seriously—as seriously as we can take any thoughts. The immensely difficult trick is to do so without taking *ourselves* seriously, because one could argue that at or near the very heart of our bent wills is a determination to uphold our own dignity. Milton tells us that Satan decided to rebel against the Almighty because of his sense of "injured merit": *he* was the one who deserved to be named Messiah, not God's Son, who surely was chosen not because of his "merit," but on account of some divine nepotism. Looked at in the proper way, this idea of Satan's is simply laughable, which is what G. K. Chesterton was indicating in one of his wisest aphorisms: "Satan fell by force of gravity."

I hope the humorous aspects of this narrative have not been lost on my readers. Certainly we have met several characters who prompt smiles; but I'd like to suggest that the whole story can be seen in a comic light—at least in one particular sense.

The poet W. H. Auden writes, in a beautiful essay on Shakespeare, that there are actually two distinct genres, one might even say kingdoms, of comedy. The first he calls "classical" comedy, though it can be found in many cultures and in many periods of history. Classical comedy focuses on exposing people who think too highly of themselves or have some otherwise fantastic self-image and mocking them. "When the curtain falls" at the end of a classical comedy, Auden writes, "the audience is laughing and those on stage are in tears." The audience may laugh because they believe themselves to possess *arete*—"virtue," or more generally, "excellence"—which those on the stage so demonstrably lack.

The other kind of comedy is best illustrated by Shakespeare's plays. Take *Much Ado About Nothing*, for instance: at the end of that play we see a motley collection of people, few if any of whom have behaved especially well. They have exhibited pride, wrath, jealousy, envy, treachery—most of the deadly sins and a sizable collection of venial ones—and a great deal of what can only be called sheer stupidity, especially on the part of the male lead, Claudio. Yet they are all celebrating, joyously, a double wedding. Well, not *all*—there is one (Don John) who did everything he could to prevent these nuptials and whose hatred for all the other characters is such that he is glad to be taken from their presence. But it is clear that even Don John, had he repented of his evil and sought to be a part of the community, would have been welcome. The only other character who may be unable to enter fully into the joy of the moment is John's brother Don Pedro, a supposedly wise man who has not acted wisely and who as a consequence seems to be having trouble forgiving *himself*, though everyone else has forgiven him.

Auden calls this kind of story "Christian comedy," because it is "based upon the belief that all men are sinners; no one, therefore, whatever his rank or talents, can claim immunity from the comic exposure." This is a model of society and human nature that turns the Greek notion of *arete* on its head, because on this account the truest excellence is to know that you deserve the "comic exposure"— to know that you need forgiveness. When a play like this comes to its end, "the characters are exposed and forgiven: when the curtain falls, the audience and the characters are laughing together." If there is a proper response, a truly wise response, to the narrative of this book, it surely begins with the recognition that if *everyone* is bad to the bone—if all of us strut and fret our hour upon the stage, filled with the consciousness of our injured merit, fairly glowing with self-praise—then our condition is, first and above all else, comical.

ACKNOWLEDGMENTS

I am moved when I pause to reflect on the many people who have offered encouragement and support in the years that I have spent writing this little book. I owe a special debt to Jay Wood, with whom I talked through many, many issues that arose as I struggled to put this narrative together. I likewise drew on the expertise and judgment of several other friends—Brett Foster, Stan Jones, Tim Larsen, Dan Treier, John Wilson—and my pastor, Martin Johnson. At the very least they nodded politely and pretended to be interested when I went off on some absurd monologue about Julian of Eclanum or the origins of Oberlin College; and often they supplied corrections, clarifications, and confirmations.

On theological and historical matters I was able occasionally to consult with Mark Noll, now at Notre Dame—I liked it better when his office was one floor below mine—and Chuck Mathewes. Chuck and I also belong to a writers' group, a function of the Project on Lived Theology at the University of Virginia, convened by our friend Charles Marsh, and though this book is not directly related to that group, the time I have spent with the group's other members has been deeply encouraging to me. So let me thank, in addition to Charles and Chuck, Carlos Eire, Mark Gornik, Patricia Hampl, and Susah Holman for their interlocution.

I am very grateful to my agent, Christy Fletcher, for her commitment to this project and her sound advice along the way. This is my second book for HarperOne, and it is a pleasure to be working again with the good people there, especially my editor, Mickey Maudlin.

Most of all I am grateful—I can't even begin to say how much—for the constant love and affection and good-natured support of my wife, Teri, and my son, Wesley. To them I dedicate this book.

BIBLIOGRAPHICAL ESSAY

Research for a book of this kind has never been easier than it is today. I have depended throughout my writing on a series of online resources for primary texts and scholarly work alike. Of course, I have also had access to what used to be called "books" but what are now, increasingly, called "hard copies" of many of the primary texts in my personal library or in the library of Wheaton College, but I have nevertheless regularly used online texts because searching in them is both easy and reliable. However, since many online texts are scanned or typed from older, sometimes less reliable editions of old books, I have consistently checked my online sources against modern editions.

For instance, the standard sources for Augustine's works in Latin are several volumes in the Loeb Classical Library and, more comprehensively, that great monument of nineteenth-century scholarship the vast *Patrologia Latina* of J. P. Migne (now available online through subscription). But there is a magnificent collection of texts from an Italian site devoted to Sant' Agostino (http://www.augustinus.it/latino/index.htm). Translations of most of Augustine's major works, usually from another vast nineteenth-century project, Philip Schaff's *Select Library of Nicene and Post-Nicene Fathers*, may be found on the invaluable Christian Classics Ethereal Library (http://ccel.org/), maintained by Harry Plantinga of Calvin College. The CCEL has been my first stop in searching for theological texts from the apostolic age through the early twentieth century.

For classical literature and some later sources in the classical languages, an invaluable resource has been the Perseus Digital Library, created and maintained at Tufts University (http://www.perseus.tufts.edu). James O'Donnell's site devoted to Augustine (http://www9.georgetown.edu/faculty/jod/augustine/) contains, among many other things, the complete text of his definitive edition plus commentary of the *Confessions,* originally published by Oxford University Press in three volumes in 1992 at $125 apiece! I am continually surprised by the vast collection of literature in all the major European languages that has been amassed by Ulrich Harsch in his Bibliotheca Augustana (http://www.fh-augsburg.de/~harsch/augustana.html). Many of the public-domain English-language texts I cite here, from the letters of Sir Horace Walpole to those of Richard Edgeworth, from the meditations of Thomas Traherne to the autobiography and essays of Benjamin Franklin, may be tracked down at the massive and magnificent Project Gutenberg (http://www.gutenberg.org).

I almost do shudder, indeed, when I consider how long it might have taken me to write this book, had I lacked these resources.

ONE: Six Stories

I have found Robert Graves's two-volume *Greek Myths* (Penguin Books, 1955) both indispensable and delightful. His judgments are not always reliable, to say the least, but the breadth of his reading and his careful identification of sources allows one to discover that. It was Graves who led me to Polybius, whose *Histories* are translated in six volumes of the Loeb Classical Library, and also to the geographers Pausanias and Strabo, who have interesting things to say about the Locrian Maiden Tribute. The Tribute is given a full and detailed chapter in Dennis D. Hughes, *Human Sacrifice in Ancient Greece* (Routledge, 1991). A brief note on the Greek sense of sin in E. R. Dodds's brilliant *The Greeks and the Irrational* (University of California Press, 1951) led me to the key passages Plato's *Laws* (translated by Thomas Pangle, Basic Books, 1980). A still fine source for the various stories about Dionysos is chapter 43 of Sir James Frazer's *The Golden Bough* (twelve volumes, 1906–15, now available online at several sites). My thoughts about King David and his sin against God were shaped by reflecting on *The David Story: A Translation with Commentary of 1 and 2 Samuel* by Robert Alter (Norton, 1999). I began my studies in Chinese philosophy by consulting the invaluable *Source Book in Chinese Philosophy,* edited and translated by Wing-Tsit Chan (Princeton University Press, 1963); I also consulted Fung Yu-Lan's *Short History of Chinese Philosophy* (Free Press, 1976, 1997). The story of the Urapmin is told by Joel Robbins in *Becoming Sinners: Christianity and Moral Torment in a Papua New Guinea Society* (University of California Press, 2004).

TWO: The African Bishop

Most of what I know about Augustine that did not come from reading Augustine himself, whom I have studied for many years now, I have learned from Peter Brown, whose *Augustine of Hippo* (new edition, University of California Press, 2000) remains the best biography. But I have also consulted James O'Donnell's *Augustine: A New Biography* (Ecco, 2005) and the extraordinarily rich *Augustine Through the Ages: An Encyclopedia,* edited by Allan D. Fitzgerald, O.S.A. (Eerdmans, 1999). *Augustine's Anti-Pelagian Writings,* a translation of most of the anti-Pelagian works, was prepared by Philip Schaff in 1886, working from an early translation published in Scotland by T. & T. Clark. This collection, with a long and insightful introduction by the great American theologian B. B. Warfield, is still an indispensable resource for those interested in Augustine's controversy with the Pelagians, especially many of the writings of Pelagius and Julian of Eclanum that have survived only in quotation by Augustine. This volume may be found in the CCEL.

A good general survey of early Christian reflection on the sin of Adam may be found in *Early Christian Doctrines,* by J. N. D. Kelly, (fifth edition, Harper, 1978), and Jaroslav Pelikan's *The Christian Tradition: A History of the Development of Doctrine, Vol. 1: The Emergence of Catholic Tradition (100–600)* (University of Chicago Press, 1971). Elaine Pagels's critical treatment of Augustine may be found in *Adam, Eve, and the Serpent* (Random House, 1988), especially chapter 5. Freud's meditation on Paul is in *Moses and Monotheism* (Vintage, 1939, 1976).

THREE: Some Dreadful Thing No Doubt

Donald Justice's "The Wall," which he wrote as a student of John Berryman's at the Iowa Writer's Workshop, appears in his *Collected Poems* (Knopf, 2006).

Lady Mary Wortley Montague's letters may be found online courtesy of Project Gutenberg (http://www.gutenberg.org/etext/10590). When C. S. Lewis was writing *Perelandra* (Macmillan, 1944), he had recently delivered a series of lectures on John Milton that became his *Preface to Paradise Lost* (Oxford University Press, 1942). The two works are like bookends and are best read in conjunction with each other.

Stephen Jay Gould's "Fall in the House of Usher" is reprinted in his *Eight Little Piggies* (Norton, 1993). David Maine's *Fallen* (St. Martin's, 2005) is a wonderful idea indifferently executed. *Calendar: Humanity's Epic Struggle to Determine a*

True and Accurate Year by David Ewing Duncan (Harper, 1998) is a useful history. W. E. H. Lecky's *History of the Rise and Influence of the Spirit of Rationalism in Europe* (1865) is a tendentious but still influential history and a vivid narrative. Lecky is wrong about almost everything.

My account of the blamefest of Adam and Eve is shaped by Stanley Fish's brilliant *How Milton Works* (Harvard University Press/Belknap Press, 2001).

Most of the sources for my discussion of Augustine, Pelagius, and Julian are indicated in the notes to Chapter 2. Helpful treatments of the Eastern church's ideas about original sin may be found in *The Spirit of Eastern Christendom (600–1700)* (University of Chicago Press, 1974), the second volume of Jaroslav Pelikan's *The Christian Tradition: A History of the Development of Doctrine,* and John Meyendorff's *Byzantine Theology: Historical Trends and Doctrinal Themes* (second edition, Fordham University Press, 1987).

The history of attitudes toward baptism is briefly told in Keith Thomas's *Religion and the Decline of Magic* (Scribner, 1971) and Lawrence Stone's *The Family, Sex, and Marriage in England 1500–1800* (Harper, 1977). Robert Alter's stimulating translation of Genesis, with rich and extensive commentary, appeared in 1996 and has now been reissued as part of *The Five Books of Moses* (Norton, 2004).

FOUR: The Feast of All Souls

Eugen Rosenstock-Huessy's *Out of Revolution: Autobiography of Western Man* and *I Am an Impure Thinker* are published by Argo Books in Vermont, a function of the Eugen Rosenstock-Huessy Fund, which is in essence a highly professional fan club (started many years ago by Rosenstock-Huessy's students at Dartmouth). Argo is Rosenstock-Huessy's only publisher and has been for many years. The definitive study of the development of Purgatory is Jacques LeGoff's *The Birth of Purgatory,* translated by Arthur Goldhammer (University of Chicago Press, 1984), but my attention was first drawn to the subject by Stephen Greenblatt's *Hamlet in Purgatory* (Princeton University Press, 2001), from which I have taken an anecdote or three.

Peter Brown's *The Cult of the Saints: Its Rise and Function in Latin Christianity* (University of Chicago Press, 1982) is the definitive work on its topic. Some of the early history of the Feast of All Souls is told in *Consorting with Saints: Prayer for the Dead in Early Medieval France,* by Megan McLaughlin (Cornell University Press, 1994). The continuation of old All Souls traditions in twentieth-century

England is documented by L. H. Hayward, in "Shropshire Folklore of Yesterday and To-Day" (*Folklore* 49:3, September 1938). I learned about the Aymara people of the Bolivian highlands from "'Living the Past Another Way': Reinstrumentalized Missionary Selves in Aymara Mission Fields" by Andrew Orta, in the *Anthropological Quarterly* 75.4 (2002), and about the Chinese Feast of the Hungry Ghosts from Alan Priest's article "Li Chung Receives a Mandate," in *The Metropolitan Museum of Art Bulletin* (34:11, November 1939).

What I know about the Church of St. Mary in Fairford, Gloucestershire, I have learned from several rich visits there. What I know about Prudentius I have learned from reading C. S. Lewis's *The Allegory of Love* (Oxford University Press, 1936). The anecdote about the Duchess of Buckingham may be found in *George Whitefield and the Great Awakening*, by John Pollock (Victor, 1986) and in almost any other book or essay about Whitefield.

FIVE: A Few Words About the Devil

The film *Hellboy* draws primarily on two original graphic novels drawn by Mike Mignola: *Hellboy: Seeds of Destruction*, written by John Byrne (Dark Horse Books, 1994) and *Hellboy: Wake the Devil*, written by Mignola (Dark Horse Books, 1997). T. A. Shippey's account of evil in *The Lord of the Rings* is in his *J. R. R. Tolkien: Author of the Century* (Houghton Mifflin, 2000). I came across the story of R. D. Laing's patient in *The 21st Century Brain: Explaining, Mending and Manipulating the Mind*, by Stephen Rose (Jonathan Cape, 2005); this led me back to Laing's key works, *The Divided Self* (Penguin, 1960) and *The Politics of Experience* (Penguin, 1967); I have quoted from the latter.

SIX: The Wicked, but Not Very

The story of Amsterdam's Jews in the seventeenth century is told, briefly, in Simon Schama's *The Embarrassment of Riches: An Interpretation of Dutch Culture in the Golden Age* (University of California Press, 1988) and, from a very particular point of view, in Rebecca Goldstein's *Betraying Spinoza: The Renegade Jew Who Gave Us Modernity* (Schocken, 2006). The details of the conflict surrounding Rabbi Aboab are related by Alexander Altmann in "Eternality of Punishment: A Theological Controversy Within the Amsterdam Rabbinate in the Thirties of the Seventeenth Century," reprinted in *Essential Papers on Kabbalah*, edited by Lawrence Fine

(New York University Press, 1995). The great authority on original sin in Judaism is Samuel S. Cohon; see, for instance, his long essay on the subject in his *Essays in Jewish Theology* (Hebrew Union College Press, 1987). I have also drawn, here and elsewhere in this book, on N. P. Williams's *The Ideas of the Fall and of Original Sin: A Historical and Critical Study* (Longmans, 1927). Sir Philip Sidney's contrast between our "infected will" and "erected wit" is found in his famous *Apology for Poetry* (written in 1583). Useful editions of Pascal's *Pensées* and *Provincial Letters* are published by Penguin books, the latter with an excellent introduction by the translator, A. J. Krailsheimer; a good recent biography is *Blaise Pascal: Reasons of the Heart* by Marvin R. O'Connell and Allen C. Guelzo (Eerdmans, 1997).

John Bunyan tells his own story in *Grace Abounding to the Chief of Sinners* (1666) and every Christian's story in *The Pilgrim's Progress*, part 1 (1678). Christopher Hill's historical biography, *A Tinker and a Poor Man: John Bunyan and His Church, 1628–1688* (Knopf, 1989) is outstanding. Hill gives further context in *The Experience of Defeat: Milton and Some Contemporaries* (Penguin, 1984); the story of James Nayler is told superbly in Leo Damrosch's *The Sorrows of the Quaker Jesus: James Nayler and the Puritan Crackdown on the Free Spirit* (Harvard University Press, 1996). Various intriguing details about Christianity in England throughout the early modern period may be found in the first two volumes of Horton Davies's six-volume *Worship and Theology in England*. These are now published in a single book with the subtitle *From Cranmer to Baxter and Fox, 1534–1690* (Eerdmans, 1996; originally published in 1970 and 1975). The later volumes are just as good.

I have been prompted to think about various matters treated in this chapter and the next—from Pascal and the Jansenists to the Wesleyans and the Great Awakening—by Ronald Knox's immensely entertaining and thoroughly unreliable *Enthusiasm: A Chapter in the History of Religion* (University of Notre Dame Press; originally published in 1950). It may be, as C. S. Lewis thought, "Ronny Knox's worst book," but it is certainly his most provocative.

SEVEN: More Hateful than Vipers

An outstanding general history of the Great Awakening in its religious and cultural context is Mark Noll's *The Rise of Evangelicalism: The Age of Edwards, Whitefield, and the Wesleys* (InterVarsity, 2004). More details about the history of English Dissent may be found in Michael Watts's *The Dissenters: From the Reformation to the French Revolution* (Clarendon Press, 1985). Franklin's wry anecdote about

Whitefield's persuasive powers is in his *Autobiography,* which he worked on from about 1771 to his death in 1790. Much of the vast output of Jonathan Edwards is available online via the Christian Classics Ethereal Library (noted above); I don't know what I would have done without this resource, nor without George Marsden's nearly definitive biography, *Jonathan Edwards: A Life* (Yale University Press, 2003).

The Child in Christian Thought (Eerdmans, 2001), an anthology edited by Marcia J. Bunge, contains a number of essays that have been useful to me in writing this chapter, and indeed this whole book: "'Wonderful Affection': Seventeenth-Century Missionaries to New France on Children and Childhood," by Clarissa W. Atkinson; "John Wesley and Children," by Richard P. Heitzenrater; "Children of Wrath, Children of Grace: Jonathan Edwards and the Puritan Culture of Child Rearing," by Catherine A. Brekus; and several others. It's a treasure chest.

I have used the translation of Rousseau's *Émile* by Allan Bloom (Basic Books, 1979), which also has excellent notes. The standard biography of Rousseau, whose final volume was left unfinished at the author's death, is by Maurice Cranston and is published by the University of Chicago Press: *Jean-Jacques: The Early Life of Jean-Jacques Rousseau* (1982), *The Noble Savage: Jean-Jacques Rousseau 1754–1762* (1991), *The Solitary Self: Jean-Jacques Rousseau in Exile and Adversity* (1997). I have also consulted Leo Damrosch's recent *Jean-Jacques Rousseau: Restless Genius* (Houghton Mifflin, 2005).

A familiar guide through the mazes of French thought in the eighteenth century is Peter Gay's *The Enlightenment: An Interpretation,* in two volumes: *The Rise of Modern Paganism* (Norton, 1966) and *The Science of Freedom* (Norton, 1969). Although I have read Gay avidly, I am sometimes distracted from his exposition by the sound of antireligious axes grinding. More commanding—though from a source equally committed to a Whiggish interpretation of intellectual history in which religion is slowly and justly strangled—is Ernst Cassirer's *The Philosophy of the Enlightenment,* originally published in 1932 (English translation, Princeton University Press, 1951). A more recent, less "progressive," more expansive, and more broadly cultural version of this story is told by Charles Taylor in his magnificent *Sources of the Self: The Making of the Modern Identity* (Harvard University Press, 1989). I have not quoted often from Taylor, but his interpretation has led, perhaps governed, much of my thinking about the post-Reformation developments of my story.

On Voltaire I have consulted Roger Pearson's *Voltaire Almighty: A Life in Pursuit of Freedom* (Bloomsbury USA, 2005) and Susan Neiman's wide-ranging and powerful *Evil in Modern Thought: An Alternative History of Philosophy* (Princeton University Press, 2004).

I learned of Richard Lovell Edgeworth in Jenny Uglow's *The Lunar Men* (New York: Farrar, Straus and Giroux 2002), a group biography of some remarkable men who lived in and around the city of Birmingham, England, in the late eighteenth century. Edgeworth's daughter Maria, later a famous novelist, produced a life-and-letters, much of which is available online.

EIGHT: New Worlds

Editions of Shakespeare, Montaigne, and other such luminaries are so plentiful that I see no point in citing particular ones here. Thomas Traherne's *Centuries of Meditations* was written around 1670, but never published; it was handed along through generations of people who had no idea of its value until it turned up in a London bookstall in 1897, where an attentive scholar purchased the manuscript. It was published a decade later. Edwards's biography of Brainerd is available online via the CCEL. Adriana S. Benzaquén's *Encounters with Wild Children: Temptation and Disappointment in the Study of Human Nature* was published by McGill-Queens University Press in 2006. Peter A. Goddard's "Augustine and the Amerindian in Seventeenth-Century New France" appeared in *Church History* (67:4, December 1998); from this article I learned about Jean Rigoleuc's influential work and was led also to Anthony Pagden's *The Fall of Natural Man: The American Indian and the Origins of Comparative Ethnology* (Cambridge University Press, 1987).

Richard Holmes's biography of Coleridge appears in two volumes: *Coleridge: Early Visions, 1772–1804* (Pantheon, 1989) and *Coleridge: Darker Reflections, 1804–1834* (Pantheon, 1998). There's a wonderful account of Robert Owen, in the context of the history of socialism, in Edmund Wilson's *To the Finland Station* (1940), recently republished as a New York Review of Books Classic (2003). Several biographies of Owen are available, but I cannot recommend any of them—he is overdue for a serious and scholarly reconsideration. I discovered Southey's visit to New Lanark in Paul Johnson's *The Birth of the Modern: World Society 1815–1830* (HarperCollins, 1992).

NINE: The Confraternity of the Human Type

I learned about Charles Finney, Lane Seminary, and the Oberlin Institute from several sources, including two books by Mark Noll: *America's God: From Jonathan*

Edwards to Abraham Lincoln (Oxford University Press, 2002) and *The Scandal of the Evangelical Mind* (Eerdmans, 1995). Also helpful was James A. Morone's *Hellfire Nation: The Politics of Sin in American History* (Yale University Press, 2003). I learned about Louis Agassiz's fateful visit to Philadelphia in Stephen Jay Gould's *The Mismeasure of Man* (second edition, Norton, 1996), which was also my chief guide to the rise of scientific racism. A helpful biography is Edward Lurie's *Louis Agassiz: A Life in Science* (reprinted by Johns Hopkins University Press in 1988); Lurie also wrote an insightful early essay called "Louis Agassiz and the Races of Man" (*Isis* 45:3, September 1954). Agassiz's 1850 essay "The Geographical Distribution of Animals" may be found at http://www.wku.edu/~smithch/biogeog/AGAS1850.htm.

On the complexities of Southern thought about race and Christian theology, the invaluable guides are Elizabeth Fox-Genovese and Eugene D. Genovese's *The Mind of the Master Class: History and Faith in the Southern Slaveholders' Worldview* (Cambridge University Press, 2005) and Eugene D. Genovese's *A Consuming Fire: The Fall of the Confederacy in the Mind of the White Christian South* (University of Georgia Press, 1998). Lincoln's response to Frederick Ross is noted in Allen C. Guelzo's *Abraham Lincoln: Redeemer President* (Eerdmans, 2003).

The notion that Africans are the descendants of Ham is very old and surprisingly multifarious and is treated comprehensively in David M. Goldenberg's *The Curse of Ham: Race and Slavery in Early Judaism, Christianity, and Islam* (Princeton University Press, 2003). James Baldwin's retort in *The Fire Next Time* may be consulted in the Library of America edition of his *Collected Essays* (1998).

My concluding comments on Shakespeare's Venetian plays draw heavily on W. H. Auden's great essay "Brothers and Others," in *The Dyer's Hand* (Random House, 1962).

TEN: The Two-Headed Calf

It is my considered judgment that Rebecca West's *Black Lamb and Grey Falcon* is the greatest book of the twentieth century; it is available in a Penguin edition. The best biography of West to date is Carl Rollyson's *Rebecca West: A Life* (Scribner, 1996).

Robert Nisbet's *History of the Idea of Progress* (Basic Books, 1981) is also a neglected masterpiece, though of a different kind and a different order. It has been especially helpful as an extension and a correction of J. B. Bury's famous *The Idea of Progress: An Inquiry into its Origin and Growth* (1920). I have also consulted

Christopher Lasch's *The True and Only Heaven: Progress and Its Critics* (Norton, 1991), and, for a general philosophical reflection on a century of moral horror, Jonathan Glover's *Humanity: A Moral History of the Twentieth Century* (Yale University Press, 2001). C. S. Lewis's letter lamenting the arrival of another war is in *The Collected Letters of C.S. Lewis,* vol. 2 (HarperSanFrancisco, 2004).

Solzhenitsyn's account of his spiritual enlightenment is in the chapter of *The Gulag Archipelago* called "The Ascent"; I found it in the one-volume edition abridged and edited by Edward R. Ericson, Jr. (Harper, 1985). I also consulted Michael Scammell's massive *Solzhenitsyn* (Norton, 1986).

The God That Failed, edited by Richard Crossman, first appeared in 1949, but Columbia University Press reissued it in 2001. Whittaker Chambers's *Witness* was published by Random House in 1952 and has been reprinted several times since; Sam Tanenhaus's outstanding *Whittaker Chambers: A Biography* was published by Random House in 1997. Russell Kirk's *The Conservative Mind* has also been frequently reprinted, for instance by Regnery in 2001. My first source for Burke has been *The Portable Edmund Burke,* edited by Isaac Kramnick (Penguin, 1999); something close to his complete works is available online at Project Gutenberg (http://www.gutenberg.org/browse/authors/b#a842).

Reinhold Niebuhr's major books were originally published by Scribner, though most of them are now out of print or reprinted in the Library of Religious Ethics. Oh, for the days when a theologian was published by a major New York City trade house. Similarly, C. E. M. Joad's various "guides"—not just the *Guide to Modern Wickedness,* but also the *Guide to Modern Thought* (1933), *Guide to Philosophy* (1936), and *Guide to the Philosophy of Morals and Politics* (1938)—were published by London's Faber.

The various citations from *Time* come from that magazine's outstanding online archive: http://www.time.com/time/archive.

ELEVEN: In the Genes

The text of *Ineffabilis Deus,* like that of most papal writings and pronouncements, may be found on the Vatican's excellent Web site: http://www.vatican.va. A brief but useful overview of Pius IX's connection with Marian devotion in his time may be found in Eamon Duffy's *Saints and Sinners: A History of the Popes* (third edition, Yale University Press, 2006). The many patristic comments on Mary are summarized in the article on the Immaculate Conception in the 1910 *Catholic En-*

cyclopedia, now available online: http://www.newadvent.org/cathen/07674d.htm. A more detailed account of Mary's role in the Christian faith may be found in Jaroslav Pelikan's *Mary Through the Centuries: Her Place in the History of Culture* (Yale University Press, 1998).

A useful account of Mendel's life and work and the delayed acceptance of that work, geared toward the common reader, is Robin Marantz Henig's *The Monk in the Garden: The Lost and Found Genius of Gregor Mendel, the Father of Genetics* (Mariner Books, 2001). An excellent brief overview of the history of genetics may be found in Colin Tudge's *The Engineer in the Garden: Genes and Genetics from the Idea of Heredity to the Creation of Life* (Hill & Wang, 1994).

The rise of the eugenics movement is described briefly in Gould's *The Mismeasure of Man* (cited in Chapter 9 above), but in much more detail in *In the Name of Eugenics: Genetics and the Uses of Human Heredity* by Daniel Kevles (Harvard University Press, 1998). An absolutely fascinating account that appeared just as I was completing this book and that therefore I could not take sufficient advantage of is Nicholas Russell's *Like Engend'ring Like: Heredity and Animal Breeding in Early Modern England* (Cambridge University Press, 2007).

The full text of Indiana's forced-sterilization law may be found online as part of a comprehensive archive called *Indiana Eugenics: History and Legacy: 1907–2007*: http://www.bioethics.iupui.edu/Eugenics/index.htm.

Philip Zimbardo's *The Lucifer Effect: Understanding How Good People Turn Evil* was published by Random House in 2007; Zimbardo maintains a detailed Web site summarizing that book and outlining his current project on developing heroism at http://www.lucifereffect.com/. His article with Zeno Franco, "The Banality of Heroism," may be found there too. Michael Bywater's review of the book, "How We Make Monsters," appeared in the *Times* of London on April 1, 2007; Cass Sunstein's review, "The Thin Line," appeared in the May 21, 2007 issue of *The New Republic*. Stanley Milgram's essay summarizing the findings of his experiment, "The Perils of Obedience," appeared in *Harper's* in December 1973.

I draw heavily on Steven Pinker's *The Blank Slate* (Viking, 2002), less heavily on his *How the Mind Works* (Norton, 1999). Jerry Fodor's review of the earlier book, "The Trouble with Psychological Darwinism," appeared in the *London Review of Books* (20:2, January 22, 1998). Richard Webster's "Steven Pinker and Original Sin" may be found at http://www.richardwebster.net/archivepinker.html. Simon Blackburn's review of *The Blank Slate*, "Meet the Flintstones," appeared in the November 25, 2002, issue of *The New Republic*.

Original Selfishness: Original Sin and Evil in the Light of Evolution, by Daryl P. Domning and Monika K. Hellwig, is from Ashgate Publishing (2006).

AFTERWORD

Robert Palmer interviewed LaDell Johnson and included the story of the "big black man" in *Deep Blues* (Penguin, 1982). See also Peter Guralnick's brief meditation *Searching for Robert Johnson* (Dutton, 1989).

Mary Midgley's review of Pinker's *The Blank Slate,* "It's All in the Mind," appeared in the September 21, 2002, edition of London's *Guardian.* Richard Dawkins's *River Out of Eden* (Harper, 1996) is perhaps his best book, *The God Delusion* (Houghton Mifflin, 2006) almost certainly his worst.

Auden's essay is called "The Globe," and it appears in his collection *The Dyer's Hand,* cited above.